STUDIES IN HISTORY, ECONOMICS AND PUBLIC LAW

EDITED BY THE FACULTY OF POLITICAL SCIENCE OF
COLUMBIA UNIVERSITY

No. 325

THE CHURCH OF ENGLAND AND
SOCIAL REFORM SINCE 1854

THE CHURCH OF ENGLAND AND SOCIAL REFORM SINCE 1854

BY

DONALD O. WAGNER, Ph.D.

NEW YORK

COLUMBIA UNIVERSITY PRESS

London: P. S. King & Son, Ltd.

1930

1108910

To
MY FATHER

PREFACE

THE Church of England during the nineteenth century seemed to have an unhappy faculty for putting its worst foot forward. In theological matters it was most in the public eye when party strife was bitterest and recrimination most violent. From time to time it defended privileges that seem almost indefensible and resisted changes that were not only popular but inevitable. Sometimes, however, faults were attributed to the whole Church which only a part of it possessed. On more than one occasion the well-advertised misdeeds of a few clergymen brought undeserved blame upon all. Moreover, there were always plenty of critics who seemed eager to interpret their actions in the worst possible light. As a result the quiet but fruitful labors of many churchmen were often lost sight of. To a certain extent this is true even of the Christian Socialists, and historians usually treat the movement as a temporary aberration of churchmen which came to an end shortly after 1850. Quite in the approved manner two writers of great repute dispatch it with a single sweep of their rhetoric: it had, they say, " more body and more passion than ' Young England ' but not a very much longer life." The narrowness of this view is patent to anyone who has read A. V. Woodworth's excellent but neglected little study of the movement.

It is not the writer's purpose to rehabilitate the Church as an agency of reform. He desires merely to state its position with regard to some of the typical problems of the nineteenth and twentieth centuries, whether that position happens to have been admirable or the reverse. General attitudes and

7

organized efforts will be given precedence over the activities of individuals; if certain well-known figures are passed over it will sometimes be because they have contributed nothing distinctive, not because they have been overlooked. The work does not pretend to be exhaustive even within those limits. Many questions occur, many ramifications suggest themselves which require further investigation. The writer has sunk a shaft at intervals, but much excavation still remains to be done.

In preparing this book interviews with leading English churchmen helped to remedy the deficiencies of an outsider, and the writer owes much to the kindness of Bishop Charles Gore, Dr. Percy Dearmer, Fr. Paul Bull, formerly chairman of the Church Socialist League, the Rev. P. T. R. Kirk, general director of the Industrial Christian Fellowship, Dr. W. R. Matthews, dean of King's College, London, Sir Wyndham Deedes, head of Oxford House, the Rev. Claude Jenkins, Librarian of Lambeth Palace Library, and Miss Maude Royden. Valued criticism of the manuscript was supplied by Professors W. W. Rockwell, H. F. Ward, and F. J. Foakes Jackson of Union Theological Seminary. At every stage Professors R. L. Schuyler and C. J. H. Hayes of Columbia rendered valuable aid, and their careful reading of both the manuscript and the proof prevented many a mistake. Finally, thanks are due the indulgent library staff of General Theological Seminary, who often waived the strict rules of library procedure and so made much of the writer's work pleasanter and more rapid.

CONTENTS

PAGE

CHAPTER V

The Reformers Organize: 1877–1895

CHAPTER VI

Conquest of the Church: 1877–1914

CHAPTER VII

War and Reconstruction

CHAPTER VIII

CHAPTER I

INTRODUCTION

1800-1854

CHRISTIANS have always been in agreement as to the ultimate social ideals of Christianity, but they have been far from unanimous as to the proper means of realizing them. The church has therefore often found it convenient to preach the ends without specifying the means, a course of action sometimes reprobated by reformers as useless or actually harmful to society. No one would deny that at least occasionally the mere inculcation of " charity ", " brotherhood ", or " fellowship " leads to thoroughly desirable changes in human conduct, and so gives the church some right to be called an agency of reform. Still, its intentions in this respect are certainly clearer and its services more definite if, instead of leaving the details of a better society to the individual conscience, it criticizes the existing order and suggests methods of improving it. In what follows, both the general and the specific teaching of the Church of England will be treated of, but for the most part Christian ideals will make their appearance only when reformers translate them into programs of action.

The main narrative runs from 1854 (when the first Christian Socialist organization was dissolved) to the present. The situation at the beginning of this period is best explained however by a preliminary sketch of the Church's social position and attitude during the preceding half-century, when the chemism of industrial revolution was precipitating a series of new and flinty problems in the current of English life.

11

THE SOCIAL BACKGROUND OF THE CLERGY

The social viewpoint of churchmen in the early nineteenth century was not entirely the result of inspiration; in fact it showed quite plainly the effect of mundane circumstances. Class associations, economic interest, the relationship between Church and State, and theological doctrine had an influence which cannot be ignored; and a discussion of these factors with reference to the clergy will help to explain the social outlook of the laity as well.

1. Class Associations

In 1800 both the Church and the general population of England were predominantly rural. The social importance of this fact lay in the community of interests and the possibility of mutual understanding it implied. The clergy as a class were most familiar with the outlook, problems, and conditions of life of that section of the people whose interests, from a democratic point of view, should have been uppermost in the state.

Industrial change, however, threatened shortly to reverse the balance of population in favor of the towns and to make the problems of town life the chief concern of the people. Unless the Church kept pace with this general movement it would find itself on the whole out of contact with the majority. In fact, a serious lag was already evident. Using the figures for church accommodation in 1801 as an indication rather than an exact measurement of this deficiency, we find that while the larger towns (i. e., those of 10,000 and over) contained 41 per cent of the population, they had only 30 per cent of the total number of church sittings.[1]

---

[1] *Parliamentary Papers, Accounts and Papers,* 1852-3, vol. 89, p. cxli. The *Parliamentary Papers* will hereafter be referred to by their subtitles: *Reports of Commissioners, Reports from Committees,* or *Accounts and Papers.*

Rather tardily, but with growing vigor, churchmen applied themselves to the problem. Societies were formed with the object of increasing the number of parish clergy and of bringing the gospel to the unchurched, building funds multiplied, and quaint edifices rapidly appeared which exemplified the efficiency and taste of the machine age. Between 1801 and 1858 £11,000,000 were contributed toward the erection of 3,150 churches.[1] Thus by 1851 the larger towns had 38 per cent of the church accommodation. But they now contained 51 per cent of the population.[2] In Staffordshire as late as 1861 it was reported that the manufacturing districts had 70 per cent of the county's inhabitants but only 36 per cent of its clergy.[3]

The rural or rather the non-industrial character of the Church was intensified by the rigidity of diocesan organization. Before the advent of great industry almost every large town was an administrative center of the Church, and the problems of urban life were, in theory at least, directly under the eye and the solicitude of a bishop. But many of the industrial towns had far surpassed the old cities in size and in the complexity of their problems long before they acquired resident bishops. Until the bishoprics of Ripon and Manchester were founded, in 1836 and 1847 respectively, the episcopate had not been increased since the time of Henry VIII. The delay was perhaps as detrimental to the Church as it was to the towns. Some relief was coming, it is true, from the closer attention of bishops to diocesan affairs—absenteeism was no longer part of the uncriticized natural order—and diocesan boundaries were redrawn by the Established Church Act of 1836, but the new situation was fully recognized and dealt with only toward the end of the century.

[1] *Reports from Committees*, 1857-8, vol. ix, p. 15.

[2] *Accounts and Papers*, 1852-3, vol. 89, p. cxxxix.

[3] *Report of the Proceedings of the Church Congress*, 1867, p. 20.

The associations of the clergy were rural.   They were also aristocratic.   Taste, education and often birth placed the clergy almost if not quite on a plane of equality with the gentry.   They were educated in most cases at Oxford or Cambridge, where a few poor students lingered only as curious survivals of medieval generosity.   Between 1834 and 1853 the two Universities supplied more than 9,000 of the 12,000 candidates for ordination.[1]   In 1815 eleven of the twenty-six bishops were of noble birth and ten had been tutors to the aristocracy.[2]   As Guizot observed to Bishop Samuel Wilberforce when the latter visited him at Val Richer, the chasm between the clergy and the upper class, so evident in France, was non-existent in England.   " I know," said the historian, " that I could not have stayed for a single week in a country house like this in England without meeting the rector of the parish.   But here, there is not a curé within the whole district whom I could ask to my table."   The bishop appears to have been so pleased with the compliment that he utterly missed the snobbery of the remark.[3]   Wilberforce himself, pleading for additional endowments in 1864, set forth the advantages of a " gentleman clergy ".   " It is of the first moment," he said,

that the leaders of thought should find their equals in education, in thinking, among the ministers of the English Church.   It is of the utmost moment that men in high rank should find standing beside them in the ranks of the Church their equals in birth and their fellows in education, and, if anything, it is still more desirable that the poor of England should be ministered to by English gentlemen.   What we mean by gentleman

[1] *Convocation of Canterbury, Lower House,* " Report on Deficiencies of Spiritual Ministration," 1872, p. 28.

[2] E. Halévy, *History of the English People in 1815,* p. 345.

[3] A. R. Ashwell and R. G. Wilberforce, *Life of the Right Reverend Samuel Wilberforce,* vol. iii, p. 357.

is just this—it is the habit of putting self down and of exalting those to whom he is ministering.[1]

But the intimate connection between the clergy and the governing class had its weaknesses. It was admitted on all sides that the Church had lost its hold upon another social class. In 1843 Henry Edward Manning, who had not yet transferred his talents to a broader theater, drew attention to the fact in a charge to his archdeaconry of Chichester. "There is one class, I admit," he said,

among whom [the Church] has still to mature and extend its spiritual rule—I mean the middle class. . . . It is not penetrated by the pastoral ministry—as the upper by kindred and association, and the lower by direct instruction and oversight. It is, therefore, open to the inroads of sectarianism, and to theories of all kinds—social, religious and economical.

Several letters in *The British Magazine* confirmed this opinion. One of them advised churchmen to stand less upon their dignity and to associate freely with those of middle station, whose "pert forwardness" and "affectation of gentility" would no doubt disappear if social barriers were lowered.[2] According to *The Guardian* the restricted influence of the Church was directly attributable to the social position of the clergy:

The relations of the Anglican clergy to the different ranks of the nation is too much what one might have expected. With the aristocracy they are very influential. . . . Over country labourers, the natural vassals of the landed gentry, they have power, but not what they ought to have. With all their charities, their industry, their integrity, their genuine sympathy with the poor, the personal respect which they command, they do not sweep a country population along with them, as seems

[1] Ashwell and Wilberforce, *op. cit.*, p. 155.
[2] *British Magazine*, vol. 24, pp. 390-4; vol. 27, pp. 377, 510.

frequently done by a less earnest, educated, and able Dissenting preacher. . . . That the Church has lost its hold on trade is too generally acknowledged to require illustration.[1]

2. *Economic Interest*

The financial arrangements of the Church were related in a variety of ways to the social outlook of clergymen. It is not uncharitable to suppose that those who sought office mainly for profit were likely to contemplate the existing order in a mellow, golden light. William Lamb (later Viscount Melbourne), who was certainly no ascetic, considered the advantages of an ecclesiastical career but finally chose the law as the more honorable if not the more lucrative profession.[2] Ambitious men no doubt still find scope for their acquisitive propensities in the Church, but the system of pluralities which flourished at the beginning of the last century makes it somewhat easier to isolate the motive at that time. The bishop of Lichfield and Coventry, for example, accused William Pitt of neglect and contempt for offering him the unremunerative see of Salisbury, and suggested that the deanery of St. Paul's (to be held in plurality, of course) would help to salve his wounded feelings. When Pitt rebuked him, he apologized for what may have seemed to be a lack of " due and proper respect." [3] Nepotism and the use of high connection to secure rich livings are some test of this motive also.[4] William Cobbett dedicated his *Legacy to Parsons* to Bishop Blomfield, who had conferred a prebendal stall and two rectories upon his son.[5]

---

[1] 10 Dec., 1856, p. 937.

[2] W. M. Torrens, *Memoirs of the Rt. Hon. William Lamb, Second Viscount Melbourne,* vol. i, pp. 48-9.

[3] Earl Stanhope, *Life of the Rt. Hon. William Pitt,* vol. ii, p. 128.

[4] S. Walpole, *History of England since 1815,* vol. i, p. 51, gives a long list of such appointments.

[5] *Legacy to Parsons,* p. 7.

Absenteeism usually accompanied pluralism. In 1830, when reform was in the air, it was estimated that out of a total of 10,550 benefices, from 3,500 to 6,000 furnished stipends to non-resident incumbents.[1] In certain cases, however, it was necessary for a clergyman to possess more than one living to secure a decent income, for 800 places returned less than £50 a year each and 4,000, less than £150.[2]

The clergy derived their income chiefly from tithes and endowments. They were expected, therefore, to guard vested rights. Even an amateur churchman (in the best sense) like Gladstone could remark in 1865, " The Church of England is more likely to part with her faith than with her funds," echoing Voltaire.[3] But the obverse aspect must not be forgotten. The possession of an independent income protected lazy or incompetent clergymen from the consequences of their neglect, but it secured to the man of unorthodox opinions a corresponding freedom of thought and action. A complementary safeguard (or abuse) was security of tenure. Once appointed, a clergyman could be removed only with great difficulty. His office and emoluments constituted almost a freehold tenure in the eyes of the law.[4]

In a reforming age, such an antique and disorderly system offered churchmen little protection against the chill, searching gale of rationalism. Jeremy Bentham in his analytical way drew up a long list of Vices of the Church.[5] The *Black*

---

[1] Walpole, *op. cit.*, vol. v, p. 259.

[2] W. L. Mathieson, *England in Transition*, p. 130.

[3] John Morley, *Life of Gladstone*, vol. ii, p. 162. Voltaire: " Le clergé anglicain a retenu beaucoup de cérémonies catholiques, et surtout celle de recevoir les dîmes avec une attention très scrupuleuse."—*Oeuvres*, vol. xxii, p. 95.

[4] O. J. Reichel, *Elements of Canon Law*, p. 207.

[5] *The Book of Church Reform, edited by One of his Disciples*, 1831.

Book [1] attacked ecclesiastical corruption with an eloquence equal to its inaccuracy.   So an act of 1836 redistributed episcopal revenues, and the abuse of pluralities was extinguished in 1838.   Two years later sinecure restories in the gift of the crown or ecclesiastical corporations were surrendered or compounded for, and the capitular establishments were reduced.   The resulting surplus went to increase the value of poor livings. [2]   But some 5,000 humble parsons continued to raise large families on less than £150 a year.   For it was proper to mulct the chapters for the benefit of the needy, but to disturb the private property of lay patrons would have been anarchical.   Nor is it recorded that middle-class radicals ever lost their tempers over the fact that a great part of the tithe was paid to lay impropriators. [3]

3. *Church and State*

The third general influence upon the social action of the clergy sprang from the relation of the Church to the State. This relationship held two interesting possibilities for social reform: it opened avenues of direct political action to the Church, while it subjected the clergy in a degree to partisan influence.

Convocation, the national synod and the equal of Parliament for certain purposes, remained in a state of suspended animation from 1717 to 1852 with just sufficient vigor to address the crown at the opening of Parliament, and is thus

[1] Attributed to John Wade. (*Dictionary of National Biography*, vol. xx, p. 416.)

[2] W. L. Mathieson, *English Church Reform*, pp. 133, 149; Halévy, *op. cit.*, p. 210.

[3] W. N. Molesworth, *History of England*, vol. i, p. 390. *Cf.* Newman's complaint in Tract 59: "Of these endowments far more than half are at this day in the hands of laymen who may be of any religion or none, and do not consider themselves obliged to spend one farthing of it in the cause of God."

outside the picture. Twenty-six bishops in the House of Lords, however, had opportunities for service which were enhanced by the modest talents of their fellow-members. " They [the bishops] sat in Parliament," as one of them observed, " not to make the Church political, but to make the State religious." [1]

But the bishops could scarcely be called free agents. Prince Albert himself drew up a set of definite though somewhat conflicting parliamentary rules for Samuel Wilberforce on his elevation to the see of Oxford:

A Bishop ought to abstain *completely* from mixing himself up with the politics of the day, and beyond giving a general support to the Queen's government, and occasionally voting for it, should take no part in the discussion of state affairs (for instance, Corn Laws, Game Laws, Trade or Financial Questions, &c. &c.); but he should come forward whenever the interests of Humanity are at stake, and give boldly and manfully his advice to the House and Country (I mean questions like Negro Emancipation, improvement of the health of the towns, measures for the recreation of the poor, against cruelty to animals, for regulating factory labour, &c. &c.).[2]

But there were more serious limits to the bishops' independence in Parliament. Prime ministers undertook to secure a " general support of the Queen's government " by appointing members of their own party to the episcopal bench. Political loyalty rather than supreme ability often determined a clergyman's fitness for promotion. This is best illustrated by Melbourne's appointments. Wordsworth, said Melbourne, must be " entirely Liberal "; Longley's opinions ought to be " of a Liberal character, particularly with respect to reform of the Church "; Arnold of Rugby failed to qualify: " What

[1] *Church of England Magazine*, vol. iv, p. 402.
[2] Ashwell and Wilberforce, *op. cit.*, vol. i, p. 276.

have Tory Churchmen ever done for me that I should make them a present of such a handle against my government?"[1] Lord John Russell went farther. In the Reform Bill of 1832 he had arranged to his own satisfaction the homage due to the powers of earth; he felt no less competent to judge the proper tribute to heaven. Tractarians were introducing "the sensual or symbolic worship of the Church of Rome." In making his appointments he therefore patronized their opponents.[2]

But the tenure of ministries was limited: churchmen held for life or until voluntary retirement, and a government could be certain of the political allegiance of none except its own creations. Bishops, then, had great opportunties, and they did not necessarily represent the views of the party in power, but their political predilections must correspond to some extent with the viewpoint current in governmental circles.

The lower clergy had no direct influence in Parliament. They were excluded from the House of Commons and until the Restoration had not been able even to vote in parliamentary elections. Very frequently, however, they were appointed justices of the peace. In this capacity Mr. and Mrs. Hammond found them generally zealous partisans of the established order and useful instruments of oppression in the years following the French Revolution.[3] Mr. and Mrs. Webb, on the other hand, have little but praise for the parson magistrates. Clergymen were "among the foremost to recognize that the magistrate . . . had duties in protecting the helpless, and in raising the standard of life of the people." They investigated houses of correction and county jails, and advocated prison reform. "It was a clerical justice of Hampshire—the Rev. Edmund Poulter—who drew up the able and

[1] W. M. Torrens, *op. cit.*, vol. ii, pp. 181, 225, 226.

[2] S. Walpole, *op. cit.*, vol. v, p. 280.

[3] J. L. and B. Hammond, *The Town Labourer*, p. 269.

elaborate report on the whole question of the labourer's position, which the assembled Justices of that county adopted in 1795." Even the " judicious Paley " (who turned author and so condemned himself to lasting infamy among reformers) had some title to that epithet as a justice of the peace, a position " for which he was peculiarly fitted by sagacity and insight." [1]

The position of clergymen as legislators and magistrates has some bearing on the attitude and opportunities of the Church in regard to social reform. But the evolution of a theory as to the relationship between Church and State came in the end to have perhaps greater significance from our point of view. The political philosophy of the Oxford Movement was a declaration of independence in theological matters which, as we shall see, could not fail to have important consequences for the social interests of the Church.

4. Theological Doctrine

As the last of a series of general influences which helped to determine the attitude of churchmen toward reform, the social principles, explicit or implied, of the various schools of theology must be considered.

The Evangelical or new low church party was the most active if not the most numerous section of the Church from the end of the eighteenth century until the rise of the Oxford Movement. John Wesley was its spiritual father and the child continued to exhibit the characteristic defects or excellences of its parentage. Possible flaws in its doctrine were not hard to discover. The emphasis which Evangelicals placed on faith as necessary to salvation and on the future life rather than the present might have grave social consequences.

[1] S. and B. Webb, *English Local Government: Parish and County*, pp. 352, 355. Paley's unfortunate essay was "Reasons for Contentment Addressed to the Labouring Part of the British Public."

Morality might be relaxed and social obligations forgotten. Wesley himself felt it necessary to deny that in praising faith he disparaged good works.

Men of deeper reflection [he admitted] are apt to say, " I lay no stress upon any other knowledge, but the knowledge of God by faith. . . . We are saved by faith, by faith alone." . . . But some men will say, with the Apostle James, " Show me thy faith without thy works; " (if thou canst, but indeed it is impossible) " and I will show thee my faith by my works." [1]

In point of fact practical morality issued from the pens of Evangelicals in a fluent if sometimes turbid stream. " We can admire their energy," said Sir Leslie Stephen, " though we cannot read their books." Yet the books were read, and in quantities—a witness, perhaps, to the power of religious enthusiasm.

But were the virtues taught by Evangelicals likely to promote reform? Some appear to have favored quite the opposite. Quiescence and submission were recommended to the poor. John Newton, one of the most popular of the exhorters, wrote " On the Advantages of a State of Poverty." Poverty, he said, keeps those of evil inclinations from great wickedness because it requires money to be bad grandly. It is a consoling thought, too, that the religious sincerity of the poor cannot be impeached, for it is plain they have nothing to gain by affectation. They are free from the sins of self-importance and attachment to the world. " If poor believers consider the snares to which their rich brethren are exposed, they will rather pray for and pity than envy them." [2] " A Christian," said Henry Venn, another moralist, " must be *meek*." He was solicitous that the children of the poor should be taught the necessity of labor—to support

---

[1] *Works*, " On Charity ", vol. vii, p. 51.

[2] *Letters*, pp. 255-6. This book is really a collection of sermons.

themselves, he added with unwitting humor, " by honest industry or some liberal profession." [1]

Such sentiments were not, however, confined to Evangelicals. They seem to have been the common property of churchmen irrespective of party. But sometimes the moral duty of submission is given a definitely Evangelical bias. Thus, the joys of salvation are a recompense for the ills of this world. But faith is indispensable to salvation, and it can often be inspired only by misfortune. Hence man should accept the divine bargain and submit to adversity in return for the promise of future bliss. Patience " is a duty because else the course of this world as a world of probation could not go on." [2] God, said Hannah More, " strengthens the virtues of his servants by hardening them under the cold and bracing climate of adverse fortune . . . when they cannot be attracted to him by gentler influences. . . Our gracious Father knows that eternity is long enough for his children to be happy in." [3]

The doctrine of resignation can be regarded as one aspect of the individualistic element in Evangelicalism. Man assumed personal responsibility for his lot and in so doing triumphed over it. Why, therefore, some might ask, disturb the material conditions which make this exhibition of faith possible? Such anti-social logic could be strengthened by reference to the Evangelical conception of religion as in large part a personal and mystical relation between men and God which had little concern with the things of this world.

But the principle of individual responsibility is capable of other applications. In fact Bishop Westcott, himself a Broad

[1] *The Complete Duty of Man*, pp. 224, 235. This was one of the most popular books of the period.

[2] *Church of England Magazine*, vol. ii, p. 353. The quotation is from " The Advantages of Christian Contentment as Opposed to a Spirit of Covetousness," by the Rev. Edward Scobell.

[3] *Works*, vol. viii, p. 367.

Churchman, in later days held that the " personal responsibility for work " taught by Evangelicals was one of the two
basic factors of Christian Socialism.[1]   If the poor perfected
themselves through poverty, the rich could do so through
voluntary asceticism.   The form this would take seemed pre-
ordained, for the obligations of wealth were set forth in the
Bible, and the Bible was to Evangelicals both the fountain of
doctrine and the literal word of God.   Thus it was made
doubly hard for them to avoid the problem of the needle's
eye.   John Wesley seems to have deliberately anathematized
wealth, although his language is not always clear.   It is not
forbidden to provide for one's family, for the conduct of a
business, and for the discharge of debts, he said.   But the
poor have a claim to all the rest.   St. Paul thundered against
all those " that will be rich."

Must we not . . . rank among those that desire to be rich, all
that, in fact, " lay up treasures on earth? " a thing as expressly
and clearly forbidden by our Lord, as either adultery or
murder. . . . We exhort you, in the name of the Lord Jesus
Christ, to be " willing to communicate; " . . . to be of the same
spirit . . . with those believers of ancient times, who remained
steadfast . . . in that blessed and holy *fellowship*, wherein
" none said that anything was his own, but they had all things
common." [2]

Later writers took a more lenient stand.   Desire for wealth
rather than wealth itself constituted the sin.   If without covet-
ing riches one attained them it was a sign of God's approval—
" to call you up to a higher station, who was content in your
own, and to entrust you with more talents to improve for
his glory." [3]   Liberal charity was of course enjoined.

[1] *Presidential Address* (to the Christian Social Union), 1895, p. 11.

[2] *Works*, vol. v, pp. 366-7, 376; vol. vii, p. 1.

[3] Hannah More, *Works*, vol. ix, p. 275; also *cf*. Henry Venn, *op. cit.*,
p. 315.

But if wealth was condoned, Evangelicals would see that its enjoyment was strictly limited. Wilberforce revived the " Society for the Reformation of Manners "—of the poor, as it turned out; but Hannah More attacked the vices of the rich. Employment of hairdressers and mantua-makers on Sunday—which deprived them of both church and rest—, card-money, Sunday concerts, and Sunday newspapers, all were forbidden. " It is no less absurd than cruel, in such of the great as lead disorderly lives, to expect to prevent vice by the laws they make to restrain or punish it, while their own example is a perpetual source of temptation to commit it." [1]

Emotionalism has long been regarded as the hall-mark of Evangelical religion. In the eighteenth century deistic churchmen had regarded " enthusiasm " as a distinctly vulgar emotion. But the fermentation had worked upward until the highest ranks of society felt the delightful stirrings of religious fervor, a sensation they had long ceased to expect. The danger was, of course, that the effervescence would spend itself in erecting a chapel and letting the spirit explode harmlessly among the stars. As we have seen, a conditional surrender had already been made to wealth: if practical and devoted leaders among the clergy were not forthcoming, the submission might become absolute. By 1830 it was apparent that the less irksome course was being followed.[2] Perhaps one evidence of this is the fact that as Evangelicalism became a fashionable success the disciples of Wesley who remained true to the Church of England failed to secure the popular following which distinguished Methodism. In 1840 Lord Shaftesbury,[3] distressed over the opposition to a bill for

---

[1] Hannah More, *Works,* vol. xi, " Thoughts on the Manners of the Great," " On the Religion of the Fashionable World."

[2] Sir James Stephen, *Essays in Ecclesiastical Biography,* p. 170.

[3] He did not succeed to the title until 1851, being known until then as Lord Ashley. To avoid confusion, however, he will be referred to throughout as Lord Shaftesbury.

remedying the condition of chimney-sweeps, said, " I find that Evangelical religionists are not those on whom I can rely.   The Factory Question, and every question for what is called ' humanity ', receive as much support from the ' men of the world ' as from the men who say they will have nothing to do with it! " [1]

Yet " enthusiasm " could on occasion serve the most practical ends.   No better example presents itself than the agitation against the new Poor Law of 1834.   Bible in hand, Richard Oastler, a churchman, and J. R. Stephens, a Methodist minister, conducted their campaign with all the fervor of a " revival ".   " It was a Wesley-Whitefield crusade again. The appeal was to the same class of people, the methods were the same, only the object was different." [2]   The emotional appeal thus undoubtedly sustained and sharpened the zeal of deeper spirits; the sacrifices of some of the leaders— Shaftesbury included—cannot be fully explained without it.

It would be wrong to estimate the relation of Evangelical doctrine to reform without considering the works of those who professed it.   If it seemed to act as a social anaesthetic in many cases, the simple fact remains that Evangelicals were more active in ameliorating abuses of the time than any other group within the Church.   Indeed, the theoretical statement of their aims frequently did them something less than justice. William Wilberforce held that " the greatest measure of temporal comforts and spiritual privileges " was assured by the existing order, but he wished to revise that order in effect by destroying slavery and the powerful slave interest in England. Shaftesbury called himself a conservative, yet he helped to initiate social democracy by legislative action.   Instances of this kind show that Evangelical churchmen did not rely

[1] E. Hodder, *Life and Work of the Seventh Earl of Shaftesbury,* vol. i, p. 300.

[2] Mark Hovell, *The Chartist Movement,* pp. 88-9.

solely on the regenerating effect of the gospels to achieve their ends.   Ardent philanthropists, politicians when it suited their need, moralists who found a place in their catechism for everything from cosmetics to cosmology, why did they yet remain aloof from many of the organized reform movements of the time?   The limitations of their religious viewpoint do not seem to be a full explanation.   One is tempted to allow greater weight to two other factors: their class affiliations, which have already been alluded to, and the stigma of irreligion which attached to most of the contemporaneous reform movements.[1]   It is said of Granville Sharp, " He learned to love the Quaker, to be kind to the Presbyterian, to pity the Atheist, and to endure even the Roman Catholic." [2] The characterization would do for most of his Evangelical friends, who strove to promote co-operation, at least among Protestant sects.   But they regarded atheists with aversion instead of pity.   In " The Loyal Subject's Political Creed " Hannah More denounced an unholy alliance:

> I *think* Heaven's punishments are due
> To Atheism and Sedition too;
> I think for these 'tis God's own sending,
> And *not* because our laws want mending.[3]

The Oxford Movement was not without respectable ancestry.   In a sense it continued the High Church traditions of the preceding century and many of its tenets had been formulated by a group of divines a generation before.[4]   But

[1] W. G. H. Cook (*Political Science Quarterly*, vol. xxxix, p. 439) mentions five infidel papers which supported parliamentary reform.

[2] Stephen, *op. cit.*, p. 313.

[3] *Works,* vol. ii, p. 100; C. E. Raven, *Christian Socialism*, pp. 14 *et seq.*; W. L. Mathieson, *England in Transition*, p. 156.

[4] F. W. Cornish, *The English Church in the Nineteenth Century*, vol. i, p. 65.

the Tractarians speedily found themselves charged with Romanism and Popery, a criticism which some of them eventually justified. The Catholic doctrine and the controversy which it aroused are said to have had several adverse consequences for social reform—they are charged with having alienated the masses from institutional religion, " diverted the attention of the Church from the crying needs of the time into meticulous and often unedifying arguments upon matters of archeology," and encouraged indiscriminate attacks upon Liberalism.[1]   The first charge rests either on prejudice or on a very limited observation of the facts.   To prove or disprove it would require a lengthy study which cannot be undertaken here.   The other two, however, need a little further clarification.

It is admitted even by apologists that the Tractarians for the most part did not concern themselves with specific abuses.[2] But to assert that " fifty years were wasted in lawsuits over regeneration and ritual, vestments and incense, and the precise meaning of sixteenth century rubrics " is to give a wrong impression of this aspect of their system.[3]   Without pressing the point that both parties to a controversy must share the responsibility for it, ceremonial was—to the Tractarians— something more than an adventure in antiquarianism.   It was the necessary accompaniment of a central idea—" the visible Church ".   The Church for them was something more than the aggregate of believers.   It had a corporate existence and a body of truths which must be defended, even against the state.   It operated, therefore, as a social bond.   When

---

[1] J. A. Froude, *Short Studies* (fourth series), p. 21; Raven, *op. cit.,* p. 19; Morley, *op. cit.,* vol. i, p. 163.

[2] C. L. Marson, *God's Co-operative Society*, pp. 70-71.

[3] C. E. Raven, *op. cit.,* p. 21.   Mr. Raven pays his respects to the corporate idea, but in the writer's opinion underestimates the significance of its relation to ceremonial so far at least as the Tractarians were concerned.

the principle of solidarity was assaulted clergymen must boldly intervene. " It is said that the Clergy should abstain from politics. . . Are we to speak when individuals sin, and not when a nation, which is but a collection of individuals? " [1] And the clergy speak with the greater assurance because through ordination they possess apostolic authority.[2] The Tractarians opposed Liberalism in its early Victorian sense. " Pride of intellect " and " false liberty " ran counter to their notions of authority. The Reformation which they were trying to explain away was a principal source of Liberalism. Too conscious of the unorthodox philosophy behind most projects of reform, they looked askance at changes which we are accustomed to regard as thoroughly desirable. Pusey, referring to the emancipation of the West Indian negroes, speaks callously of " paying twenty millions for a theory about slavery." [3] Tractarians were pretty sure to anathematize any attempt to meddle with the privileges of the Church. On the other hand some phases of early nineteenth-century Liberalism seem less admirable than formerly, and we can sympathize with the Tractarians' distrust of utilitarianism and laissez-faire.[4] Their antipathy is expressed in unmistakable terms. *The British Magazine,* an organ of the Oxford Movement, attacked Harriet Martineau's version of Malthus for teaching us

to see our fellow-creatures suffer and die. . . . It need not be argued that the bad management of others has taught the poor to be improvident. The fact that they are so, and that they suffer dreadfully, is enough. The cure for their improvidence, and

[1] Tracts 2 and 11; J. H. Newman, *The Arians of the Fourth Century,* fourth ed., p. 259.

[2] Tract 1.

[3] Morley, *op. cit.,* vol. i, p. 103, quoting Liddon's *Life of Pusey.*

[4] J. A. Froude, *op. cit.,* p. 154; J. H. Newman, *Letters and Correspondence,* p. 179.

the relief from its present evils, must go hand in hand. It may not be easy to devise such remedies; it is very easy to cut the knot, and say, " Do nothing for them." [1]

Tractarians proposed nothing new in the way of direct action in social matters. For this the academic nature of the movement was in part accountable. A good deal of energy was consumed in disputes about ritual for which the party was not entirely to blame. But the conception of the Church as a society of believers with mutual obligations, capable of existing independently of the state, and having sufficient authority to regulate the activities of its members, political— when moral issues were involved—as well as religious,— this conception was to have the greatest influence on the attitude of the Church toward reform during the succeeding period. It was not, indeed, entirely barren of results even before 1850.

The Young England party flourished in the early 1840's at the period when Tractarianism was in full vigor. The group derived its importance not from numbers but from the social standing of its members, the novelty of its political philosophy, and the patronage of Disraeli. Young men, some of them fresh from Cambridge, they entered public life with an exalted notion of the social mission of the aristocracy. The brilliant and temperamental George Smythe, and Lord John Manners, artless and idealistic,[2] were the leading figures, apart from Disraeli. They had come under the influence of the Oxford Movement through acquaintance with Frederic William Faber, a friend of Newman, and rapidly assimilated whatever it offered to undermine Radicalism and to fortify paternalism. Disraeli devoted two novels, *Coningsby* and

---

[1] Vol. iii, p. 95.

[2] Manners was the author of the unforgettable couplet:
　　" Let wealth and commerce, laws and learning die,
　　　But leave us still our old Nobility ! "

Sybil, to an exposition of the principles of Young England as he interpreted them. "The Church," he said, "was in theory, and once it had been in practice, the spiritual and intellectual trainer of the people," and he wished to use it as a principal means of putting his theories into effect.[1] For some years Young England was a force to be reckoned with in English politics, and its spirit remained after the party had dispersed. Tractarianism thus early contributes to a movement for social and political reform, and also to the future success of Disraeli. "It is not fanciful to imagine," says his biographer, "that through the influence of Faber and Young England the Oxford movement helped to shape the policy of Queen Victoria and her favorite Prime Minister a generation later." [2]

The Broad Church party was in some respects a reincarnation of the eighteenth-century school of Paley and Butler. The anxiety of men like Arnold, Maurice, Stanley, Hampden, and others to make religion reasonable by discarding or reinterpreting troublesome doctrines continues the rationalistic attitude of their predecessors. This relaxation of dogma in time perhaps served to keep many within the Church who might otherwise have found the new developments in science and historical criticism disturbing, and so preserved or enlarged the audience to which churchmen might broach their theories of social reform. Yet it must be admitted that the advantage before 1850 was prospective rather than immediate. Evangelicals and Tractarians equally abhorred the new policy of concession where it was impossible to convince, Broad Churchmen were not particularly charitable in defending themselves, and the only effect seemed to be the addition of a new disrupting element to the Church.

[1] *Lothair,* General Preface (1870).

[2] W. F. Monypenny and G. E. Buckle, *Life of Benjamin Disraeli,* vol. ii, chap. 6; Harry Graham, *Splendid Failures,* chap. on George Smythe.

But the first requisite of a reforming party is to be aware of the currents of thought and the needs of its time. Since Broad Churchmen had freed themselves to an extent from tradition and authority they had to discover principles of action in contemporary thought and practice. Unlike Evangelicals or Tractarians, they were not easily frightened by words. Dean Milman did not scruple to compare Abraham to an oriental sheik.[1] Arnold discovered some justice in Cobbett's viewpoint and even attempted to imitate his *Political Register*. " Liberalism " and " Conservatism " meant nothing to him as political parties—he was ready to support the one which seemed to represent progress.[2] Maurice was content to be called a socialist.

The consequence of this eclecticism in searching out the truth is well illustrated in the function which Broad Churchmen assigned to the Church in the regeneration of society. Milman would have the clergy serve their parishioners, " lead the model family of order, of peace, of piety, of contentedness, of resignation in affliction, of hopefulness under all circumstances," and abandon attempts at exerting their authority.[3] Arnold, appealing to the example of the prophets Isaiah, Jeremiah, Amos, and Habbakuk, fulminated against the craven advice that clergymen should preach subordination and obedience—" I say, God forbid they should." [4] Since the machinery of the state was beginning to be used for reform it was natural that he should look upon the close co-operation of Church and State as indispensable. The result is his curious theory of their identity, in which he applies " the principles of the Gospel to the legislation and administration of [the] state."

[1] Cornish, *op. cit.*, vol. i, p. 186.

[2] A. P. Stanley, *op. cit.*, vol. i, pp. 75, 284, 403; vol. ii, p. 19.

[3] H. H. Milman, *Savonarola, Erasmus, and Other Essays*, pp. 442-3.

[4] A. P. Stanley, *op. cit.*, vol. i, p. 284.

I cannot understand what is the good of a national Church, if it be not to Christianize the nation and introduce the principles of Christianity into man's social and civil relations, and expose the wickedness of that spirit which maintains the game laws, and in agriculture and trade seems to think that there is no such thing as covetousness, and that if a man is not dishonest, he has nothing to do but to make all the profit of his capital that he can.[1]

Stanley accepted his political theory with reservations.

It is not so much that Church and State are one as that the Church, in its highest sense, is equally above both Church and State—represented in different ages, sometimes more by the one, sometimes more by the other.

Like Arnold, he believed that Christianity ought to impregnate "all a man's relations with life, all his opinions ".[2]

Maurice assigned a balancing function to Church and State separately.

The State, I think, cannot be Communist; never will be; never ought to be. It is by nature and law conservative of individual rights, individual possessions. To uphold them it may be compelled (it must be) to recognize another principle than that of private property; but only by accident; only by going out of its sphere, as it so rightly did in the case of the factory children. But the Church, I hold, is Communist in principle; conservative of property and individual rights only by accident; bound to recognize them, but not as its own special work, not as the chief object of human society or existence.[3]

The Broad Church movement produced men who were worldly enough and courageous enough to apply their beliefs

---

[1] Stanley, *op. cit.*, vol. i, pp. 27, 51, 276.

[2] R. E. Prothero and G. G. Bradley, *Life and Correspondence of Dean Stanley*, vol. i, pp. 384, 184.

[3] F. Maurice, *The Life of Frederick Denison Maurice*, vol. ii, p. 8.

to current social problems. Maurice and Kingsley as promoters of Christian Socialism will demand attention later on. Of all Broad Churchmen interested in reform, however, Thomas Arnold occupied the most strategic position. More important still, he knew how to use it. As headmaster of Rugby he shaped the opinions of younger men and his ideas bore fruit in the generation of Thomas Hughes and Arthur Stanley.[1] Never entering the battle like the Christian Socialists or proposing anything radically new, he was intensely alive to the evils of his day and stood always ready to pass judgment on schemes of amendment, usually deciding in favor of the newer views. So he approves the abolition of slavery in the West Indies, and in 1829 writes a pamphlet on " The Christian Duty of Conceding the Claims of the Roman Catholics." " At one time," he wrote, " I had the notion of going over there [to Ireland] and taking Irish pupils, to try what one can could do towards civilizing the people, by trying to civilize and Christianize their gentry." He lectured at mechanics' institutes, carefully avoiding any appearance of condescension. The Reform Bill of 1832 won his qualified approval: he did not consider it in any sense millennial. In the same way he accepted the new Poor Law in principle, but in 1839 agreed with the Chartists that it had done more moral harm than good. Chartism itself he believed to be founded upon a reasonable dissatisfaction. " It fills me with astonishment to see anti-slavery and missionary societies so busy with the ends of the earth, and yet all the worst evils of slavery and heathenism among ourselves." He proposed a society " for calling attention to the condition of the lower orders." [2]

The temper of Broad Churchmen was in no sense revolutionary, however completely they had divested themselves

---

1 Cornish, *op. cit.*, vol. i, p. 190.

2 Stanley, *op. cit.*, vol. i, pp. 73, 234-5, 395; vol. ii, pp. 133, 147, 175.

of an unreasoning fear of reform. Besides the events of 1830 and 1848 on the continent, agricultural disturbances and Chartism in England constantly reminded them of the uncouthness and intemperance of popular movements. An undercurrent of mistrust sometimes crops out in Arnold's writings. What the " lower people " need, he thinks, is moral rather than political improvement. " I would, therefore, carefully avoid exciting political violence in them." He tries to be cautious in dealing out subversive ideas to his students, and in a course in history passes over the French Revolution as too delicate a subject for the immature. There is a certain grim humor in his description of his own position. " It is really too great a folly to be talked of as a revolutionist, with a family of young children, and a house and income that I should be rather puzzled to match in America, if I were obliged to change my quarters." His radicalism, he protested, was conservative. " There is nothing so revolutionary, because there is nothing so convulsive to society, as the strain to keep things fixed." [1] But Arnold does not stand alone. Kingsley, too, knew how to be cautious. The author of *Cheap Clothes and Nasty* is almost unrecognizable in the parson who dispenses a sedative bromide like the following to his flock: " It is just as easy to sell one's soul for five pounds as for five thousand. . . I do not see that rich people are at all more unjust about money than poor ones." [2]

The foregoing pages have (it is hoped) indicated the social significance of Evangelical, Tractarian, and Broad Church principles. But the conscience of churchmen was stirred not only by their reading of Anglican doctrine but by the teachings and accomplishments of Dissenters. The " Nonconformist conscience " busied itself with prison reform, the abolition of slavery, education, temperance, immorality in

[1] Stanley, *op. cit.*, vol. i, pp. 293, 282-3.

[2] *Village Sermons and Town and Country Sermons*, p. 355.

literature and art, and almost every other problem of the century. In some instances, notably temperance, the Church of England merely followed the leadership of the sects, sometimes protestingly and at a distance, but often without contributing any ideas distinctly its own. The Evangelical party was to some extent the vehicle of dissenting influence within the Church. But the full history of this influence has its place in the social history of the Free Churches rather than in that of the Church of England.

So far we have been concerned with the environment, material and intellectual, which molded the opinions and governed the actions of churchmen in the field of social relations. It remains to sketch the rôle played by the Church in the adjustment of specific problems of conflict during the first half of the nineteenth century.

THE SOCIAL ACTION OF THE CHURCH

1. Education

If widespread education is accepted as basic to any scheme of reform in which something more than unreasoning acquiescence is expected of the general population, the Church of England must be given its share of credit for providing this foundation. Yet it is safe to say that so far as this aspect of education was considered at all it did not appeal very vividly to the majority of churchmen.

Education had always been looked upon as a function of the national Church, and since about 1700, through the efforts of the Society for Promoting Christian Knowledge, a movement had been in progress to provide free instruction for the masses. As the idea became more widely accepted, the Society for Bettering the Condition of the Poor (founded in 1796) turned its energies in that direction, and a plan of education on a national scale was definitely adopted when in 1811 the National Society for Promoting the Education of

the Poor in the Principles of the Established Church came
into existence.[1]   As the names of two of these societies indicate, the members believed that education ought to be firmly
grounded in religion.   This idea was brought to perfection
in the Sunday schools.   Thus an admirer says of the latter,

Religion pervaded it all.   Every part of the work seems to be
religious work, distribution of sponges, slates, books.   They
taught the alphabet to shambling urchins as in the glow of
eternal things; cyphered a sum in glory; gave a lesson in
grammar or dictated a line in spelling as if Christ Himself
presided over it.[2]

Education was given either in daily schools for children
or in Sunday schools for children and adults.   Aside from
religion the curriculum usually consisted of little beyond the
three R's, and reading and writing were generally considered
sufficient.   Some, like Hannah More, even objected to the
teaching of writing as leading to fanaticism.[3]   The intention
of the patrons of Church schools was almost wholly conservative.   " A system of moral and religious instruction,
connecting the rising generation with our civil and ecclesiastical establishment, is not only the first and most beneficial
act of charity, but the wisest and most politic measure of the
state." [4]   A note of patronage and charity in the bad sense
rings through the utterances of churchmen.   Francis Place
was careful to exclude the words " poor " and " laboring
poor " from the by-laws of the British and Foreign Schools
Society,[5] but no such delicacy troubled the Church organiza-

---

[1] Cornish, *op. cit.*, vol. i, pp. 95-6.

[2] W. J. Bain, *A Paper on the Early History of Sunday Schools
Especially in Northamptonshire*, p. 18.

[3] J. L. and B. Hammond, *The Town Labourer*, p. 58.

[4] *Christian Observer*, vol. ii, p. 180, quoting the nineteenth report of
the S. B. C. P.

[5] Graham Wallas, *Life of Francis Place*, p. 95.

tions. Teachers as well as students were to be impressed with the duties of their station. The principal of St. Mark's Training College said that " to produce schoolmasters for the poor, the endeavour must be, on the one hand, to raise the students morally and intellectually to a certain standard, while, on the other hand, we train them to lowly service." [1]

Nevertheless even such a thoroughly safe type of education might bring unexpected or unwished-for results. Malthus considered it " a great national disgrace that the education of the lower classes of people in England should be left merely to a few Sunday schools supported by a subscription from individuals, who of course can give to the course of instruction in them any bias which they please." [2] But once the " lower classes " were taught how to read no one could answer for their tastes. Cobbett's *Political Register* or Paine's *Age of Reason* were likely to be as popular as Venn's *Complete Duty of Man.* Churchmen would have been strangely lacking in intelligence if they had not seen the danger involved—they deserve some credit for taking the risk. Some of the country clergy were truly conservative. They looked upon all education as of doubtful value. Hannah More was considered a dangerous radical in Somerset.[3]

Churchmen and Nonconformists were unable for the most part to co-operate in education. Each group maintained its own schools. Even the Sunday School Union with which the Church associated itself proved unsatisfactory to the Tractarians and the connection had to be broken in 1843.[4] And if the private orthodoxies of the sects made it difficult for them to work together voluntarily, they were no less dis-

[1] Cornish, *op. cit.,* vol. i, p. 202.

[2] *Principle of Population* (third ed.), vol. i, p. 418.

[3] Cornish, *op. cit.,* vol. i, p. 86.

[4] *The Encyclopedia of Sunday Schools and Religious Education,* vol. i, p. 260.

trustful of a yoke imposed by the state. Brougham's education bill of 1820 had to be withdrawn because he tried to combine religion in a neutral form with state education, and Hume's proposal of 1843 met defeat because he attempted to separate them. In 1843, again, the educational clauses were dropped from the factory act principally because of Nonconformist disapproval. The only recourse for the present seemed to be state contributions to existing agencies. In 1839 the government succeeded in appointing—not without resistance—a committee of the privy council to distribute such grants.[1] Although the educational efforts of the Church and other private agencies had been considerable, " it was said in 1837 in the House of Commons that 49 per cent of the boys and 57 per cent of the girls—13 and 14 years old— could not read, and that 67 per cent of the boys and 88 per cent of the girls could not write." [2] It seemed evident to many that private efforts, however zealous, were inadequate. If state aid was necessary the Church must share the blame for obstructing it.

2. State Intervention

While the Church was applying itself more or less successfully to the moral and intellectual elevation of the people through education, other schemes of reform engaged its attention, either to be welcomed or to be opposed. We may divide these proposals into plans which involved governmental intervention for the benefit of the weaker members of society and those which were designed to encourage self-help either directly, or indirectly by the removal of legal obstacles to it.

[1] Hodder, *op. cit.*, vol. i, p. 457; Walpole, *op. cit.*, vol. iv, p. 185; Cornish, *op. cit.*, vol. i, pp. 98, 210.

[2] Walpole, *op. cit.*, vol. vi, p. 393.

(a) The Poor Law

The state had recognized since the time of Elizabeth a responsibility for the continued existence if not the comfortable maintenance of its able-bodied as well as its helpless poor. But the system of relief had been perverted into a caricature of benevolence. It had demoralized the working class—particularly agricultural labor — by disguising exploitation under the mask of charity. The large landholders reaped the benefits of this policy and willingly shifted the burden of supporting the laborers onto the rest of the community. A reformed Parliament, however, could hardly permit this condition of affairs to continue, sentiment toward the landed class being what it then was. A Commission on the Poor Laws accordingly set out in 1832 not so much to investigate the existing system as to accumulate evidence against it, and to bring in proposals for reform. Blomfield, bishop of London, and Sumner, bishop of Chester, represented the Church, but the most active members of the Commission were Sturges Bourne and Nassau Senior.[1] The philosophy which underlay the recommendations of the Commission seems to have been Malthusianism with a slight—a very slight—tincture of old-fashioned benevolence. Lord Althorp in supporting the scheme admitted that any system of poor relief was "contrary to the strict principles of political economy."[2]

The Poor Law of 1834 passed both houses of Parliament unopposed except by a few conservatives and radicals. Cobbett fought the proceedings at every step, although he admitted the evils of the old system.[3] But the difficulties of the government really began when the law was securely on the

[1] Walpole, *op. cit.*, vol. iii, p. 441; G. Slater, *The Making of Modern England*, p. 99.

[2] G. Nicholls, *History of the English Poor Law*, vol. ii, p. 263.

[3] G. D. H. Cole, *Life of William Cobbett*, chap. 25.

statute book. A period of trade depression added the protests of workmen of the towns to those of rural laborers, and organized attempts to prevent introduction of the new system occurred in various parts of the country. Among churchmen, Richard Oastler was one of the most energetic agitators against the law, and the clergy themselves were sometimes moved to protest. What became known as the " Andover scandal " was brought to light by a clergyman of that town who exposed the cruelties practiced in the local workhouse. This created such an impression that its influence was felt for a long period and even caused a defeat of Peel's government in the heat of the Corn Law struggle in 1846.[1] We also find the clergy of Petworth joining magistrates and landholders in a petition to parliament protesting against the local administration. The deserving poor man was denied relief unless the whole family went to the workhouse where husband and wife were regularly separated. The petitioners believed that large families might be aided by receiving some of the children only into these institutions. They " are deeply interested in [the] diminution [of the poor rate], but wish not to see that diminution brought about by a system of injustice and oppression." [2]

Another feature of the system particularly exasperated the clergy. In presenting a petition from Macclesfield to the House of Lords for repeal or alteration of the law, Bishop Philpotts denounced the practice of preventing inmates of workhouses from attending the parish church.[3] The matter had already been brought to the attention of the Poor Law Commissioners by a letter from the clergy of twenty-six out

[1] S. Walpole, *op. cit.*, vol. iv, p 365; G Nicholls, *op. cit.*, vol. iii, pp. 368-70. The complaint was that insufficient food was causing depraved appetites among the inmates.

[2] *British Magazine*, vol. x, p. 356.

[3] *Ibid.*, vol. x, p. 85.

of the thirty parishes in the Eastry Union. "We are aware," they said, "that the service is performed once on every Sabbath by the chaplain at the Union Poorhouse; but we fervently hope that this may not be considered a sufficient reason for their being prevented from attending the house of God at another hour on that sacred day." The Commissioners replied in a spirit consistent with the tenor of the act which had created them.

The legislature having confided to the Commissioners the important task of maturing and carrying into operation the Workhouse system, they have devoted the most anxious attention to the devising of such regulations for these establishments as shall, on the one hand, provide for the poor a certain refuge from destitution and on the other shall render these asylums less eligible than the dwellings of the independent labourer— or of those who, by industry and forethought, may secure for themselves a provision for their old age—and the Commissioners have arrived at the conclusion that these objects cannot be obtained if those who take refuge in the Workhouse are allowed to quit its precincts and return to them again, unless they go out with the *bona fide* intention of procuring the means of support by their own labor, or through the assistance of others.

The petitioners had pointed out that the church was only a furlong's distance from the workhouse and that " some person might be appointed to attend the paupers this short distance, and prevent their going elsewhere, and so abusing the liberty, if extended to them." But reason (or what passed for it) triumphed over sentiment and the " Bashaws of Somerset House " were immovable.[1]

As a later writer saw it, the Church in criticizing the poor law " used its influence to aggravate the irritation of the

[1] *British Magazine*, vol. x, pp. 157-8, 188-9.

masses, and to enhance an agitation which it should have endeavoured to see allayed." [1]

(b) Labor Legislation

If criticism of the poor-law administration was largely unavailing, reformers were more successful in gaining the reluctant intervention of the state to improve the conditions of labor. Legislation to this end was confined to restricting the employment of women and children in the period under review.[2] One of the earliest subjects of agitation had been the use of children as chimney-sweeps, a matter in which churchmen had displayed considerable interest. An ineffective act was passed in 1788 dealing with the subject. The bishop of Durham in 1799 protested against the practice of compelling chimney-sweeps to cry their masters' trade in the streets. The Society for Bettering the Condition of the Poor, a Church organization, endeavored to awaken the humanity of the masters, but without much success.[3] In spite of a good deal of activity and the submission of many bills, no further legislation was obtained until 1834 when apprenticeship of children under ten years of age was forbidden. In 1803 a Society for Superseding Climbing Boys had been established and had distributed many sweeping machines *gratis* but it had encountered much opposition from interested parties. The bishop of Winchester as president commented in 1838 on the " inhuman practice " which resulted in disease and in unemployment at the age of fifteen or sixteen.[4] From 1840 onward Lord Shaftesbury applied

[1] Walpole, *op. cit.*, vol. iv, p. 367.

[2] B. L. Hutchins and A. Harrison, *History of Factory Legislation*, chaps. 1-6; J. L. and B. Hammond, *The Town Labourer*, chaps. 8-9.

[3] J. L. and B. Hammond, *The Town Labourer*, pp. 180, 184; Hodder, *op. cit.*, vol. i, pp. 295 *et seq.*

[4] *Church of England Magazine*, vol. iv, p. 11, supplement.

himself to the evil, but it was not until 1875 after several more ineffectual measures had been passed that an act introduced by himself finally ended it.[1]

The hesitant experiments of the state in factory legislation before 1830 seem not to have commanded much support among churchmen. With the entrance of Lord Shaftesbury upon the field, however, the movement received a large infusion of religion. He was, in his own words, " an Evangelical of the Evangelicals," and all his utterances were charged with the faith that was in him. " I am satisfied," he said in 1884, " that most of the great philanthropic movements of the century have sprung from them [the Evangelicals]," and he was as ready to welcome the co-operation of Methodists as of Anglicans. His social attitude is summed up in the words " Christianity is not a state of opinion and speculation. Christianity is essentially practical." [2]

It is not the purpose here to detail the campaign for adequate protection of women and children in industry, but to indicate the assistance which Shaftesbury and his allies received from other churchmen. Richard Oastler, of course, again rendered invaluable aid as a popular agitator, although Shaftesbury accused him of " dogging his [Shaftesbury's] latter years " in Parliament because Oastler thought he was too willing to compromise.[3] *The British Magazine,* also, attacked the entire factory system in 1833, but was pessimistic about the results of legislation so long as parents were ready to sacrifice their children. " If factories cannot exist without these evils, is there anyone—even the veriest Utilitarian that breathes—who will dare to say that they ought not to be swept off the face of the earth, which they pollute and

[1] Hodder, *op. cit.,* vol. iii, pp. 157-8.
[2] *Ibid.,* vol. i, p. 327; vol. iii, p. 3.
[3] *Ibid.,* vol. ii, p. 211.

poison?" [1] This was after the lurid disclosures of Sadler's committee, which is accused of having overstepped the limits of strict truth in its humanitarian enthusiasm.[2] In 1841 the Rev. Henry Christmas placed his journal, *The Church of England Magazine,* at Shaftesbury's disposal.[3] At the very beginning of the Ten Hours' struggle, G. S. Bull, vicar of Bierly near Bradford, had thrown himself into the agitation with devotion and effect. It was he who had been deputed to ask Lord Shaftesbury to take Sadler's place as chairman of the Select Committee of 1831 when Sadler was defeated for reëlection to Parliament. For a short time during 1832 and 1833 he edited, in collaboration with Charles Walker, a weekly journal, *The British Labourer's Protector and Factory Child's Friend.* In 1837, with Oastler and J. R. Stephens, he preached adequate factory inspection before crowded meetings in the manufacturing districts.[4] The Young England party, too, gave their support to Shaftesbury. A clergyman of great influence who took a deep interest in factory legislation was Samuel Wilberforce, bishop of Oxford, to whom the Central Short Time Committee representing the operatives of the West Riding sent a vote of thanks for his exertions.[5] Shaftesbury himself praised the attitude of the bishops in general toward the Ten Hours Bill of 1847.[6]

[1] *British Magazine,* vol. iii, p. 318; vol. iv, p. 565.

[2] *Cf.* W. H. Hutt's article "The Factory System of the Early Nineteenth Century" (*Economica,* March, 1926, p. 78) in which the accuracy of the committee's report is challenged.

[3] Hodder, *op. cit.,* vol. i, p. 363.

[4] Hutchins and Harrison, *op. cit.,* pp. 33-4, 46, 58; Hodder, *op. cit.,* vol. ii, p. 209. Bull's periodical is listed in J. B. Williams' *Guide to the Printed Materials for English Social and Industrial History,* vol. ii, p. 191.

[5] Monypenny and Buckle, *op. cit.,* vol. ii, p. 235; Ashwell and Wilberforce, *op. cit.,* vol. i, p. 390.

[6] Hodder, *op. cit.,* vol. ii, p. 193.

Yet Shaftesbury accused the majority of the clergy of indifference to his projects.   Few ministers of any denomination aided him in the Ten Hours' campaign, "at first, not one,
except the Rev. Mr. Bull; . . . and even to the very last,
very few, so cowed were they (or in themselves so indifferent) by the overwhelming influence of the cotton lords.   I
had more aid from the medical men than the divine profession." [1]   There may have been other reasons why Anglicans
remained aloof.   Theological differences often made political
co-operatin difficult, and Shaftesbury's affiliations with Nonconformists no doubt cooled the enthusiasm of members of
his own Church for his projects.   He himself was probably
not entirely guiltless in this respect, for he ignored the Christian Social program of Maurice and Kingsley, an attitude
which was very likely due to his distaste for Broad Church
doctrine.   Yet Shaftesbury remained a devout churchman,
and his unremitting labor in the cause of reform could not
but reflect credit on Anglicanism as a whole.

3. Self-Help

One of the most penetrating observers of modern Germany
has pointed out the striking contrast between German and
English social policy during the nineteenth century.[2]   German
solicitude for the working class was a continuation of the
traditional paternalism which undertook to solve the concrete
problems of labor by state intervention, whereas in England
more confidence was placed in voluntary associations.   These,
if given proper legal encouragement, might be left to work
out the details of a better social order in the heat of conflict,
the state assuming the rôle of a benevolent umpire.

[1] Hodder, *op. cit.*, vol. i, p. 346; vol. ii, p. 209.
[2] W. H. Dawson, *The German Empire*, vol. ii, pp. 41-2.

(a) Trade Unionism

Trade unions, which were organizations of this character, fought their battle for recognition and secured moderate benefits for their members during this period, without any conspicuous opposition or aid from the Church. William Wilberforce, however, no doubt voiced the opinions of a certain number of churchmen when he denounced labor combinations as a " general disease in our Society " and urged the passage of the notorious act of 1799. It therefore seems like poetic justice to find the clergy, magistrates and other philanthropic citizens of Leicester threatened in 1816 with indictment for criminal combination by the neighboring manufacturers because they raised a fund to support workers who could not secure employment at the full rate of wages.[1] The Christian Socialists very much later seem to have been the first churchmen to give trade unionism any active support.

(b) Political Reform and Chartism

During the years 1829 to 1842 old-fashioned trade unionism was in a state of decline.[2] The working class deserted the pedestrian methods of economic warfare and grasped at the more alluring instruments of political democracy. The Reform Bill of 1832 was far from satisfactory to the workers. It displeased the Church also, though for an entirely different reason. Anglicans realized that with the admission of the middle class to political rights, a swarm of Dissenters would be let loose upon the Establishment. " The attitude of the Church of England in regard to the First Reform Bill may be summed up in a single sentence. There was but one class opposed to the Bill with anything like unanimity—the

[1] J. L. and B. Hammond, *op. cit.*, p. 117; S. and B. Webb, *History of Trade Unionism*, p. 94.

[2] S. and B. Webb, *History of Trade Unionism*, p. 112.

clergy of the Church of England." [1]   The Church was little
more sympathetic when electoral reform arrayed itself in the
unconventional garments of Chartism.   And as the Church
looked askance at Chartism, so the Chartists were restrained
by no false notions of decorum in criticizing the Church.   The
adjurations of the clergy to obey lawful authority, to fear
God and honor the king, were answered by vigorous description of the Church as " old mother hypocrisy ", " Super-
stitious Old Hog ", and " a system of vile priestcraft ".   A
sentimental attachment to the good old days of paternalism
and yeoman virtue characterized both the Oxford Movement
and the wing of Chartism led by O'Connor and O'Brien, but
the similarity of ideals was obscured by the haze of conflict.
Nevertheless individuals within the Church—for example,
Thomas Arnold and Lord Shaftesbury—admitted that the
agitation sprang from just grievances, while a small group of
churchmen actively participated in it. [2]   Above all, the dying
flicker of Chartism set off Christian Socialist energies in
1848.

(c) Friendly Societies

Combined action on the part of the working classes was
not limited to political associations.   Many felt that something might be gleaned from the existing order by establishing
Friendly Societies for the practice of the middle-class virtues.
The Friendly-Society movement appears to have received considerable encouragement from churchmen.   To a generation
which professed to believe that the sad condition of the
pauper was traceable to his own negligence, friendly or provident societies and savings banks had the aspect of a social

---

[1] W. G. H. Cook, " Electoral Reform and Organized Christianity in
England " (*Political Science Quarterly*, vol. xxxix, p. 488).

[2] H. U. Faulkner, *Chartism and the Churches*, pp. 18, 28-9, 35, 59
et seq., 74; Hodder, *op. cit.*, vol. i, p. 323.

panacea. "No reasonable doubt can be entertained," said *The Christian Observer,* "that the most effectual plan to render the laboring classes industrious, sober and frugal is to induce them to depend on their own exertions." It was reported that the Farthinghoe Clothing Club had wiped out head-money paid to able-bodied laborers, reduced the parish expenditure, and eliminated illegitimacy.[1] The salutary effect which the presence of such a society would have on the less thrifty was explained by the vicar of Clapton:

Your readers have only to imagine A, who has *not* deposited, seeing a sack of coals shot into B's (his next door neighbor), who has it every fortnight during the winter without anything *then* to pay for it, to understand how easily the inclination to deposit may be created in the poor, and continued in them.[2]

But if a society enlivened its rather unromantic activities by surrounding them with mystic ritual and secret oaths it was likely to suggest class war and revolution to timorous clergymen. For this reason "pulpit and press . . . rang with denunciations" of Forestry, Shepherdry, Druidism, and Oddfellowship. But in 1834 when the esoteric rites were replaced by "new 'lecture' books, more after the style of prize essays on the virtues," even these lodges became respectable.[3] Thus when the "Curate of a Market Town" wrote doubtfully to the *British Magazine* about the propriety of admitting benefit societies in their regalia to the church a correspondent replied in defense of the practice. Evidence of the thawing climate in ecclesiastical circles is the action of the vicar of Leeds, W. F. Hook (later dean of Chichester),

[1] *Christian Observer,* vol. iv, p. 241; vol. xx, p. 490; *British Magazine,* vol. i, p. 478.

[2] *British Magazine,* vol. iii, p. 59.

[3] J. F. Wilkinson, *The Friendly Society Movement,* pp. 27, 29.

who in 1837 joined a lodge which had been denied the use of the church by his predecessor.[1]

(d) The Co-operative Movement

More far-reaching plans of co-operation met with a less certain reception from the Church.   The schemes of Robert Owen at first enjoyed a measure of approval.   As a philanthropic manufacturer he was invited to attend a meeting of notables to consider relief of distress in 1816.   This conference, which was graced by the most august names, elected him to its permanent committee, the archbishop of Canterbury, at that time a friend of his, being chairman.   Owen's report to this committee contained the germs of his later theory of communism although it was stated in terms moderated to the prejudices of his colleagues.   They appear not to have been alarmed at his proposal to establish co-operative communities for the relief of the unemployed, but feeling that consideration of such a scheme was beyond their competence advised him to present it to the newly created parliamentary committee on the poor laws.   Here he met with humiliating neglect, and in revulsion against it cast aside useless diplomacy.   Openly declaring an opinion he had long privately held, he assailed religion as the great obstacle to social betterment.   Up to this time (1817), as his biographer says, " he had appealed to the Government and the upper classes for favour, and had received a good measure of sympathy.   The opposition had come not from the Church, but from the Political Economists . . . and the Radicals." [2] His attack on religion was enough to have alienated the clergy, but his growing socialism and newer morality made reconciliation impossible.   Eventually the vociferous Bishop Philpotts condemned him and all his works.   A contempor-

---

[1] *British Magazine*, vol. xx, pp. 408-9; Wilkinson, *op. cit.*, p. 29.
[2] G. D. H. Cole, *Robert Owen*, pp. 133-148.

ary cartoon portrays the shrinking *New Moral World* being chased by four Old Women (the bishops of Exeter and London, the archbishop of Canterbury, and the duke of Wellington).[1]

(e) Christian Socialism

Much as the Church disliked Owen's theology, it had already sanctioned his sociology in a tepid way by approving Friendly Societies. It now surprised the critics who had taunted it with sterility by giving birth to Christian Socialism.[2] The movement began unobtrusively and grew by accretion of men and ideas. J. M. Ludlow, F. D. Maurice, and Charles Kingsley were its original promoters, and the principal later adherents were Thomas Hughes and E. V. Neale. Two of the three founders were clergymen and the movement retained its distinctly clerical aspect.

Although most of the early members were relatively obscure,—Maurice being the only one who had in 1848 anything like an established reputation,—Christian Socialism was by no means an isolated movement. Currents of reforming opinion flowed into it from many quarters. In Maurice it possessed a leader of the Broad Church party. Hughes and Arthur Stanley introduced the philanthropic tradition of Thomas Arnold. The Young England Party furnished a recruit in the person of Edward Ellison. The literary revolt against economic liberalism touched it through Carlyle's friendship with Maurice, who had married the sister of John Sterling.[3] Ruskin himself later on lectured in the Christian Socialist Working Men's College.

[1] F. Podmore, *Robert Owen*, p. 504.

[2] The fullest account of the earlier phase of Christian Socialism is to be found in C. E. Raven's *Christian Socialism, 1848-1854*. Lujo Brentano's *Die christlich-soziale Bewegung in England* is the brief work of another admirer.

[3] *Dictionary of National Biography*, vol. xiii, pp. 98-9.

Maurice in 1848 was professor of English literature and history at King's College, London. He had known Kingsley since 1844, and as chaplain of Lincoln's Inn had made the acquaintance of Ludlow, a young lawyer who was making the cause of the poor his real vocation. It was at Maurice's suggestion that Kingsley first called upon Ludlow. The visit occurred on 10 April, 1848, and the two men went to see the Chartists return from their futile demonstration on Kennington Common.[1] With this as an object lesson the three friends issued a " Proclamation to the Workmen of England ", written by Kingsley and signed " A Working Parson ". The manifesto was a declaration of sympathy and a warning against violence. It assured the workers that " almost all men who have heads and hearts " knew their wrongs were real and their complaints justified. But " do not humbug yourselves into meaning ' license ' when you cry for ' liberty.' " There is " no true freedom without virtue " and " no true industry without the fear of God and love to your fellow men." [2]

The friends soon made it plain that their sympathy was of a practical sort. They set up a night school for workingmen which enlightened the teachers perhaps as much as it educated the scholars. The school met with some difficulties at first but it eventually overcame them and furnished employment for the increasing band of workers who gathered about the original three.

Such a narrow field of activity however did not give scope enough for the enthusiasm of the group, and plans of industrial co-operation became increasingly attractive. The impetus toward practical action along these lines was given

[1] *Dictionary of National Biography*, vol. xi, p. 175; vol. xiii, p. 98; second supplement, vol. ii, pp. 487-8.

[2] F. E. Kingsley, *Charles Kingsley, his Letters and Memories of his Life*, vol. i, pp. 117-19; C. E. Raven, *op. cit.*, p. 107.

by Ludlow who on a visit to Paris in 1849 had been impressed with the apparent success of the *associations ouvrières* founded on the principles of Buchez. Maurice at first withheld his consent from the new project, and it was only when the rest decided to go on without him that he yielded. Steps had already been taken to sound out working-class opinion as to the special needs of labor. Beginning on 23 April, 1849, a series of weekly discussions took place between the associates and workingmen which had at least the effect of breaking through the reserve of both groups.[1]

Meanwhile the leaders were giving publicity to their opinions through the press, a medium in which their talents showed to the best advantage. The proclamation of 1848 was followed by the appearance of a periodical called *Politics for the People* which continued for three months and was then succeeded by a series of occasional *Tracts on Christian Socialism.* When the limitations of the *Tracts* became apparent, *The Christian Socialist,* a penny journal, was launched, the circulation of which rose from 1,500 the first year to 3,000 the second.

Only with some hesitation did the group adopt the unsavory word " socialist " to describe their principles. The decision to do so was reached when Maurice urged that entire frankness would save them many arguments in the future. "Anyone who recognizes the principle of co-operation as a stronger and truer principle than that of competition has a right to the honour or the disgrace of being called a socialist," he said. While the words " Christian Socialism " had been used before,[2] the consequences of their adoption in

---

[1] C. E. Raven, *op. cit.,* chaps. 2-4.

[2] G. J. Holyoake (*History of Cooperation,* p. 539) says "the term ' Christian Socialism' first appeared as the title of a letter in the *New Moral World* of November 7, 1840." This is not quite the earliest use, for they occur in the title of a book by T. H. Hudson, *Christian Socialism Explained and Defended and Compared with Infidel Fellowship, especially as propounded by Robert Owen, Esq.,* published in 1839.

this case were far-reaching. Not only did it indicate the purposes of the group, but it focussed the attention of critics as well as sympathizers upon them.

Among the writers outside the group of leaders who contributed to the cause were Samuel Wilberforce, Archbishop Whateley of Dublin, and A. P. Stanley. But the literary genius of the movement was Kingsley. In him were combined the fluency, the dogmatic assurance and the easy emotionalism of a perfect propagandist. His " Letters of Parson Lot " and the tract *Cheap Clothes and Nasty* established his reputation as a pleader. His moralizing novels *Alton Locke* and *Yeast* in which he attacked the problems of industry and agriculture won him recognition also as an artist.[1]

Having accepted the principle of co-operation, the Christian Socialists constituted themselves a Society for Promoting Working Men's Associations and subscribed the necessary funds to set up a co-operative tailoring shop. The establishment employed a dozen men at first, the number being later doubled. Seven more associations rapidly followed this one, and the movement eventually included organizations of builders, cobblers, bakers, smiths, piano-makers and needle-women. Workshops were set up not only in London but in the provinces as well.

Some more effective central authority soon appeared necessary. Maurice at first objected to what seemed to him the substitution of machinery for Christian brotherhood, but he finally submitted to the judgment of his friends. A constitution for the Society of Promoters was accordingly drawn up which surrendered the executive functions to a Council of Promoters acting in concert with the Central Board of members of the workers' associations. As long as the local associations remained financially indebted to the Promoters

[1] Raven, *op. cit.*, chap. 5.

the Council was to have a veto on the acts of the local managers. It was also agreed that the associations should not establish equality of wages. But profit-sharing was required, and the working day was to be not more than ten hours, with a Sunday holiday. In the work of organization and finance Ludlow and a recruit of 1850, E. V. Neale, had an indispensable part. A barrister of large means, Neale, while not an orthodox Christian, was thoroughly convinced of the need of industrial reform and supported the co-operative associations with his personal effort and his money to the extent of £60,000.[1]

While the Christian Socialists were cultivating their own particular corner in the field of social reform they found opportunities of contributing to other phases of the working-class movement. Investigation of the tailoring trade incidental to the establishment of their first workshop revealed the extent of the government's responsibility for sweated labor in the making of uniforms for the army, police, postmen and convicts. *The Christian Socialist,* therefore, attacked the system of contracting which made these conditions possible, and petitions were circulated for the purpose of moving Parliament to action. This was but a part of the general condemnation of sweated labor which Kingsley so forcefully expressed in *Cheap Clothes and Nasty.*

It was natural that the Christian Socialists should feel a lively interest in experiments similar to their own. The temporary discouragement which trade unionists experienced after a series of unsuccessful strikes about 1850 caused them to turn to producers' organizations as an alternative method of bettering their condition.[2] Typical of these ventures was the operation conducted by the Amalgamated Society of

---

[1] Raven, *op. cit.,* chap. 6 and pp. 225-31.

[2] Beatrice Webb, *The Cooperative Movement in Great Britain,* pp. 124 *et seq.*

Engineers. In 1850 this newly formed trade union called upon the Christian Socialists for financial aid in founding a co-operative iron-works. The project failed of realization for the time being due to the weakened condition of the Society following the lock-out of 1852. When the scheme was revived two establishments were actually set up with the help of the Christian Socialists, only to meet with almost immediate failure.[1] A like fate overtook similar but independent experiments on the part of plush-workers, silk and velvet weavers, tailors, hatters, and boot-makers. These adopted the Christian Socialist associations as their models. The consumers' co-operative movement in Lancashire also began at this time to enter the field of production. This may have been partly due to the energetic campaign carried on in that district by Ludlow, Hughes and Neale in 1850-1851.[2] But this establishment differed from the type favored by Christian Socialists in keeping the control of the business in the hands of the consumers rather than entrusting it to the employes.

While the Christian Socialists believed that in producers' associations lay the real solution of industrial problems they were not indifferent to the achievements of consumers' associations. Their interest expressed itself first in an attempt to introduce the Rochdale idea to the south of England, where it had not yet taken root, by the establishment of a store in London. An effort was also made (not indeed for the first time) to federate the existing isolated stores on a national basis. To this end a central agency was founded to supply goods at wholesale to local stores, a Co-operative League was organized to disseminate information and to expedite communication between persons interested, and a general conference of co-operators was called in 1851 to

[1] Raven, *op. cit.*, chap. 7.
[2] Beatrice Webb, *op. cit.*, p. 125.

which all known societies were invited and to which twenty-eight responded.[1]

One of the serious handicaps of the co-operative movement thus far had been its weak position before the law. The expense of registration was heavy, and societies possessed limited rights over corporate property and lacked protection in dealing with non-members. The Christian Socialists therefore began an agitation for adequate legislation on the subject. A parliamentary committee was appointed to consider the matter, and the Christian Socialists gained a preliminary victory when John Stuart Mill as a witness before the committee gave his unqualified approval to producers' associations. Parliament was less responsive; the Liberal government of Russell opposed the desired legislation. The Derby ministry of 1852 however expedited its passage and Slaney's Act, as it was called, removed most of the disabilities which hampered co-operation. The limited liability of members was not, however, secured.[2]

In 1854 the Christian Socialists as a group ceased to participate in the co-operative movement. The Association of Promoters turned over their duties to the executive committee of Working Men's Associations. There appear to have been several reasons for this action. Promotion of the workers' associations had been a severe financial burden and it was felt that those already in existence should now be able to look after themselves. Furthermore, the results so far had not been very encouraging. The workshops had shown weaknesses which if not congenital had so far kept them in precarious health. The passage of Slaney's Act also seemed to make less necessary the maintenance of the societies in a state of tutelage. Finally, the interests of Christian Socialists were once more centering on education.[3]

---

[1] Raven, *op. cit.*, chap. 8.

[2] *Ibid.*, chap. 9.   [3] *Ibid.*, pp. 302-7.

Something more ambitious than the night school was projected. For some time the desirability of an educational center for members of the associations and other workingmen had been apparent. Accordingly the Hall of Association was converted to this use. Two types of lectures were arranged, hand-bills being distributed to announce the new venture. One course was intended for entertainment and included such diverse subjects as Shakespeare's historical plays, Robert Burns, architecture, entomology, astronomy and vocal music. The other courses, for more serious instruction, consisted of series of lectures in grammar, English history, French, book-keeping, and singing.

All this was preliminary to the final stage which was inaugurated after Maurice resigned his post in King's College. The religious differences which led to his virtual dismissal set him free to work out the scheme of a Working Men's College. In February, 1853, he submitted a plan to his associates. It was agreed to with certain modifications. Maurice then delivered a number of public lectures for the purpose of interesting persons who might be willing to contribute money or time to the project. A building which had housed the now defunct Needlewomen's Guild was taken over and in November, 1853, the College opened with an enrollment of 176 students. Courses were offered in grammar, geometry, arithmetic, algebra, the historical geography of England, and the law of partnership. Maurice himself lectured on Political Terms Illustrated by English Literature, The Reign of King John Illustrated by Shakespeare's Play, and, on Sundays, the writing of St. John. The later history of the College will receive attention further on.[1] But one cannot leave the subject without remarking the radical nature of a plan which provided advanced education for men who

[1] *Infra*, pp. 113-117.

had not received the preparatory instruction usually believed necessary.[1]

Along with Slaney's Act, the Working Men's College proved to be one of the indisputably successful projects of the Christian Socialists. The value of their other experiments is more open to question. The co-operative associations in which they had placed so much faith and sunk so much money one by one dropped by the wayside. Among the reasons given for their failure are inefficient management, hard times, the too generous assistance of Neale, lack of capital. Mrs. Webb has attributed it to a more fundamental defect—the elimination of the entrepreneur while the profit-making motive was retained, and this in a small-scale enterprise.[2] Ludlow, Hughes, and Neale, however, kept their faith to the end and it is interesting to observe that the producer-co-operative idea has again become popular in a modified form as guild socialism. The criticism of Mrs. Webb has been answered by the charge that it is based at least partly on a misconception. Mr. Raven denies that the profit-making motive was advocated by Christian Socialists and holds that there is no fundamental difference between the conduct of a small enterprise in this respect and a large one. He notes also that competition of the societies was to be prevented through price control by a central board. He is inclined to lay more stress upon the unsettling effect which the persecution of Maurice had upon the movement, as a cause of its failure.[3]

Beyond the concrete results of Christian Socialism there are others which may be fully as important but which are harder to estimate. For one thing it raised a clamor of opposition within the Church, especially on the part of the

[1] Raven, *op. cit.*, chap. 9.

[2] Beatrice Webb, *op. cit.*, p. 167.

[3] Raven, *op. cit.*, pp. 317-20.

religious press. With the illogicality which sometimes accompanies religious controversy the condemnation of Broad Church theology as it was found in the writings of Maurice was transferred to the social theories which he advocated.[1] The question was also vividly posed as to how far the Church ought to identify itself with definite schemes of economic reconstruction, a dispute which still divides Anglicans. To an outsider like Holyoake the association of religion with schemes of industrial co-operation was incomprehensible. "Christianity may be true and sacred in the eyes of a co-operator, but he cannot well connect the special doctrines of Christianity with those of Co-operation. When Mr. Pitman associated anti-vaccination with Co-operation the incongruity was apparent to most persons."[2]

Small as was the number of churchmen who identified themselves with Christian Socialism, it is probable that the increasing interest which the Church exhibited in matters of reform after the 1850's was largely due to their example. And finally, the movement contributed to a better understanding between the Church and the working class by bringing the two into more intimate contact through the co-operative movement and the workers' college.

It is hazardous to summarize the inchoate mass of opinion and effort which makes up the attitude of the Church toward social reform during the period just reviewed. After all, the vast majority of clergy and laity were silent so far as history is concerned and their evil as well as their good deeds are buried with them. But it seems fair to say that the Church directly and as an organized body had a distinctly minor part in the readjustment of society made necessary by

[1] Raven, *op. cit.*, p. 370.
[2] G. J. Holyoake, *op. cit.*, p. 538.

the contemporaneous industrial changes. Individuals performed excellent service but there was a lack of coordinated effort until the appearance of Christian Socialism. There was, of course, no central body for the exchange of views such as dissenting sects possessed — Convocation survived only as a formal body until its reconstitution in 1852. On the other hand, organizing ability was not wanting in other fields. The missionary and educational bodies achieved notable results. Nor did the Church suffer from a lack of first-rate ability. The power to understand was there, but seemingly not the will to listen.

When all is said, the control of Church affairs continued to be in the hands of a class, and of a class moreover which was little conversant with the special necessities of the new order. A long process of contact and education was needed before the requirements of the situation could be brought home to them. Obstacles to a better understanding slowly disappeared as the Church became less a career and more a service. The Oxford revival and the Broad Church movement had already demonstrated the vitality of Anglicanism: it remained to turn this energy into definitely social channels and so complete its significance.

CHAPTER II

THE CHURCH ASSEMBLIES AND SOCIAL REFORM:
1854-1877

DURING the quarter-century which elapsed between the dissolution of the Christian Socialist Promoters' Association in 1854 and the founding of the Guild of St. Matthew in 1877 there existed no organized group within the Church whose declared purpose was a thorough-going reform of economic and industrial institutions. This deficiency does not, however, imply an absence of interest in the topic or in social matters generally on the part of the Church, although they lingered darkly in the wings while theological controversy occupied the center of the stage. Aside from this negative character, however, the period derives a certain unity from the fact that it witnessed (1) the establishment of a group of quasi-governing bodies within the Church, (2) the last phase of the earlier Christian Socialist movement, and (3) the metamorphosis of the agricultural laborer from a submissive instrument of farming into an economic protagonist and a political force. These are the nuclei about which it is proposed, in this and the two following chapters, to group the social activities of the Church.

THE NEW CHURCH BODIES

As we have already noticed, one of the serious difficulties in dealing with the present subject is the absence, before 1850, of any effective organ which assumed to represent the Church of England as a whole. Within a decade or so after

62

1850, however, several representative bodies began to operate which did much to remedy this defect. Two of these, Convocation and the Lambeth Conference, were exclusively clerical; the others contained members of the laity.

The reasons for this sudden development of conciliar action are to be found not in any quickening of interest in social problems but rather in events which seemed to threaten the unity and even the existence of the Church. It was a time when Dissent and unbelief were questioning her most sacred privileges on one side while Rome was attracting her children on the other. It was also a time when the Pope, whose authority had presumably expired under Elizabeth, established a hierarchy of bishops and showed that he still had the power to shock. Since the state had been unable or unwilling to pacify and protect, argued men like Samuel Wilberforce, let the Church take a hand in governing herself.[1] "It is a reproach sometimes thrown out against our Church," said a leading Church paper, "that while professing to be Episcopal, she is, in fact, Presbyterian. . . . Every parish seems almost a distinct and complete unit in itself, and to be a microcosm self-sustaining, self-involved, and self-sufficient."[2] Moreover, theological disputes might be carried on with less rancor and expense by conferences than by piping ritualist parsons through the Court of Arches at £10,000 apiece.

There were, of course, other motives besides pacification and defense. The Church Congress was partly inspired by the success of the British Association for the Advancement of Science and the new Social Science Congress.[3] Further-

---

[1] Ashwell and Wilberforce, *op. cit.*, vol. ii, p. 136; *Hansard*, 1851, vol. 118, col. 534.

[2] *Guardian*, 16 July, 1862 (leader).

[3] *Report of the Proceedings of the Church Congress* (hereafter referred to here as "*Church Congress*"), 1861, p. iv.

more, the interest and aid of the laity might be stimulated by participation in conferences on terms of equality with the clergy.[1]

The discussions in the new assemblies give us for the first time a means of judging the general trend of opinion in the Church with respect to social questions. But the personnel and organization of these bodies were such that the attitude of the rank and file had to be expressed for the most part indirectly or not at all. The Lambeth Conference, which met first in 1867, was composed solely of bishops—of the British, colonial, and American churches. Convocation had a somewhat broader basis. Largely through the pertinacity of Bishop Samuel Wilberforce and the agitation of Henry Hoare, a layman, the southern branch, meeting as the Provincial Synod of Canterbury, was gradually restored to life between 1847 and 1852.[2] The Convocation of York had no such energetic person as Wilberforce to promote it—had even the open hostility of its archbishop to contend with—consequently it transacted no business of importance until 1859. In each assembly the upper house was composed of the bishops of the province.[3] The lower house included deans and archdeacons ex officio, proctors for the cathedral chapters, and representatives of the parish clergy. Many of the clergy and laity rebelled against this arrangement, because it excluded the laity from the chief governing body of the Church and left the lower clergy under-represented. For example, a petition in 1865 sponsored by Wilberforce notes

[1] *Chronicle of Convocation, Province of Canterbury* (hereafter referred to as "*Convocation of Canterbury*"), 1863, p. 1406.

[2] *Convocation of Canterbury*, 1847-57, preface, pp. x-xi.

[3] In the Convocation of York, the bishops and lower clergy, though nominally and constitutionally two separate houses, sat and transacted business together from 1864 to 1884, when the arrangement was ended on account of friction. (E. H. Thomson, *William Thomson, Archbishop of York*, ch. 14.)

that at present the ex officio members of the Lower House of Convocation of Canterbury are eighty-two in number, while the Proctors for the Chapters and the parochial clergy together number only sixty-seven, that of these last twenty-five Capitular Proctors represent not more than 130 capitular clergy of whom a large proportion, as Deans and Archdeacons, are themselves already ex officio members of Convocation, while the whole body of parochial clergy, believed to exceed 10,000, return only forty-two Proctors.

Dean Stanley considered the bishops alone or the Universities more representative of the Church than Convocation.[1]

Motives of prudence no less than justice required that laymen be admitted to the councils of the Church. A place was accordingly found for them in the Church Congress and the diocesan conferences. These bodies, however, had no official status. Participation in the Church Congress, which met annually from 1861 onward, was voluntary for clergy and laity. The members heard a prearranged list of addresses and spoke their minds decorously in ten-minute speeches after the formal papers had been delivered.[2] The diocesan bodies were virtually duplicates in little of the Church Congress, although the bishop presided and the members—besides a few nominated by the bishop or sitting ex officio— were elected by rural deaneries. Neither the Church Congresses nor the diocesan conferences, however, were perfect cross-sections of the Church. So much is indicated by the organization of special meetings for workingmen from 1867 onward. Speaking at the meeting of 1872, Bishop Bickersteth of Ripon quoted a revolutionary statement of the archbishop of York: " We will give up our Congress Hall one

[1] Ashwell and Wilberforce, *op. cit.*, vol. ii, pp. 154, 161, 232, 376-7; *Convocation of Canterbury*, 1847-57, p. 125; 1865, pp. 1980, 1959.

[2] A. J. B. Beresford Hope, *The Place and Influence in the Church Movement of Church Congresses*, p. 4.

evening for the purpose of inviting the workingmen to come and hear what we have to say about Church matters." Some had doubted its wisdom, but Bickersteth was " glad to have the opportunity of meeting them face to face in this hall, and of giving them the opportunity of hearing those who have come hither for the purpose of discussing matters which affect the interests of the Church." Perhaps it was slightly mortifying to his sense of benevolence that Bishops Wilberforce and Fraser told the audience that the men themselves should have done the talking.

Furthermore, members of the diocesan conferences were chosen by the rural deaneries not only in proportion to population but also according to social position. Earl Nelson deplored the fact that workingmen were not encouraged to co-operate with the clergy along with other classes.

Even in our Church Conference [1] [he said] where the laity have been elected, and a great many most useful people of the middle classes have come forward, and are working . . . there is not a single representative of the class that I want to have represented. . . . We talk about it, but we entirely fail in getting the description of men that the class leaders of the Nonconformists are taken from.

Women, of course, were not competent to assist such weighty deliberations. They might attend, but, as Beresford Hope said in 1874, "happily there has never been a claim from any one to address the gathering." [2]

Before 1850 the single place where churchmen met officially to debate questions of general interest was the House of Lords. Along with the newer organizations the little enclave of twenty-six bishops formed a barometer of

---

[1] *I. e.*, diocesan conference.

[2] Beresford Hope, *op. cit.*, p. 4; *Convocation of Canterbury,* "Report on Diocesan Conferences," 1882, p. 34; *Church Congress,* 1863, p. 246; 1872, pp. 75-6, 346 *et seq.*

Church opinion in general.[1] How accurate it was depends partly upon the motives which governed prime ministers in the selection of spiritual lords. Gladstone furnishes the completest catalogue of virtues that were to be looked for:

Piety. Learning (sacred). Eloquence. Acumen. Power. Faithful allegiance to the Church and to the Church of England. Activity. Tact and courtesy in dealing with men. Knowledge of the world. Accomplishments and literature. An equitable spirit. Faculty of working with his brother bishops. Some legal habit of mind. Circumspection. Maturity of age and character. Corporal vigor. Liberal sentiments on public affairs. A representative character with reference to shades of opinion fairly allowable in the Church.[2]

The best evidence of Liberal sentiments might be one's chairmanship of Gladstone's electoral committee. Thus Archdeacon Jacobson is said to have become bishop of Chester.[3] Palmerston also was in some degree guided by political considerations. True, "'if a man is a good man,' he often said, ' I don't care what his political opinions are.'" But he added, "' Certainly I had rather not name a bishop who would make party speeches and attacks on the Government in the House of Lords.'" It is sometimes assumed that Palmerston was the trusting disciple of Lord Shaftesbury in these matters. But something else is involved besides the confidence of a father-in-law. Perhaps Palmerston did not " know in theology Moses from Sydney Smith " and had only recently heard of the Tractarians, but Shaftesbury always considered his relative's political position in making his recommendations, and took care to satisfy the latter's

---

[1] This does not include the four Irish bishops, who did not concern themselves with English social questions.

[2] Probably written during his first administration, 1868-1874. Morley, *op. cit.*, vol. ii, p. 431.

[3] Hodder, *op. cit.*, vol. iii, pp. 194 *et seq.*

particular friends.[1] Disraeli's motives were also somewhat mixed. By refusing to promote Samuel Wilberforce he sacrificed his High Church inclinations to a fear of losing Conservative votes.[2]

What, indeed, was a conscientious statesman to do? Especially when he had to trim his sails to the hints, requests, commands, almost querulous complaints of the " Illustrious Individual who now sits upon the Throne " ? Queen Victoria's letters bristle with optimistic suggestions on how to distribute Church patronage.   There is a Mr. Blunt, Lord Hertford's son-in-law, " not remarkable in any way," who would be glad for a stall at Worcester.   Mr. Duckworth, a special friend of one of the princes, should have a canonry at Westminster.   Austerely she criticizes the appointment of a brother of Disraeli's elderly nymphs to a canonry of York: " For the *future* she would wish Mr. Disraeli to try and select, for canons and high places in the Church, people whose literary or other merits point them out for promotion, rather than merely from their birth. . . . Merit and true *liberal* broad views should be the recommendation." [3]   It is well known that the queen forced the promotion of Tait to Canterbury against Disraeli's choice of Ellicott.[4]

Political appointment will be condemned or justified according to the point of view.   " If Prime Ministers," says a writer in *The Commonwealth,*

had not braved scandal by appointing bishops whom Convocations would have excommunicated if they had had the chance

[1] Hodder, *op. cit., loc. cit.* and vol. ii, p. 505; vol. iii, p. 191; *cf.* Guedalla, *Palmerston,* p. 420.

[2] Monypenny and Buckle, *op. cit.,* vol. iii, p. 268.

[3] *Letters of Queen Victoria,* second series, vol. i, p. 545; vol. ii, pp. 341, 370, 374.

[4] *Ibid.,* vol. i, pp. 545 *et seq.*

to do so, it is quite certain that the Established Church as a national institution would have perished under a storm of well-merited obloquy. . . . It is through the refusal of the State to acquiesce in the proscription of minorities, through the promotion of men like Tait, Temple, Stanley, and Thirlwall, who were all in their day hated and feared by the clerical majority, that the Church retained its hold upon the nation.[1]

The task of prime ministers was not an easy one; they had to conciliate the queen, their political followers, the various shades of opinion in the Church, the Universities, and their own consciences. On Disraeli at least the responsibility did not sit too heavily. Confronted with the necessity of creating five bishops, to say nothing of a crowd of deans and canons, he writes blithely to his secretary in 1868, " I don't know the names and descriptions of the persons I am recommending for deaneries and mitres. . . Send me Crockford's Directory; I must be armed." [2]

If bishops had been selected with the hope that they would take little part in legislative affairs (and there is no evidence that this was the case), the expectation would in the majority of instances have proved correct. From 1850 to 1875, of almost seventy individual bishops who were entitled to sit in the House of Lords twenty, so far as the records show, never uttered a word in debate and nineteen others, whose episcopates averaged nine years, spoke less than half a dozen times each. The archbishops of Canterbury and the bishops of London were the most consistently active in debate. The bishops of Hereford remained totally silent. Individual parliamentarians like Samuel Wilberforce of Oxford (later translated to Winchester), Ellicott of Gloucester and Bristol, and Thomson of York spoke frequently on a rather wide

---

[1] 1911, p. 198.

[2] Monypenny and Buckle, *op. cit.*, vol. v, p. 57.

range of subjects, while certain others such as Magee, Goodwin, and Waldegrave pressed measures in which they were particularly interested upon the attention of the House. At the most liberal estimate not more than five or six out of twenty-six bishops were active legislators.[1] The reasons for this relative neglect of what would seem to be one of their most valuable functions are various. The cares of administration in a large see (it was recognized that the number of bishops was clearly insufficient at this time), expense, and the distance from London may have been decisive in many cases. Again, in a test of strength the entire episcopal bench could be easily swamped by the inert surrounding masses. Perhaps, too, a certain sense of inferiority oppressed them. Personal merit is not always comfortable in the presence of hereditary right. The debates on life peerages which occurred in the 'fifties can not have tended to allay such a feeling. Even in 1890 if it came to a brush, " ' noble lords' do not like other ' noble lords ' being sat upon by bishops," said Magee. Bishops, even more than Lord Shaftesbury, may have felt, as he confided to his journal, that " the House of Lords is terrible; there is a coldness, an inattention, and an impassibility which are perfectly benumbing." [2]

After this somewhat detailed account of the original purposes and personnel of the Church assemblies (including the officially spiritual part of the House of Lords), it is hoped that the record of their social interests may not too much resemble a mortuary decorated with a Corinthian façade. Yet it must be admitted that by far the greater part of their attention was occupied with subjects unconnected with or only indirectly related to social reform. Doctrine and forms of ritual, clerical discipline, foreign missions, Church finance,

[1] These facts are drawn from *Hansard*, 1850-1875.

[2] J. C. Macdonnell, *William Connor Magee*, vol. ii, p. 289; Hodder, *op. cit.*, vol. ii, p. 425.

Protestant reunion, and kindred topics touch social reform remotely if at all. Others of an intermediate nature are more significant. Such was the question of extending the Church's influence among the neglected classes. This, however, was discussed chiefly in terms of evangelistic missions, multiplication of churches and clergy, forms of lay co-operation, greater efficiency of organization, abolition of pew rents, etc. It would not be far wrong to say that three-fourths of the record deals with such matters.[1] The Lambeth Conference, important as were its later expressions on social questions, never got beyond strictly ecclesiastical topics in the single meeting held during this period.

Nevertheless almost every social problem which arose during these years appeared somewhere for discussion or at least received passing notice. Church assemblies (and the bishops in Parliament) considered the relations between capital and labor, the condition of the worker at his task (under which may be grouped slavery, abuses in factories, mines, etc., agricultural gangs, and Sunday labor), charity organization, immorality (prostitution, seduction, and the circulation of obscene books), what may be called social welfare (housing, hospitals, benefit and friendly societies, prisons, and recreation), and lastly temperance and education. The opinions expressed by members of the Church assemblies on most of these topics can be taken account of more conveniently in other connections. But the interest displayed in temperance and education so far outstripped that shown in all the rest that the total activities of the Church in these two matters will be dealt with here.

[1] As shown in *Hansard, Reports of the Convocations of Canterbury and York, Reports of Church Congresses.* Summaries of the activities of diocesan conferences are given in *Convocation of Canterbury,* 1872 and 1881, and *Convocation of York,* 1883.

THE CHURCH AND TEMPERANCE

In the eighteenth century political supremacy still remained with the aristocracy and economic control gravitated toward the bourgeoisie, but preeminence in drinking was rapidly passing to the working classes. If drunkenness could have been achieved only by long and expensive application to port wine and claret, it must have remained an enviable privilege of the rich. But the growth of a native gin manufacture placed a cheap and effective means of self-destruction in the hands of the masses. Measures to cope with this alarming innovation were rather slow in arriving. The first licensing and excise act (1729) touched the pockets of the farmers and so was repealed in 1733. Several further experiments in legislation led to the act of 1751 which, says Mrs. George, " really did reduce the excesses of spirit drinking." But conditions at the end of the century, though greatly improved, were still " appalling." [1]

The idea of an organized temperance movement appears to have originated in America, whence it passed to Ireland in 1829. The agitation began in England about the same time, probably as a result of contact with a spontaneous movement in Scotland. Meanwhile Parliament was engaged in further attempts at regulation. A licensing act of 1828 having failed to bring the desired results, the famous Beer Acts were passed in 1830. It was expected that the latter would encourage the revival of primitive and innocuous habits of drinking. They repealed the duties on beer and left the sale of beer and cider almost uncontrolled in shops where more potent beverages were prohibited. It is sufficient to say that the sociological experiment was unsuccessful except in providing a point of departure for temperance propaganda in succeeding years. [2]

[1] M. Dorothy George, *London Life in the XVIIIth Century*, pp. 26-43.
[2] Dawson Burns, *Temperance History*, vol. i, pp. 19 *et seq.*, 45 *et seq.*, 79.

Almost from the beginning the temperance movement secured adherents in the Church of England. The London Temperance Society (a non-sectarian body) owed its formation in 1830 to William Collins, and it was speedily patronized by high dignitaries of the Church. Bishop Blomfield of London presided over its first great public meeting. Other churchmen appeared on the list of vice-presidents.[1]

The future, however, seemed to lie with a more uncompromising form of the agitation. The moderate pledge exacted by the London Temperance Society required abstinence from distilled liquors only. But more ardent devotees would not tolerate any concession to what they felt to be a disreputable if ancient habit. Stern Protestants, who cast suspicious eyes upon enthusiasm for monasticism in the Church of England, found an outlet for their ascetic impulses in total abstinence. The principle appears to have received its first real impetus from a society at Preston which has a special claim to the notice of history because it originated the word " teetotal." Societies on a national and international footing appeared. Fired by the example of prohibition in Maine, the United Kingdom Alliance for the Total and Immediate Suppression of the Liquor Traffic strove to convert a somewhat phlegmatic Parliament. Father Matthew after signing up Irishmen by the tens of thousands and temporarily reducing the consumption of spirits by forty per cent came to England where he achieved much honor but little practical success.[2]

For a time the history of total abstinence in the Church of England reproduced that in England as a whole. At first individual parish clergymen formed district organizations of their own. When some broader affiliation appeared to be desirable a clerical conference at which the dean of Carlisle presided met in 1862. Among other things it was resolved

---

[1] Burns, *op. cit.*, p. 43; Cornish, *op. cit.*, vol. ii, p. 99.
[2] Dawson Burns, *op. cit.*, vol. i, pp. 137, 191, 360.

that, considering the influence of the clergy and the force of their example in their respective circles, it appears to this Meeting that their adoption and open avowal of the principle of Total Abstinence would be one of the most effectual means of checking the deplorable evils resulting from the drinking customs of the day.

A list of 250 abstaining clergy was drawn up, corresponding secretaries were enlisted in 25 dioceses, and the Church of England Temperance Reform Society was under way. For the attainment of its objects it relied upon " the establishment of Parochial Temperance Associations, the circulation of suitable information, the delivery of Sermons and Lectures, and the holding of Public Meetings throughout the country." While the lyrist of the United Kingdom Alliance in uncomplicated verse was attributing the success of Samson and Cyrus the Persian and the comparative failure of Alexander the Great to their attitude on the liquor question, the *Church of England Temperance Magazine* invoked the shade of Hector.[1]

But the Church as a whole had by no means capitulated to " teetotalism." The subject was aired at a number of Church and diocesan conferences. The Rev. H. J. Ellison, although one of the moderates, drew the most extravagant picture of a temperate England: " The parochial clergy can go far to say ' If it were not for this drink, poverty and rags would come to an end; poor rates would scarcely exist; union workhouses and pauper lunatic asylums would lose two-thirds of their inmates; the education question, the working man's dwelling question and many others would settle themselves.' " Occasionally a bishop like Stanley of Norwich supported the cause. But the list of skeptics is longer. Bishop Fraser, for example, feared it might produce moral astigmatism.

[1] Church Congress, 1862, pp. 230 *et seq.*; *Church of England Temperance Magazine*, October, 1862, pp. 1-4; June, 1865, supplement, p. 4; Dawson Burns, *Temperance Ballads*.

I say that the clergyman who abjures port-wine, but loves turtle soup, is not doing much to mend the manners of the age. And I venture to say further, that the clergyman who does not himself make a god of his belly, yet allows his wife and daughters to make gods of their backs, is no better.

Wordsworth recommended a later temperance society because it did not require total abstinence or " venture to condemn as evil any of God's creatures." Evangelicals were supposed to be the chosen advocates of the cause, but the venerable *Christian Observer,* spokesman for the party, hesitated to make it a point of faith and remarked that the Christian religion was one of temperance, not asceticism. Shaftesbury considered a friendly glass of wine a beneficent institution. To him, compulsory sobriety became less attractive as the law became more stringent. He objected to the entry of police officers into coffee and confectionery shops. America, the source of inspiration for some, was already a horrible example to others. Bishop Fraser adverted to it in terms strikingly modern:

It may be said that the Maine Liquor Law is effective in America; but American feeling is liable to momentary impulses, which is apt to carry it off the legs of reason. When I was there the Maine Liquor Law was simply non-effective . . . and at New Haven, in the state of Connecticut, the Provost-Marshal told me that it was a common phrase of people going to take a drink, " Come, let us violate the law."

Bishop Magee attacked the permissive bill of 1872 on the ground that it neglected the rights of minorities, and let slip a statement which he never succeeded in quite explaining away: " If I must take my choice . . . I should say it would be better that England should be free than that England should be sober." [1]

[1] *Church Congress,* 1862, pp. 230 *et seq.*; 1864, pp. 194, 196; 1871, p. 420;

It may be said, however, that the Church while skeptical of total abstinence and prohibition fully admitted the need for reform. The Convocation of Canterbury signalized its entry into the field of social reform by a voluminous report on intemperance in 1869. The debate which preceded the appointment of the investigating committee shows the range of opinion represented. Members of the C. E. T. R. S., especially Archdeacon Sandford, were responsible for initiating the discussion and helped to draw up the report. This may partly account for the drastic nature of some of its recommendations. After the examination of a body of evidence which compared favorably in bulk with the product of a parliamentary commission, it was found that the direct cause of intemperance was the too lenient licensing act of 1830. Indirect causes were: the practice of transacting business at public houses, the use of such places as rendezvous for benefit clubs, part payment of wages in drink— "generally prevalent in rural districts at harvest time"—, and the custom of indulging in drinking-bouts at marriages, christenings, and funerals. The results were increased mortality, crime, pauperism, waste of money and grain, and inefficiency in public services such as the army and navy. As a remedy the report considered legislation imperative. It advised the repeal of the licensing act of 1830 and the suppression of beer-houses, the strict regulation of public houses and a reduction in their number, Sunday closing and earlier closing on week days, enforcement of penalties for drunkenness on licensed persons and offenders, refusal of license to public houses for music and dancing, prohibition

Dawson Burns, *Temperance History*, vol. i, p. 179; *Convocation of Canterbury*, "Reports of Diocesan Conferences," 1881; J. H. Overton, *Christopher Wordsworth, Bishop of Lincoln*, p. 191; *Christian Observer*, Oct., 1873, pp. 775 *et seq.*; Hodder, *op. cit.*, vol. iii, p. 324; *Hansard*, vol. 159, col. 165 (1860); vol. 211, col. 85 (1872); *Convocation of York*, 1874, p. 16.

of their use as committee rooms on election days, and a special inspecting police; lastly, the repeal of duties on tea, coffee, chocolate, and sugar, and local option on the regulation of the drink traffic. As collateral aids for the working population it recommended

the encouragement of Cottage allotments, Night Schools for Adults, Parochial Libraries, Workmen's Clubs and social gatherings — whether for mutual instruction or amusement — in which kindly intercourse and sympathy between the different classes of society may be promoted; more comfortable, commodious, and healthy Dwellings for working men—implying an abundant supply of light, ventilation, and water—it being well known that a craving for intoxicating liquors is created and increased by the closeness, damp, and discomforts inseparable from the miserable and crowded apartments in which many of them lodge.[1]

Several points about this report deserve notice. It attained a fairly wide circulation — 5,000 copies of the first edition were published.[2] The question of proper housing was intimately associated with intemperance, a relationship which had been previously pointed out in the Church Congress and in the pages of the *Guardian*.[3] But while the report called attention to the responsibility of employers in this and other matters it left the question of wages and the whole economic position of the worker conspicuously untouched. One other omission is significant—neither total abstinence nor prohibition was mentioned.[4]

[1] *Convocation of Canterbury*, 1867, p. 6; 1869, pp. 241, 257-61; "Report on Intemperance," 1869.

[2] Dawson Burns, *Temperance History*, vol. ii, pp. 112-13.

[3] *Guardian*, 9 Dec., 1857, p. 933; *Church Congress*, 1864, p. 196.

[4] The Convocation of York presented a similar report in 1874. Among other things it found that "the amount of intemperance varies considerably in different localities, but is always in proportion to the rate of wages." (Quoted by Canon Ellison in the *Report of the House of Lords Committee on Intemperance* (1877), Question 8733).

The report, in fact, was a step toward the reconciliation of extreme and moderate reformers. As yet the Church of England possessed no official temperance society. Contrasting English with American churches, the historian of the movement remarks the tardiness of Dissenters as well as Anglicans in setting the seal of authority on these efforts. In 1872, however, when Cardinal Manning was organizing the Roman Catholic Total Abstinence League, H. J. Ellison, vicar of Windsor, proposed to the C. E. T. R. S. the admission of non-abstainers to its membership.[1] One reason for the decision to accept this advice was perhaps the increasingly remote likelihood that total abstinence would become popular with members of the Church. Only some six or seven hundred clergy out of four thousand abstaining ministers of all denominations accepted the principle.[2] Early the next year a union of the C. E. T. R. S. and the Manchester, Chester, and Ripon Diocesan Temperance Societies took place on the basis of co-operation between abstainers and non-abstainers. Archbishop Tait presided at the inaugural meeting of the new organization, which received the title, " The Church of England Temperance Society ". Since that time it has been the official nucleus of temperance promotion.[3]

The labors of Convocation and the arrangement of terms of co-operation among reformers were reflected during 1876 in the attitude of bishops in the House of Lords. Spiritual lords had so far shown only a mild inclination toward tem-

---

[1] G. P. McEntee, *The Social Catholic Movement in Great Britain,* p. 62; Cornish, *op. cit.,* vol. ii, p. 104.

[2] Dawson Burns, *Temperance History,* vol. ii, p. 193. The figures for the Church seem to be substantially correct. In 1865, according to the *Church of England Temperance Magazine,* there were 555 abstaining clergy. (Supplement, 1 June, 1865).

[3] Dawson Burns, *Temperance History,* vol. ii, p. 189; *Convocation of Canterbury,* " Supplementary Report on Intemperance," 1876.

perance — their enthusiasm even now was admirably restrained. A memorial on the subject signed by ten thousand clergy, although it was too resounding to be overlooked, was not authoritative enough to be obeyed. The petitioners asked for legislation and received a parliamentary committee. Moving " that a select committee be appointed for the purpose of inquiring into the prevalence of habits of intemperance, and into the manner in which those habits have been affected by recent legislation and other causes," Archbishop Tait voiced the opinion that it would afford an opportunity of testing the reports of Convocation, to whose conclusions he did not commit himself. He saw, however, some incongruity in supplementing schools with workhouses and lunatic asylums. Bishop Goodwin, supporting the motion, considered the matter to be properly a lay subject. He permitted himself an excursion into psychology with the opinion that while men could not be made temperate by act of parliament, they could be made intemperate by it. He had in mind among other things the practice of granting grocers' licenses. Bishop Magee again asserted his attachment to freedom which, he said, the workers since their adoption of trade unionism had shown too much inclination to renounce. Two logical extremes presented themselves to him—free licensing with severe penalties for drunkenness, disorder, and adulteration, or complete prohibition. The latter would not be an infringement of liberty, because the state had the right to forbid the sale of " any article whatever which it believed to be injurious," but public opinion in England would not support such a remedy. A permissive bill (equivalent to local option in America) still filled him with apprehension. After all, " it was to the elevation of the sanitary, social, religious, and moral condition of the poor far more than to laws respecting the licensing of public houses that we must look for the suppression of intemperance." Lord Salisbury

reminded the House that it was still an open question whether
the English government should " correct . . . the action of
Providence in the creation of alcohol," but ministers accepted
the archbishop's proposal.[1]

A committee of fifteen including five bishops immediately
began to collect evidence.[2]   They examined witnesses for
over two years and eventually presented a long report with a
tail of some twenty recommendations.   They advised numerous modifications of the licensing laws, some measure of
local control, changes in the hours of closing, etc.[3]   But the
interest manifested by the Lords in their Report was not
commensurate with its bulk.   Bishops seem to have dropped
the matter completely.   It faintly reverberated in 1880 when
the earl of Onslow asked whether the government intended
to follow up the Report by legislation, but the question was
not raised again for some time.[4]

THE CHURCH AND EDUCATION

While the Church somewhat slowly clarified its position
with regard to the temperance movement, education was a
subject in which it felt thoroughly at home and to which the
various Church assemblies reacted with marked vigor.   The
National Society had extended its ministrations throughout
the country, contributions from the laity increased, and the
number of scholars in Church schools multiplied.   It was no
longer a question whether education was desirable.   The
problem had now become one of increased efficiency and

[1] *Hansard*, 1876, vol. 230, col. 715 *et seq.*

[2] Tait, Magee, Temple, and Goodwin were first named.   Thomson was
added later.

[3] *Reports from Committees*, 1877, vol. xi; 1878, vol. xiv; 1878-9, vol. x.
(Reports from the Select Committee of the House of Lords on
Intemperance.)

[4] *Hansard*, 1880, vol. 253, col. 1366.

universalization. Secondary and higher education for the masses could hardly be successful until elementary education had reached the poorest child in the remotest village, and it is with the latter branch that we shall be concerned here. The student of reform is bent upon discovering whether the Church retarded or advanced the cause of sound general education. If we consider the legislation of the years 1850 to 1880 as representing the movement of average public opinion, the attitude of the Church toward these measures may afford some answer.

The controversy which centered about the report of the Royal Commission on Popular Education of 1861 and its sequel, the Revised Education Code of 1862, illustrates the conflict of opinion as to what constituted efficiency in education. The Commission was the result of a compromise. Disappointed in his earlier attempts to secure legislation, Sir John Pakington fell back upon the last resource of a reformer, and Palmerston's government in 1858 accepted his proposal of a Royal Commission " to inquire into the present state of Popular Education in England, and to consider and report what changes, if any, are required for the extension of sound and cheap Elementary Instruction to all classes of the people." [1]

The commission, headed by the duke of Newcastle, labored for three years and extracted seven volumes of evidence from clergymen, educators, and reformers.[2] Perhaps the most detailed examination of the existing situation conducted on the ground was that of the Rev. James Fraser, later Bishop of Manchester, who has appeared before [3] and in other capacities will appear frequently hereafter. In their con-

[1] *Hansard*, 1858, vol. 148, col. 1184 *et seq.*

[2] *Reports from Commissioners*, 1861, *Popular Education (England)*, vol. xxi, parts 1-7.

[3] *Supra*, pp. 74-5.

clusions the Commissioners proposed to extend the benefits of elementary education by doing away entirely with the provisions of the old Education Code which made government grants partly dependent on local voluntary subscriptions. This would prevent poorer districts from being excluded from state aid.[1]

But it was around the new method of distributing these grants that argument raged.   The Commissioners believed that every school should attain a minimum of " efficiency " before it received assistance.

We have been obliged to come to the conclusion [they said] that the instruction given is commonly too ambitious and too superficial in its character, that (except in the very best schools) it has been too exclusively adapted to the elder scholars; and that a main object of the schools is defeated in respect of every child who, having attended for a considerable time, leaves without the power of reading, writing, and cyphering in an intelligent manner.[2]

The school inspectors ought thereafter to examine the scholars individually in the three R's.   Part of the grant should be apportioned accordingly and the rest distributed on the basis of attendance.   To critics of this simple plan the Commissioners replied,

We believe that to raise the general character of the children, both morally and intellectually, is, and must always be the highest aim of education; and we are far from desiring to supersede this by any plan of a mere examination into the more mechanical work of elementary education, the reading, writing, and arithmetic of boys below ten years of age.   But we think that the importance of this training, which must be the foundation of all other teaching, has been lost sight of.[3]

[1] *Reports from Commissioners*, 1861, vol. xxi, p. 318.

[2] *Ibid.*, part 1, p. 295.

[3] *Ibid.*, part 1, p. 321.

Another defect of the old system (which the Commissioners placed at the head of their list) was the expense entailed upon the central office by the complicated method of apportioning the grants.[1]

Almost before the ink of the report was dry, Robert Lowe, vice-president of the Committee of Council on Education, sallied forth with a Revised Code based upon its recommendations. On a most vital point he even went beyond it and proposed that grants should be made exclusively on the basis of individual examination in the three R's. Introducing his creation to the House of Commons, he said it must be recognized that eighty per cent of the children attending school were below eleven years of age. Nor was it desirable to keep them longer, for, as the Commissioners said,

Independence is of more importance than education, and if the wages of the child's labour are necessary either to keep the parents from the poor rates or to relieve the pressure of severe and bitter poverty, it is far better that it should go to work at the earliest age at which it can bear the physical exertion than that it should remain at school.

What was even free education compared to five or six shillings a week in wages? The Code fixed a minimum not a maximum of education, but after all, said Lowe, " we do not profess to give these children an education that will raise them above their station and business in life; that is not our object, but to give them an education that may fit them for that business." His praise of individual examination was unqualified. " The principle of examination is a jealous and engrossing principle. It supersedes all others, because it includes all conditions necessary to success, and those conditions imply all which constitute excellence in a school." But the financial aspect had an irresistible appeal.

[1] *Reports from Commissioners*, part I, p. 313.

I cannot promise the house that this system will be an economical one, and I cannot promise that it will be an efficient one, but I can promise that it shall be either one or the other. If it is not cheap it shall be efficient; if it is not efficient it shall be cheap.

The epigram was telling, but the truth of the dilemma (fortunately for him) could be proved only by experience.[1]

The ears of Parliament were somewhat less sympathetically attuned to the Report and the Revised Code. Spencer Walpole brought forward a long list of modifications, some of which the government felt it necessary to accept. As a result the revised edition of the Revised Code which finally went into operation in 1862 provided that, as before, grants should be made only to schools conducted by some recognized religious denomination or to those which included Scripture reading as part of the curriculum. The inspectors of Church of England schools must be approved by the archbishop of the province and were removable at his pleasure.[2] Grants were to be made partly dependent on attendance if a certain general standard was maintained, but the larger portion was to be distributed on the basis of individual examination. Scholars in the highest class must be able to read "a short paragraph in a newspaper, or other modern narrative", write a similar one from dictation, and in arithmetic do "a sum in practice or bills of parcels." As had previously been the rule, certificated teachers must be employed, but they no longer received direct grants from the government.[3] Special aid for night schools, instruction in drawing, and the purchase of books was discontinued. Grants for building and fitting up schools were mercilessly cut. As a result state expenditure on education fell from £813,000 in 1861 to

1 *Hansard*, 1862, vol. 165, col. 207.

2 Provided by order in council in 1840.

3 *Accounts and Papers*, 1862., vol. 52, pp. xvi-xliv.

£636,000 in 1865. Not until 1869 did it again reach the earlier figure.[1] The substance of Lowe's Code was thus realized in spite of the Committee of Council's sober assertion that examination presupposed a judgment on the general standard of excellence in a school and did not supersede it.[2] " Payment by results " was firmly entrenched in the British educational system.

The opinion of churchmen as to the need and manner of educational reform was by no means so unanimous as that of the Newcastle Commission. Some thirty clergymen testified before the Commission on the state of education and the possibility of improving it.[3] The majority favored the existing system. One or two like Frederick Temple, master of Rugby (the future archbishop of Canterbury), attacked it as paternalistic. If parents were quite unable to pay for the education of their children, he believed that free education should be provided by the wealthy rather than by the state. The witnesses placed the desirable age at leaving school somewhat higher than the Commissioners believed it possible to expect. Sentiment was more divided on the comprehensiveness of the curriculum. A number of the witnesses regarded the three R's and an introduction to religion, together with some vocational training, as virtually all that was essential. Echoes of a past age filtered through the remarks of the Rev. Samuel Earnshaw.

It is not desirable [he said] too much to elevate the taste of the class of people whose life is to be passed amid a perpetual occurrence of rebuffs, rough usage, and coarse work. . . . And too much refinement of the taste shows itself, as I have in many

[1] M. E. Sadler and J. W. Edwards, *Summary of Statistics, Regulations, &c., of Elementary Education in England and Wales, 1833-1870*, p. 526.

[2] *Accounts and Papers*, 1863, vol. 47, p. xviii.

[3] The following statements are generalized from the testimony given in parts 5 and 6 of the Commission's report.

cases observed, by *creating a distaste for the ordinary work of the lower class, and a too eager desire to obtain a living by other means than labor*; and leads to dissatisfaction, talking, and speech-making at trade-unions, neglect of work, and misdirected and mistaken efforts to live by other means more refined but less useful and proper than ordinary work.[1]

The greater number, however, marked out a more extensive schedule for the schools. Grammar, history, geography, music, even geometry and botany, carried weight with them.

Could the efficiency of education be increased? Most of the witnesses believed so. But it was rather by an intelligent application of the present system than by radical changes in method. If examination in the three R's should be found to drive out other subjects, the advocates of a broader education must necessarily have opposed it. The testimony showed that even under the existing code certain inspectors made use of the individual examination. This was vastly different, however, from making the government grant depend almost wholly upon such tests. The Rev. Samuel Best denied that a few things learnt thoroughly were better than a general acquaintance with a number of subjects; the outline acquired at school could be filled in later on.

The opponents of individual examination seized the opportunity for criticism when the Revised Code appeared. Sir James Kay-Shuttleworth (former secretary of the Committee of Council) had set off the first gun before the Royal Commission. " The tendency of such a system would be this, instead of examining the general moral relations of the school and all the phenomena which meet the eye, the attention of the inspector would be concentrated necessarily upon some two or three elements of education." [2]   W. E. Forster,

[1] *Reports from Commissioners*, 1861, vol. xxi, part 5, pp. 184-5.

[2] Frank Smith, *Life and Works of Sir James Kay-Shuttleworth*, pp. 258 *et seq.*

criticizing the Revised Code, admitted the desirability of " payment by results ", but thought that examination should not be the sole criterion. Surely attendance at a well-equipped school, discipline, and religious training were results worth paying for. The case was stated with greater breadth by Bishop Wilberforce in the House of Lords. The new examination, he said, would be an inspection

in the most mechanical part of their [the scholars'] training. . . . Your object is not to teach in these schools mere mechanical drudgery, but to give the children an opportunity of raising themselves intellectually and morally above the level which is too often found in their cottage homes. But by degrading the examination from an inquiry into the moral and intellectual tone of all the schools into a test examination of each individual child in the most mechanical part of its training, you prevent the schools from being the true enlighteners of these children. To say that under such a system you are going to pay for results is a most fallacious way of putting it, because, in fact, you are going to pay for the poorest results, and to take the very worst criterion of the progress of education.[1]

Lord Granville, the government leader, who strove to imitate the darting lightness of Puck but whose wit more resembled the aimless but irritating sallies of a mosquito, in reply caricatured Wilberforce's plea for highly educated inspectors : " I must think that for the mere examination of a small school intended for the working classes it is not absolutely necessary to employ senior wranglers and first-class men from Oxford." He discreetly left mechanical results unconsidered.[2]

Aside from inducing the children to stay longer at school churchmen had few new suggestions to offer in place of the government's plan for increasing the efficiency of inspected

[1] *Hansard*, 1862, vol. 166, col. 92; vol. 165, cols. 990-1007; Bishop Tait fully agreed with Wilberforce (col. 1493).

[2] *Hansard*, 1862, vol. 165, col. 1010.

schools. They professed themselves to be generally satisfied with the quality of instruction offered. The obvious modern method of attracting a better fitted class of people to the teaching profession by paying higher salaries was therefore almost entirely overlooked. Yet the wages of schoolmasters and -mistresses ranged between the modest limits of £50-90 and £30-60 a year respectively. The Rev. James Fraser was almost alone in proposing a moderate increase of salary.[1]

Experience alone could tell whether the sanguine expectations of Robert Lowe or the forebodings of Bishop Wilberforce were correct. It is worth noting that after two years of trial only a third of the clerical inspectors who reported in 1865 and 1866 expressed themselves as distinctly satisfied with the Revised Code. The rest were neutral or opposed.[2] Later writers have supported the hesitation of the clergy and confirmed the predictions of Wilberforce. The Revised Code has been described as degrading education to " parrot work " in the three R's and reducing the level of instruction.[3] The teachers had been accused of polishing up their bright students to the injury of the less brilliant majority. They accepted the rebuke and neglected them. " The subsequent history, during nearly thirty years, of English elementary schools is the gradual undoing of the mischief wrought by the Newcastle Commission and Robert Lowe." [4]

Beside the problem of raising the standard of education England had to deal with the parallel question of making it as widespread as possible. It was also fully recognized both by clergy and laity that efficiency in part depended upon regular attendance at school. The simple way to make at-

[1] *Report of the Royal Commission*, part 2, p. 118.

[2] *Accounts and Papers*, " Reports of the Committee of Council on Education," 1865, vol. 52; 1866, vol. 27.

[3] H. B. Binns, *A Century of Education*, p. 186.

[4] J. W. Adamson, *A Short History of Education*, p. 309.

tendance universal and regular was to make it compulsory. The Newcastle Commission and the government, however, both rejected this solution. Four of the clergymen who testified before the Commission favored it but a larger number were opposed. Sentiment in the Church swung toward it in the course of the next fifteen years. In 1869 the Education Union, which included in its membership all the bishops and archbishops, pronounced itself favorable to compulsion. Convocation took up the question of education in 1870 but aside from Canon Woodgate who still regarded compulsory attendance as impossible the members were silent on the topic.[1] When the Education Bill of 1870 appeared in the House of Lords, Bishop Temple approved the modest efforts of the government in that direction, while Bishop Ellicott unwillingly accepted them.[2] In 1875 the National Society announced that compulsion was the one thing lacking. Means of enforcing attendance were not complete, however, until the passage of the Education Act of 1880.

The commonest objection to the " voluntary "[3] system of education was that it fell short of being universal. In answer to this Churchmen could cite an increase in enrollment and contributions which showed no signs of slackening. Between 1851 and 1866 the number of scholars registered in Church schools rose from 930,000 to 1,500,000. Expenditures on Church schools were £875,000 in 1847 and £1,-180,000 in 1868.[4]

---

[1] Cornish, *op. cit.*, vol. ii, p. 277; *Convocation of Canterbury*, 1870, p. 175.

[2] *Hansard*, 1870, vol. 203, cols. 841, 1189.

[3] " Voluntary " here of course has no reference to voluntary attendance but to the setting up of schools on private initiative supported wholly or in part by voluntary contributions, tuition fees, and endowments.

[4] *Accounts and Papers*, 1852-3, vol. 90, pp. cxxiv, lvii; 1868-9, vol. 47, pp. 269 *et seq.*; *Convocation of Canterbury*, 1870, " Report on Elementary Education," p. 16.

Even if a place were provided for every child, however, it might be argued that religious scruples would prevent many parents from sending their children to denominational schools. William Lovett was not alone when, in his disillusioned old age, he wrote,

The working classes are still compelled to pay and obey at the mandates of exclusive legislators—Catholics, Jews, and Dissenters—are in England still compelled to support a Church whose rule they hate and whose doctrines they abhor. Education is still regarded by vast numbers as a means of filling Churches and Chapels instead of a glorious instrument of human elevation.[1]

How far Churchmen would go toward removing these suspicions appears in the reception they gave legislation with that end in view.

A bill dealing with endowed schools was introduced in 1860. Four bishops commenting on the scheme in the House of Lords agreed with Archbishop Sumner's declaration that he " desired to preserve the foundation as it stood at present . . . whilst he allowed individual parents to enjoy all the advantages of the school without any sacrifice to which their consciences may be opposed." He objected to any scheme which would take the government out of the hands of the trustees and in particular to the clause which provided that the Court of Chancery might issue a summons to show cause why a conscience clause should not be inserted in any plan of reorganization. Wilberforce proposed that the conscience clause be made permissive.[2] A new Endowed Schools Bill in 1869 provided that parents might withdraw children from religious instruction. Archbishop Thomson objected to this on the ground that it would permit

[1] *Life and Struggles*, preface, p. xxxi (written 1876).
[2] *Hansard*, vol. 156, cols. 1210-21, 712.

idle boys to work on the sympathies of their parents. He also rejected the provision which gave parents the right to protest against the persistent teaching of any religious doctrine (outside the regular service) of which they disapproved. It would, he said, be a source of annoyance to teachers. Harold Browne disagreed with the first objection — " the parents ought, no doubt, to have a right to object to the special spiritual lessons "—but he supported the second for reasons similar to Thomson's. Ellicott differed with both of his colleagues. There ought, he said, to be some provision against " a sort of illicit teaching of the worst kind, and he for one could not tolerate that sort of proselytizing." [1]

The question of religious tests at the Universities was a perennial bloom. When according to custom a bill appeared in 1867, Bishop Jeune attacked the provision which admitted Dissenters to the governing bodies of the Universities, while he acknowledged their right to scholarships, honors, and degrees. He believed the test to be so lax that it would permit professors to " avow any of the forms of belief " prevalent in Germany. The bill was shelved with the assistance of four bishops, two voting in favor of its continuance.[2] More comment was drawn forth by the bill of 1870 which removed religious restrictions on the distribution of University emoluments. " I not only regret," said Bishop Mackarness, " that it should be necessary to bring in a measure for the abolition of tests, but I regret that it was ever necessary to enact them." The burden of criticism had now shifted to the point where bishops were trying to protect the Christian rather than the sectarian character of the Universities and to prevent religious instruction from being excluded. An amendment to the latter effect was carried, ten bishops voting Aye, four, No. But only Wordsworth and Ollivant spoke

---

[1] *Hansard*, vol. 197, cols. 1878 *et seq.*
[2] *Ibid.*, 1867, vol. 189, cols. 61 *et seq.*

in favor of a test which would have shut out non-Christians altogether.[1]

The Endowed Schools Act of 1869 (mentioned above) in its conscience clause anticipated a more important piece of legislation.   Article 7 of the Elementary Education Act of 1870 required that schools receiving government grants must not compel students to attend Sunday schools or religious worship within the school, and that any such instruction must take place at the beginning or end of the daily session. While the act was in embryo, bishops did not venture to attack the principle of the conscience clause.   They rather confined themselves to objections which would have weakened its force.   Goodwin and Jackson opposed posting the regulations in the schools.   Ellicott, while acquiescing in the measure, found much to criticize.   A conscience clause he regarded as unnecessary—" the clergy already acted with few exceptions as if there was a most binding one."   He opposed the relegation of religious instruction to the beginning or end of the session and in this was supported by Wordsworth.   Only Temple and Gilbert accepted the clause without reservations.[2]

Convocation was forewarned of what might be expected of the bill of 1870.   The synod of Canterbury in discussing its probable terms occupied itself chiefly with the conscience clause.   The trend of sentiment was distinctly favorable to the clause although a respectable number of diehards held out to the end.   A committee appointed to consider the bill recommended that " in all cases of sustentation grants, and in all cases of future building grants, the managers of Church Schools need not decline Parliamentary aid if only the principle be recognized of perfect liberty of distinctive religious teaching in the schools on the part of managers, combined

[1] *Hansard*, 1870, vol. 203, cols. 214 *et seq.*
[2] *Ibid.*, vol. 203, cols. 841, 1162 *et seq.*

with perfect liberty of declining such teaching on the part of parents." They could not recommend the religious " time-table " if this meant " rigidly to prohibit religious influence at other times." [1] The Convocation of York also issued a report and passed a resolution " thankfully acknowledging the general spirit of earnestness and fairness in which the bill is conceived, and while reserving its judgment upon some points is prepared to accept the Regulations for the conduct of Public Elementary schools laid down." [2]

A determination to be fair is poor armor for anyone who, in quest of a summary statement of the Church's contributions to educational reform, plunges into the hail of claims, denials, accusations, and rebuttals which beset this most controversial subject. One is fortunate to emerge with a few facts which have the semblance of truth.

With reference to increased efficiency in the schools, we have seen that the clergy stood for a higher leaving age than the state authorities regarded as necessary. Churchmen in 1861 also upheld a broad cultural education in opposition to the three R's of the Education Department. A similar progressive attitude marks the education report of the Convocation of Canterbury in 1870. Pointing out omissions in the bill of 1870 it noted the absence of provision for a future supply of teachers, state schools in connection with the army, navy, and other governmental institutions, technical education, the education of neglected children whose parents were neither vagrants nor criminals, a local education authority in places where facilities for education were satisfactory, and pensions for teachers. [3]

---

[1] *Convocation of Canterbury*, 1870, pp. 107-175, 413-418; " Report on Elementary Education," pp. 28-9.

[2] *Convocation of York*, 1870, p. 167.

[3] *Convocation of Canterbury*, " Report on Elementary Education," 1870, p. 30.

No one argued against universal education, but was the policy of the Church calculated to attain that object? In the matter of compulsory attendance the Church seems at least to have kept pace with the movement of public opinion. It officially recognized religious scruples to the extent of acquiescing in the conscience clause. What the atmosphere in individual schools was, however, we have small means of knowing. One thing is certain—the Church endeavored to keep education in religious hands, not only in the case of elementary schools but also in the case of the Universities and the endowed schools. This appears to be one of the reasons for its opposition to supporting the schools by local taxation. Rating was suggested as a means of supplementing voluntary contributions where the latter were inadequate. But churchmen argued that it would discourage such donations and proposed instead larger grants from the central government.[1]

Whether denominational education prevented any considerable number from taking advantage of its facilities, is a matter for argument. Secularists claimed that it did. Churchmen testified to the contrary.[2] Lord Shaftesbury charged that the issue was being used as a stalking-horse by the enemies of the Church.[3] To this it might be replied that the accommodation in Church schools always exceeded the registration by a wide margin. But there are other and what seem to be better ways of explaining the failure to make full use of the existing facilities. So long as the economic

---

[1] *Convocation of Canterbury*, "Report on Elementary Education," 1870, pp. 18, 32. *Hansard*, 1870, vol. 203, col. 841. The Education Union was founded in 1869 to offset the secularist Birmingham League whose object was the introduction of rating. (Cornish, *op. cit.*, vol. ii, p. 227.)

[2] *Report of the Royal Commission* (1861), part 5, pp. 124 *et seq.*, 128 *et seq.*; *Convocation of Canterbury*, 1870, p. 110.

[3] *Hansard*, 1870, vol. 203, col. 843.

exploitation of children continued, a great number were likely to be denied proper schooling. And in the absence of compulsion, it was a long and difficult process to educate parents in the advantages of education. Perhaps Canon Riddell struck very near the truth when he said, " I do not think the present system fails at all on the religious ground. It fails because the employers of labor think it their interest to employ children at an age at which they ought not to be employed. It fails because parents are indifferent to it. It fails because in many places where Government aid is most needed, Government aid is not granted." [1]

There was another reason for non-attendance, one less honorable to the Church. A faint odor of charity and social inferiority clung about the voluntary schools. Teachers themselves were visited with the painful condescension of the clergy. To be successful, said one of the inspectors, the the teachers must feel at home with the poor—" we do not want a high standard of culture in the teacher; it is *possible,* in fact, that the standard realized by him may be too high." [2] It may be significant that a frugal but self-respecting middle class long continued to educate its children in private schools.

THE CHURCH ASSEMBLIES AGAIN

We have seen that the Church assemblies became forums where social problems were discussed and even where programs were formulated. But these bodies varied widely among themselves in the scope of their social interest during the third quarter of the century. The mixed lay and clerical bodies were more responsive to current social questions than either Convocation. Both the diocesan conferences and the Church Congress showed a tendency to broaden their dis-

---

[1] *Convocation of Canterbury,* 1870, p. 171.

[2] *Report of the Royal Commission* (1861), part 5, p. 135.

cussions as they grew older. But most of the bishops in the House of Lords sat wrapped in dignified silence while Lord Derby and Lord Granville fenced over some of the greatest issues England had to face. What was the principle on which bishops exercised their parliamentary function? Were Irish land reform, legalization of trade unions, protection of savings banks and Friendly Societies, extension of the suffrage, and revision of the judicial system less vital to public welfare or of less concern to the Church than temperance and the crowded dwellings of working-men? The logic of ignoring the former and periodically agitating the latter is not apparent. It may lie in the respect for a tradition which the young Church assemblies were fortunate enough not to possess.

The Church assemblies owed their existence and whatever vitality they possessed largely to the personal efforts of a few individuals. Perhaps their chief promoter was Bishop Samuel Wilberforce. He it was who performed the delicate task of framing the encyclical of the first Lambeth Conference. The revival of Convocation tested his resources to the utmost. It was not easy to pacify Lord Aberdeen, the Prime Minister, who refused to consent tacitly to the revival: " Do you think I am going to tolerate them [the bishops] by a side-wind because the Archbishop is a poor, vain, weak, silly creature who [sic] they can bully with impunity? " But the diplomacy of Wilberforce triumphed in the end, and Convocation rose somewhat unsteadily to its feet in 1852. The invalid still, however, needed careful nursing—it might expire from a lack of business. Wilberforce, therefore, was in constant attendance, and during a period of twenty-two years moved or seconded two-thirds of the resolutions in the Canterbury House of Bishops. The Church Congresses also owe something to Wilberforce. Before his death in 1872 he had spoken or presided at four or five of them, and early in their history had tamed an exuberance which might have been fatal by checking their tendency to pass resolutions.[1]

The Church produced few great parliamentarians during the nineteenth century, but Wilberforce was one of them. Unlike most of the bishops, he appeared and spoke regularly in the House of Lords. What is more unusual, his speeches are worth reading after the lapse of seventy years. His thoughts on education and his attitude toward labor have already been noticed. He also frequently aired an amiable prejudice inherited from his father—a hatred of slavery— and whenever the slave trade flaunted itself he dealt it a vigorous blow.[2] In the breadth of his social interest, if we take parliamentary activities as a measure, he far surpassed the other bishops of his time. Without minimizing Wilberforce's contributions in the least, it may be said that reading the speeches of his episcopal brethren is too often like shaking a bag of bones—all we hear is the clatter of dead theological disputes.

[1] Ashwell and Wilberforce, *op. cit.*, vol. ii, p. 161; vol. iii, pp. 229-30, 236-7, 51; *Convocation of Canterbury*, 1874, p. 33.

[2] *Hansard*, 1852, vol. 122, cols. 382, 387; 1854, vol. 135, col. 122; 1858, vol. 150, cols. 1700, 2195; vol. 151, col. 70; 1859, vol. 152, cols. 178, 929; 1869, vol. 194, col. 477; 1873, vol. 215, col. 1781.

CHAPTER III

Problems of Town Life and Labor (1854-1877)
The Christian Socialists

Since the Church assemblies devoted only a minor share of their attention to social reform, it devolved upon individual churchmen to carry the standard of religion farther into this field. The relation of the Church to the problems of the industrial population must therefore be described in terms of individual contacts and efforts. Now and again the assemblies acted as forums of discussion, but never during this period—except with regard to temperance and education—did they undertake to crystallize the views or assume the leadership of the Church in such matters.

WORKERS AND SETTLERS IN THE SLUMS

In the absence of official guidance and as a prelude to organized action, it was evident that more of the class who were responsible for Church policy ought to familiarize themselves with social problems through intimate contact with the working class. Churchpeople could acquire this personal knowledge either by joining the new monastic organizations engaged in philanthropic work or by taking up their residence independently in the slums. In earlier years it was chiefly clergymen who chose the latter alternative; later on a growing number of prosperous laymen followed their example. The importance of this intermingling of classes became fully evident only after the period with which we are now dealing had passed. Nevertheless we must briefly consider its beginnings at this point before describing the rôle of churchmen—and especially Christian Socialists—in the great reforms of the period.

98

Tractarians early admitted a fondness for conventual life. One could improve the soul by withdrawing from the world. But in doing so one might be closer to humanity than before. For the secular benefits of monasticism had been part of its justification in an earlier age, and they could be cited no less effectively in the present. Indeed, with an overwhelming majority of the Church suspicious of " Romanism ", it was perhaps a condition of success if not of survival that the active rather than the contemplative side of monasticism should be emphasized.

Moreover, although it was felt to be a little monstrous that men should pledge themselves to remain perpetually celibate, virtuous women often had no choice in the matter. The conventions of society had already established for them the first rule of the cloister, and it was to be expected that most of the recruits to monasticism in the Church of England would be women.[1] Under the tutelage of Pusey and with the assistance of Lord John Manners, Gladstone, and other laymen a small group of women began the religious life in 1845 in a house near Regent's Park, London. From then on sisterhoods became acknowledged centers of Church activity. In pursuit of the devotional ideal they sometimes fell foul of the Evangelical conscience, but the benefit of their ministrations to the neglected won them a growing toleration. It was not long indeed before the irreconcilables themselves offered alternatives. Orders of deaconesses not under vows began in 1879, but they were anticipated by the " Mildmay " organizations of women, instituted by the Rev. William Pennefather in 1860, who interested themselves in almost every branch of charitable work.[2]

[1] R. W. Sockman, *The Revival of the Conventual Life in the Church of England in the Nineteenth Century*, p. 105.

[2] H. P. Liddon, *Life of Edward Bouverie Pusey*, vol. iii, chap. 1; Cornish, *op. cit.*, vol. ii, pp. 78-81.

The sisterhods carried their labors into the most wretched quarters of the cities and among the class which Victorian society seldom referred to except by euphemisms. "Fallen" women became their particular concern. In the crowded districts of the cities, under the hands of women, "ragged" and industrial schools, lodging-houses, soup-kitchens, hospitals, and orphan asylums opposed the forces of indifference and neglect. It is customary for reformers to describe these charitable efforts as the ambulance service which despairingly collects a few broken victims of capitalist brutality. But however small their practical results in proportion to the need, they at least indicated a sharpening sense of social responsibility.[1]

Anglican communities of men never became as numerous or as intimately associated with the poor as did the orders of women. Without taking vows, however, men like Lord Shaftesbury and the Christian Socialists were viewing poverty at close range, and during this period the squad of veterans received a growing number of recruits.

The town clergy, especially in London, were coming more and more to appreciate the evils of slum life, not the least of which was its imperviousness to religion. Among the clergymen who chose to occupy themselves with the needy majority instead of the respectable minority was William Champneys, rector of Whitechapel from 1837 to 1860.[2] Another, less fortunate than Champneys—who lived to be dean of Lichfield—, was Alexander Mackonochie. The victim of a now forgotten Ritualist *cause célèbre,* he had to quit his living; not, however, before winning the respect of a great body of his poorer parishioners. The chief cause of his downfall was probably his interference with Jewish sweatshops in the

---

[1] Cornish, *op. cit.,* vol. ii, pp. 71-4; R. W. Sockman, *op. cit.,* p. 125.

[2] *Dictionary of National Biography,* vol. x, pp. 36-7.

East End. Workingmen ordinarily had little to do with Convocation, but a petition signed by 14,000 who opposed his removal was presented to it in 1876. Archbishop Tait pronounced them " excellent fellows " but disregarded their petition. Associated with Mackonochie as a curate was Septimus Hansard, one of the original promoters of Christian Socialist workingmen's associations.[1] Hansard later on removed to Bethnal Green. It was there that the young and enthusiastic Stewart Headlam, whose career as a reformer falls within a later period, came to him as a curate in 1873. Hansard was a friend of Dean Stanley and is described as a " reverent " broad churchman. He endeavored to improve the board-school system, and secured a museum for his parish.[2]

John Llewelyn Davies, whom we shall have occasion to notice in connection with the Christian Socialists, held cures successively in Limehouse, Whitechapel, and the poorer district of St. Marylebone. He was a member of the first London school board and author of the famous Cowper-Temple Clause of the Education Act of 1870.[3]

Here and there a layman too was coming out to see for himself the squalor of the East End. Edward Denison lived there for a short time after 1869. " He did not stay long nor accomplish much, but as he breathed the air of the people he absorbed something of their sufferings, saw things from their standpoint, and, as his letters and memoirs show, made frequent suggestions for social remedies." Edmund Hollond followed him, and it was at Hollond's suggestion that perhaps the best-known workingman's parson made

[1] *Convocation of Canterbury*, 1876, pp. 181 *et seq.*, 243; *Economic Review*, vol. vi, p. 313.

[2] F. G. Bettany, *Stewart Headlam*, pp. 34-40.

[3] *Contemporary Review*, June, 1916, pp. 782-8.

Whitechapel the field of his labors.[1]   Samuel and Mrs. Barnett took up their residence at St. Jude's in 1873.   The founder of Toynbee Hall began his pastorate in unpropitious circumstances in the midst of a poverty-stricken and filthy district, but within a year he had set in motion a machinery of adult schools, maternity classes, penny bank, and poor relief, not to mention concerts, oratorios, and other entertainments, which makes the astonished reader wonder how he found time for the cherished months abroad of which he wrote with so much gusto.   In his own mind the temporal welfare of his parishioners was strictly subordinate to their spiritual welfare, but he knew that " the walls of degrading and crippling poverty hid many from the light of truth."

The fastnesses of Whitechapel did not cut off Barnett from his friends.   As the companion of her sister Kate, a steady worker in the slums, Beatrice Potter (the future Mrs. Sidney Webb) first " became aware of the meaning of the poverty of the poor ", and was well-known at St. Jude's. Herbert Spencer and John Morley attended Barnett's assemblies.   Barnett was a co-worker with Octavia Hill, the energetic and somewhat eccentric apostle of housing reform and charity organization.   " What charmed his comrades at work in the East End," says Mrs. Webb, " and I speak from personal experience, was Barnett's fathomless sympathy, his ' quickness at the uptake ' of your moral and intellectual perplexities; his inspiring encouragement for your strivings after the nobler self." [2]

With a group of young and active Churchmen arming themselves for battle against a ubiquitous enemy, and secure in principles which pronounced this clearly right and that

[1] Samuel Barnett and Mrs. Barnett, *Practicable Socialism*, new series, p. 107.

[2] Mrs. H. O. Barnett, *Samuel Barnett, His Life, Work, and Friends,* vol. i, pp. 68, 106; Beatrice Webb, *My Apprenticeship*, pp. 90, 202.

indubitably wrong, it was quite safe to predict that, whatever the timidity of more dignified personages, the voice of the Church would be heard more clearly in social matters in the future than it had been in the past.[1]

CHURCHMEN AND TOWN PROBLEMS

1. Housing

One of the most difficult questions of an industrial society and one least satisfactorily dealt with has been the provision of decent dwellings for the working classes. Clergymen who dwelt in the slums naturally felt the gravity of the problem, and Samuel Barnett could claim some credit for influencing the government to bring in the housing bills of 1875 and 1879 which became the " Cross Acts ", for he had helped to enlighten the home secretary, R. A. Cross, by piloting him through the crowded hovels of the ironically named Castle Alley. In 1884 as inspirer of the East End Dwellings Company, Barnett took the matter into his own hands.[2]

---

[1] Frederic Harrison, by no means a gentle critic of the Establishment, bore witness to the changing atmosphere in Church circles. Writing to his mother, who had proposed holy orders to him, he said in 1853: " What is our Church? Do I not see it as a selfish sect—pressing on other Christians—keeping them from its schools and colleges—grasping its own wealth? Do I not see year after year a more complete estrangement from the poor? It is notorious that a poor man never by accident comes into a town church. The great mass of the poor of this city have no kind of place there: and does the Church care? . . . As a politician, I feel as sure as I am of anything that this Church cannot last a generation." He had yet to acquaint himself with the changes that were already afoot, but in 1911 he could say, still with a trace of the old suspicion, " I heartily admit that an immense rally of the Established Church has taken place in the fifty or sixty years since this furious indictment was penned. It is a moral as well as a great social revival of Church power, mainly in towns, and largely designed as a political experiment." (*Autobiographic Memoirs*, vol. i, pp. 143, 147.)

[2] Mrs. H. O. Barnett, *op. cit.*, vol. i, chap. 12; *Reports of Commissioners*, 1884-5, vol. 30, " Housing of the Working Classes, Minutes of Evidence," p. 290.

By that time, however, the evil had been singled out for treatment in a long series of experiments. These assumed the form at first of purely private undertakings. Lord Shaftesbury was almost the first in the field with his Labourers' Friendly Society (1842) later known as the Society for Improving the Condition of the Labouring Classes.[1] Patronized by the prince consort, the archbishop of Canterbury, and several bishops, the society evolved a rather grandiose scheme of central and local associations. By 1850 it had built or renovated houses for 91 families and 158 single women and lodgings for 241 workingmen. Up to 1858 £41,000 had been expended.[2] A number of similar projects went into operation about the same time but the results were pitiably small. R. A. Cross estimated in 1875 that philanthropic enterprise had so far provided accommodation for only 30,000 persons in London although the population of the city grew at the rate of 40,000 a year.[3]

In spite of the unfettered reign of an economic providence conditions showed no tendency to improve. The rector of Whitechapel in 1850 drew a gloomy picture of life in his parish. " I have administered the sacrament to a dying man in a room with sixteen beds, occupied the greater part of them by some married and single persons. . . I have visited a house in which I have counted 30 or 40 beds in one room; the tenants were absent when I went in the middle of the day; they were beggars, thieves, or vagrants, and there was no one but the dying man I was visiting, dying of consump-

1 Hodder, *op. cit.*, vol. ii, p. 154. The first housing organization seems to have been the Metropolitan Association for Improving the Dwellings of the Working Classes (1841). (J. J. Clarke, *The Housing Problem, its History, Growth, Legislation, and Procedure*, p. 72.)

2 Henry Roberts, *The Dwellings of the Labouring Classes*, p. 6; *Guardian*, 10 Feb., 1858, p. 109. The Metropolitan Association had spent £67,682.

3 *Hansard*, 1875, vol. 222, cols. 97, 177.

tion, in the room." [1]   Lord Shaftesbury described how workmen engaged in tearing down buildings for his society struck work when met by the swarms of rats which lived in the premises, and "though accustomed to that sort of thing," refused to return "until fire-engines had been introduced charged with water that destroyed those animals and pumped them out of existence." [2]   But a clear recognition of the evil sometimes went hand in hand with mistrust of state interference: "Is it not perfectly monstrous," said the High Church *British Magazine,* "to allow men to maintain these depositories of contagion and death in the midst of such a population as that of London?   It is not our business to prescribe remedies.   A little more of energy, a little more of just sense of responsibility on the part of local authorities and other influential persons, would do much to render legislative interference less necessary than many persons believe it to be." [3]

But when other remedies failed it was necessary to appeal to law.   Accordingly in 1851 Lord Shaftesbury secured the passage of two bills, the more ambitious of which permitted local authorities to erect public lodging-houses at their own expense.   The other, and as it turned out, the more effective one, provided for the inspection and supervision of lodging-houses. [4]

A subordinate housing issue revolved about the entry of railways into London.   It was customary for railroads to

[1] *Reports from Committees,* 1850, vol. 19, p. 177, "Report from the Select Committee of the House of Lords on a Bill to Prevent Sunday Trading."

[2] *Reports of Commissioners,* 1884-5, vol. 30, "Royal Commission on the Housing of the Working Classes, Minutes of Evidence," p. 3.

[3] 1848, vol. 33, p. 53.

[4] J. J. Clarke, *op. cit.,* p. 6; London County Council, *The Housing Question in London 1855-1900,* p. 1; J. W. Bready, *op. cit.,* p. 97.

buy rights of way through thickly populated territory and eject the inhabitants, who went to overtax the already crowded tenements in the vicinity.   Lord Shaftesbury in 1853 moved a new standing order of the House of Lords which would have compelled all companies seeking legislation thereafter to provide dwellings for the persons displaced. Bishop Blomfield of London seconded the proposal.   " The poor had their rights," he said,

and although they might not have rights of property, as that term was understood, yet they had rights, the enjoyment of which was as valuable to them as the rights of property to other persons. If they destroyed a rich man's residence, he was entitled to compensation, and, perhaps, it was of no consequence to him whether he removed to a distance of one mile or five miles; but if they turned a poor man out of his tenement he had no choice, he must of necessity live near to his employment, and thus was obliged to pay any price, however exorbitant, to secure shelter for himself and his family.

The committee which reported on Shaftesbury's motion reduced it to nothing more than a promise that the interest of dispossessed tenants would be considered when railway bills were framed.[1]   The advantages which were expected to result from this modest check proved to be illusory and Shaftesbury returned to the charge, supported by a new bishop of London, Tait, in 1861.[2]   Thomas Hughes almost immediately after taking his seat in the House of Commons in 1866 broached the question once more.   He quoted representatives of the railways to the effect that almost 18,000 persons were to be dispossessed in that year alone.   But the measures taken were slow enough to be easily outstripped by the agile

---

[1] *Hansard*, 1853, vol. 125, cols. 399, 408; vol. 126, col. 1292.

[2] *Ibid.*, 1861, vol. 161, col. 1074.

imagination of railway executives and the record is one of systematic evasion until 1885.[1]

Previous to the introduction of further legislation the housing situation was called to the attention of the Church Congress of 1864 by the Rev. J. E. Clarke and Canon Stowell. The former connected total abstinence with cleanly dwellings and asserted that bad living conditions were at the root of the failure of religion. Canon Stowell said the situation was " a disgrace to this Christian country," and the agricultural population lived in quarters " into which one of their squires would hardly turn his dogs, and certainly into which he would not turn his horses." [2] Before this *The Guardian* had attributed drunkenness in part to bad housing: " We talk of the hindrances to popular education, and immediately the difficulty presents itself of inculcating lessons of decency of which the homes of the children offer neither the example nor the opportunity." [3]

The Torrens Acts of 1866 and 1868 were the first attempts to apply adequate compulsion to house owners. Local authorities were empowered on application of four householders or the recommendation of the health official to require the closing or repair of houses at the owner's expense.[4] In the House of Lords both Shaftesbury and Tait supported these measures. "If such a state of things continued to exist, he [Tait] thought that all efforts to improve the condition of the population and extend education among the masses must to a great extent be rendered powerless." The evil might, he admitted, be due partly to lack of energy

[1] *Reports of Commissioners*, "Housing of the Working Classes," 1884-5, vol. 30, Report, pp. 52-3; E. R. Dewsnup, *The Housing Problem in England*, p. 19.

[2] *Church Congress*, 1864, pp. 196-7.

[3] 9 Dec., 1857, p. 933, "The Dwellings of the Poor."

[4] J. J. Clarke, *op. cit.*, pp. 7 *et seq.*

on the part of the people, but the surroundings were of themselves demoralizing.[1]

2. *Factory Legislation and Sunday Labor*

Even a Shaftesbury was unequal to the task of threading the housing wilderness with its thickets of vested interest, economic prejudice, and popular indifference. Another and more tried avenue of approach to the problems of labor remained open. He could improve working conditions if he could not improve living conditions. As always, his eyes were fixed chivalrously upon the weaker members of the working class. His successful campaign in behalf of chimney sweeps has already been mentioned. In 1861 his motion " that an Enquiry be made into the Employment of Children and Young Persons in Trade and Manufactures not already recognized by law " resulted in the appointment of the Children's Employment Commission.[2] The government measures of 1864 and 1867 called the Factory Extension Acts were the outcome of this investigation. In general their purpose was to fill the interstices of previous legislation by bringing under control establishments such as potteries, match factories, explosive plants, and workshops in which fewer than fifty persons were employed. Finally, in 1871 Shaftesbury proposed to include brickyards within the scope of the acts, being supported by Bishop Jackson.[3]

However leniently the Church regarded the current morality of employment for six days of the week, it could not agree to any invasion of the seventh. Samuel Wilberforce favored stopping the Post Office on Sunday.[4] Bishop

---

[1] *Hansard*, 1868, vol. 192, col. 907.

[2] *Ibid.*, 1861, vol. 164, col. 1875.

[3] J. W. Bready, *op. cit.*, pp. 313 *et seq.*, 323; *Hansard*, 1871, vol. 207, col. 1401.

[4] *Hansard*, 1850, vol. 109, col. 125.

Waldegrave attacked a Sunday trading bill of 1866 because it was not stringent enough.[1] Thomas Hughes submitted a number of measures to the House of Commons from 1868 onward. Bishops Ellicott and Jackson supported the bill of 1870.[2] None of these projects effected any important changes in the law, which continued to rest chiefly on a statute of Charles II.[3] Their interest lies rather in the fact that the arguments for stricter regulation were not narrowly theological in tone. The physical as well as the spiritual needs of labor received due notice.[4]

LATER HISTORY OF THE CHRISTIAN SOCIALISTS

1. Adult Education and the Working Men's College

It was only a little less evident after 1850 than it had been before that if workingmen wished to improve their condition they would have to rely mainly on their own efforts. Charity grew more effective as it became less sentimental, and the state was contributing a little in the way of education and factory laws, but self-help contained possibilities more impressive because they had not been fully explored. Christian Socialism was likely to survive under these circumstances, for its basic doctrine was self-help through co-operation.

Many writers have described the earlier phase of Christian Socialism, but few have said anything of its later career.

[1] *Hansard*, 1866, vol. 183, col. 940.

[2] *Ibid.*, 1868, vol. 191, col. 1084; 1869, vol. 194, col. 557; 1870, vol. 199, col. 677.

[3] *Cf. Reports from Committees*, 1906, vol. 13, " Report from the Joint Select Committee on Sunday Trading." A brief review of the law as it existed before 1906 is given by the permanent under-secretary of the Home Department (p. 19) and sections of the laws from 27 Henry VI. c. 5 on are printed (p. 268).

[4] *Cf.* Waldegrave on the opening of the Dublin botanical garden (*Hansard*, 1861, vol. 164, col. 25) ; *Guardian*, 4 July, 1855, p. 517.

This is because after 1854 it ceased to be an organized movement. But individual Christian Socialists still had much to contribute to adult education, trade unionism, the co-operative movement, and friendly societies. Indeed, for some years they constituted the backbone of Church influence in the labor movement.

Men never lose faith in education as a social panacea, and the working class has for a long period looked upon the instruction of adults as a primary step in social advancement. Before recounting the later history of the Christian Socialist Working Men's College it is necessary to consider the contribution of churchmen to other types of adult education.

Like many similar movements, adult education has its primitive foreshadowings which are not in the direct line of historical development. A Sunday Society of Birmingham, for example, provided classes for young men in writing, book-keeping, arithmetic, geography, and drawing as early as 1789. Of more importance were the lectures for artisans by George Birkbeck of Glasgow, begun in 1799 and continued for some years afterward. But the real center of propagation was the London Mechanics' Institution which, suggested by Robertson and Hodgskin, promoted by Birkbeck, and patronized by Brougham, Hobhouse, and Lushington, began to operate in 1823. The idea speedily took root and spread throughout the British Isles until by 1851 mechanics' institutes numbered 700, with 120,000 members and a book circulation of 2,000,000.[1] In 1861 the institutes had increased to 1,200 and the membership, to 200,000.[2]

Writing about 1850, two strong advocates of mechanics'

[1] J. W. Hudson, *History of Adult Education*, pp. 29-36; James Hole, *An Essay on the History and Management of Literary, Scientific, and Mechanics' Institutions*, p. 58.

[2] J. M. Ludlow and Lloyd Jones, *Progress of the Working Class, 1832-1867*, p. 169.

institutes had several uncomplimentary things to say about the attitude of clergymen. " The Mechanics' Institutions, established in England during the years 1824 to 1835, received the most direct opposition from that powerful section of the Community, the clergy of the Establishment." In the cities, where the influence of the clergy was relatively small, this antipathy was of little moment, but in the rural districts it was often decisive. " The squire or the clergyman is the only person who could render effectual help, but in not one instance out of a score do they look with favor upon the plan—well, indeed, if they do not oppose it as new-fangled and dangerous." " Even when disposed to aid the Institution, it is often rather in the capacity of self-elected dictator than in that of its director and friend." [1]

But the clergy were not wholly sunk in reaction. A few like Dr. Hook, the vicar of Leeds, and Bishops Whateley and Thirlwall were speedily converted. When it became apparent that the movement had too much vitality and popularity to be ignored, others set up institutions with a carefully preserved Church atmosphere. These were successful in centers such as Stourbridge, Bradford, and Wakefield, where the Establishment was strong; in other places the clergy called on Dissenters for assistance. [2]

Mechanics' institutes experienced some difficulties unconnected with the animus of clergymen. Intended for workingmen, they were in many cases appropriated by the middle class. In 1840 nineteen-twentieths of the membership of the West Riding Union was said to have been of this character. [3] Clerical witness before the Education Commission of 1858 testified that the institutes were failing to reach the

---

[1] J. Hole, *op. cit.*, pp. 92-3, 130.

[2] J. W. Hudson, *op. cit.*, p. 201.

[3] J. Hole, *op. cit.*, p. 21; Basil Yeaxlee, *Spiritual Values in Adult Education*, vol. i, p. 157.

working class.[1] The fact was that many workingmen had
no elementary education to start with. " The time which
[the worker] should be spending in the temple of knowledge
is taken up in mastering the keys of its portals." [2]   Night
schools in part supplied this need, and it was discovered by
the Education Commission that two-thirds of the 2,036
schools with 80,000 pupils were conducted by the Church of
England.[3]

Another tendency which the more earnest reformer looked
upon with disfavor was the inclination to use the institute
more as a place of amusement than of serious instruction.
Others frankly met this perhaps natural tendency by organizing working-men's clubs where recreation was made acces-
sory to education.   When the Workingmen's Club and Institute Union was founded in 1862 less than ten such clubs
existed.   In 1878 there were more than a thousand.[4]

The faults of mechanics' institutes did not, however, rest
wholly upon those who attended them.   Very often the
lectures were superficial and the arrangements unsystematic.[5]
An ingenious way out of this difficulty was offered by Lord
Arthur Hervey, rector of Ickworth, president of the Bury
Institute, and later bishop of Bath and Wells.   As early as
1855 he pointed out the desirability of calling upon the
Universities for assistance in adult education.   Nothing,
he said, would " more conduce to their conciliating to themselves the affection and support of all classes in the land."
His scheme called for travelling instructors who would visit

---

[1] *Royal Commission on Popular Education*, part 5, pp. 83, 123, 154, 166.

[2] J. Hole, *op. cit.*, p. 20.

[3] *Church Congress*, 1864, pp. 259 *et seq.*

[4] J. M. Ludlow and Lloyd Jones, *op. cit.*, p. 179; *Report of the Co-operative Congress*, 1878, p. 9.

[5] *Royal Commission on Popular Education*, part 5, p. 78, evidence of
the Rev. Samuel Best; J. Hole, *op. cit.*, p. 24.

mechanics' institutes and give a series of perhaps six consecutive lectures. He suggested that Cambridge should create four professorships, "say of Natural Philosophy, of Geology, of Astronomy, of Literature", for this purpose. The incumbents would be able to cover twenty towns a year and their stipends might consist of £20 contributions from each. He believed that the plan might well be extended to other universities.[1] " In this short pamphlet the author shows his prescience by recommending the very form in which Extension work, as we know it, was first made a reality."[2]

The idea had to wait some eighteen years for its adoption. Through the efforts of James Stuart, however, Cambridge began the experiment in university extension in 1873. Among the earliest lecturers were W. Moore Ede (afterwards dean of Worcester) and William Cunningham, the economic historian and later archdeacon of Ely.[3]

Meanwhile the London Working Men's College, pursuing its ideal of advanced education for the masses, gathered a student body almost equally divided between skilled artisans and tradesmen, with a sprinkling of the professional class.[4] Its founders had the satisfaction of seeing their experiment imitated at Oxford, Cambridge, Manchester, Wolverhampton, Salford, Halifax, and other places.[5] During the first years the Christian Socialists found no difficulty in attracting a group of instructors already well-known or on the road

[1] *A Suggestion for Supplying the Literary, Scientific, and Mechanics' Institutes of Great Britain and Ireland with Lecturers from the Universities* (1855).

[2] William H. Draper, *University Extension, a Survey of Fifty Years, 1873-1923*, p. 3.

[3] *Ibid.*, pp. 5 *et seq.*, 19.

[4] *Guardian*, 30 May, 1855, p. 422.

[5] *Ibid.*, 9 June, 1856, p. 23; B. Yeaxlee, *op. cit.*, vol. i, pp. 264-5.

to fame. Among these first teachers were Fitz-James Stephen, Godfrey and Vernon Lushington, J. F. Westlake, F. J. Furnivall, J. S. Brewer the historian, and M. E. Grant Duff.[1]

The art courses were particularly well-staffed. A conflict in theory between Ruskin and Rossetti helped to stimulate and perhaps to disconcert their classes. While Ruskin patiently explained the chiaroscuro of an egg, " Rossetti put a bird or a boy before his classes and said ' Do it; ' and the spirit of the teacher was of more value than any system." [2] For some years the Pre-Raphaelite influence predominated, Rossetti's work being continued by Edward Burne-Jones and Ford Madox Brown.[3]

Among a group of young intellectuals habitually defiant of authority, it was natural that the ideals and achievements of the College should be liberally criticized. The particular religious note struck by Maurice irritated Ruskin. " Maurice was by nature puzzle-headed, and though in a beautiful manner, *wrong*-headed; while his clear conscience and keen affections made him egotistic, and in his Bible-reading as insolent as any infidel of them all. I only went once to a Bible-lesson of his; and the meeting was significant and conclusive." [4] Frederic Harrison began teaching in 1855. While he had experienced no difficulty in arriving at fixed opinions on other difficult subjects, his religious ideas still obstinately refused to congeal. But the liberal theology of Maurice proved to him the futility of all creeds and set him far on the road toward Positivism.[5]

[1] F. Maurice, *Life and Letters of Frederick Denison Maurice*, vol. ii, p. 305.

[2] G. B. Hill, *Letters of Dante Gabriel Rossetti*, p. 88.

[3] Gertrude Burne-Jones, *Memorials of Edward Burne-Jones*, vol. i, pp. 128, 191 ; Ford Madox Ford, *Ford Madox Brown*, p. 159.

[4] *Praeterita*, vol. iii,

[5] Frederic Harrison, *Autobiographic Memoirs*, vol. i, p. 151.

Doubts as to the efficacy of the whole enterprise assailed both Harrison and Ruskin. " The classes at the Ormond Street College," wrote Harrison in 1861, " do not satisfy me. The students are mere parasites of the middle classes, not really working men. The education ends in the ordinary literary trifling." [1] Ruskin added another axiom to his collection: " I have very clearly ascertained that the only proper school for working men is of the work their fathers bred them to, under masters able to do better than any of their men and with common principles of honesty and the fear of God to guide the firm." [2]

Before retiring to the purer atmosphere of Free Thought Hall, Harrison attempted to introduce some reforms in the teaching of history. But Maurice " furiously " opposed them and clung to the venerable division of the subject into reigns of kings, threatening to resign the presidency if Harrison's system was adopted.[3]

About 1860 the College entered on a time of troubles. No longer possessing the attractiveness of novelty, it had to rely on the more solid qualities of fitness and adaptability to the purposes it served. But the standard of instruction showed a tendency to decline, while the spirit and personnel of the student-body left much to be desired. A clique of earlier students developed ideas of exclusiveness which contradicted all the precepts of brotherhood so laboriously instilled by Maurice. Hughes, horrified at the prospect of a French invasion, and intent also on advertising the College, organized a volunteer military corps which attracted men interested in uniforms rather than in intellectual culture. The establishment also suffered from administrative and financial weakness.[4]

[1] Harrison, *op. cit.*, vol. i, p. 266.
[2] *Praeterita*, vol. iii.
[3] Frederic Harrison, *op. cit.*, vol. i, p. 150.
[4] J. L. Davies, *The Working Men's College 1854-1904*, pp. 100-104.

During R. B. Litchfield's vice-principalship, from 1872 to 1875, a period of reorganization began. Faculty and students joined in working out a scheme of reform, by which the government of the College was placed in the hands of a committee consisting of the faculty and student representatives, and a more efficient system of finance was instituted. Ludlow and several others resisted these innovations but the marked progress of the College in succeeding years gradually silenced the opposition.

New men of ability began to offer their services. As early as 1866 A. V. Dicey for a short time conducted a class in logic and from 1899 to 1912 held the office of principal.[1] Mr. (later Sir) Charles Lucas was connected with the institution, first as a teacher, and later as vice-principal from 1897 to 1903. The early efforts of neither were brilliantly successful. Like Hughes, who turned his law class into a seminar in boxing, Lucas found it necessary to supplement his teaching by active participation in the Maurice Cricket Club.[2] Alfred Lyttelton, the future colonial secretary, is said to have been more fortunate as a teacher of law than Hughes. The name of Sidney Webb also appears on the roll of the faculty. After the death of Maurice in 1872 John Llewelyn Davies represented the clerical element among the founders. A man of no little capacity, his frank liberalism prevented the promotion in the Church which friends believed his due. " His own words on the subject were, that he would rather that people asked why he was not made a bishop than why he was." [3]

Thus by 1880 the Working Men's College appeared to

[1] Davies, *op. cit.*, p. 121; R. S. Rait, *Memorials of Albert Venn Dicey*, pp. 175-6.

[2] *Cornhill Magazine*, 1916, p. 425, " Llewelyn Davies and the Working Men's College," by Sir Charles Lucas.

[3] *Ibid.*, p. 422.

have reached firm ground. Frederic Harrison in 1911 stated its minimum achievement.

The College has thriven and increased on the basis of the Christian Socialism of Maurice and the muscular Christianity of Tom Hughes, as a useful and well-conducted school of secondary education on the established and moderate lines, with some Christianity, a little arm-chair Socialism, and a mild infusion of real working men.[1]

2. *Friendly Societies*

The Promoters' Association had been dissolved in 1854, but the Christian Socialists abandoned none of their original aims, although they somewhat modified their policy. As co-operators, they were naturally attracted to Friendly Societies, and their influence upon the movement was exerted chiefly through the medium of Ludlow. In an earlier chapter we have noticed the disappearance of antipathy toward these associations on the part of clergymen.

Unknown to the great public [says the historian of the movement] and devoting the silent but consistent activity of a whole life to the task, many land-owners and their wives and the country clergymen, have been labouring for these Friendly Societies, as they have laboured for many other institutions of common utility, have been preaching thrift and providence, have set an example by their conscientious co-operation in the Friendly Societies, and have succeeded in diffusing knowledge and forming character.[2]

A clergyman, the Rev. C. P. Tidd Pratt, was appointed to the office of Registrar of Friendly Societies when that position was created by the government in 1846.

---

[1] Frederic Harrison, *op. cit.*, vol. i, p. 159.

[2] J. M. Baernreither, *English Associations of Working Men*, p. 177; *Reports of Commissioners*, 1874, vol. 23, part 2. Various societies conducted wholly or partly by churchmen are referred to on pp. 70-72, 114, 169, 182-3, 187, 190, 192, etc.

These associations insured their members primarily against loss of wages through sickness, and sometimes against damage to tools or implements by fire. Occasionally they furnished medical attendance and paid the expenses of members travelling in search of work. Others acted as savings banks. These complicated functions required intelligent and honest administration if the contributors were not to suffer. But many of the directors, untrained in actuarial methods, frequently assessed insufficient premiums and made bad investments with the result that poor people often lost heavily. Various acts had been passed to remedy these evils, and registration with the government, while not compulsory, offered some sort of guaranty to the members of those societies which took advantage of it.[1]

A royal commission subjected the whole matter to scrutiny in 1871. Ludlow was appointed secretary to the commission and in 1874 drew up its final report in two thick volumes which contained a digest of the evidence and recommendations for reform. Ludlow's summary of the testimony is described as " admirable " by a later authority, and the influence of the commission " greater than many an earlier Act of Parliament."[2] While the inquiry was in progress Ludlow expressed his opinion as to the facts which had already been disclosed. He attacked some of the great commercialized societies which had been battening on the ignorance of their subscribers. " Substantially it is hardly an exaggeration to say that the system on which these great collecting burial Societies is conducted resolves itself into the very simple operation of selling half-pence for pennies."

[1] J. M. Baernreither, *op. cit.*, pp. 162, 165, 298-9. It should be said that Friendly Societies were supposed to be mutual in character, thus differing from the insurance companies, which were regulated by a different series of acts.

[2] *Ibid.*, pp. 310-11.

But true to his co-operative principles he remained averse to thoroughgoing government control. " I cannot say that I wish for this. I believe that the self-government in ordinary Friendly Societies is a precious thing in itself,—an education not to be bartered away for mere indolent safety." [1]

The sequel to the investigation was the Friendly Societies Act of 1875 (amended in 1876). Ludlow drafted the original bill. As it was finally adopted the act (38 & 39 Vict. c. 60) enlarged the privileges of registered societies, permitted the registration of societies not falling within the ordinary categories, if specially authorized (thus leaving the way open to trade unions), and closely restricted societies which employed collectors. It also provided for a Chief Registrar, to whom the registrars for Scotland and Ireland were subordinated. Ludlow received the office, which he continued to hold until 1891. He proved to be an efficient administrator and compiled valuable statistics on sickness and mortality, thus giving the societies a stronger actuarial basis. [2]

3. The Co-operative Movement

Friendly Societies attempted to provide for the vicissitudes of life. Co-operation concerned itself with the ordinary business of society. It therefore contained greater social possibilities and received a larger share of the attention of Christian Socialists. Their abortive experiments with co-operative workshops—unsuccessful at least in those particular instances—have been noticed above. [3] Two other earlier projects which had temporarily failed were brought to fruition during this period. These were the Wholesale Society and the Co-operative Union.

[1] *Contemporary Review*, April, 1873, pp. 758 *et seq.*

[2] *Dictionary of National Biography*, second supplement, vol. ii, p. 489; J. M. Baernreither, *op. cit.*, p. 324; J. J. Dent, *J. M. Ludlow* (a pamphlet by a fellow co-operator), p. 13.

[3] Pp. 54, 56.

E. V. Neale had supplied the funds for a Central Co-operative Agency where goods of high quality might be purchased at wholesale by the scattered co-operative stores. The agency was discontinued in 1852 after an existence of only two years, due to its inconvenient location in the south of England and to the societies' lack of interest in an enterprise not their own. A congress of co-operators meeting in 1853 under the auspices of the Christian Socialists proposed that some local society should enter the wholesale trade. The suggestion was adopted by the Rochdale Pioneers. But jealousy on the part of the member stores and unwillingness on the part of the Rochdale Society to continue a losing business closed the wholesale department after a brief career.[1]

The last and successful campaign for the establishment of a wholesale agency began in 1860 when a group of co-operators met near Manchester to consider the question. Another conference followed at Oldham the next year. Their conclusion was that a wholesale society must be owned and operated by the co-operatives as a group. To do this it was necessary to secure legislation which would permit the investment of co-operative funds in such an agency with reasonable security. The group corresponded with Neale for advice concerning the necessary legislation and thus put in operation the machinery which had secured the similar act in 1852.[2] Once more R. A. Slaney was called upon to introduce the measure to the House of Commons. Although during his illness a Conservative member, J. Sotheron Estcourt, stepped into the breach the result was the same and the act of 1862 opened the way for a new wholesale society. Neale drafted the rules of registration for the North of England Co-operative Wholesale Industrial and Provident

[1] Percy Redfern, *The Story of the C. W. S.*, pp. 11-15; *Report of the Co-operative Congress*, 1869, p. 39.

[2] *Supra*, p. 57.

Society, which came into being in 1863 and has continued to prosper (though under a different name) ever since.[1]

Some general oversight of the Co-operative movement had long been deemed necessary by the leaders. The Owenites had met in conference as early as 1831. Again in 1852 and 1853 the Christian Socialists had called together assemblies of this kind. Between the latter date and 1869 no such meeting had occurred in London.[2] There existed, however, a self-constituted group composed of Lord Ripon and the Christian Socialists who, in the words of Hughes, " practically settled down into a committee for advising associations, preparing and revising their rules, and obtaining amendments and modifications of the Industrial and Provident Societies Act." [3]

A meeting held on August 28th, 1868, at which Neale presided, determined to call a conference of co-operators at London. Societies for production were invited to participate. But the appeal had such a luke-warm response that it was dropped. William Pare, editor of the *Co-operator,* revived the project in 1869 and another meeting took place on April 2nd, with Neale in the chair. A committee was appointed to get in touch with the Lancashire and Yorkshire societies and a call issued to distributive organizations and trade unions as well as to producers' associations. This time the response was gratifying, and later in the year the first Co-operative Congress assembled. Evidently with the idea

[1] Percy Redfern, *op. cit.,* chaps. 3 and 4; *Report of the Co-operative Congress,* 1869, p. 40; *Dictionary of National Biography,* vol. 40, p. 139.

[2] For some years there had been a North of England Conference Association (Catherine Webb (ed.), *Industrial Co-operation,* p. 192), and according to A. D. Acland and B. Jones (*Working Men Co-operators* (1921 ed.) pp. 143-4) from 1860 to 1868 nineteen conferences were held: four in Scotland, twelve in the north, and three in the south of England.

[3] *Report of the Co-operative Congress,* 1878, pp. 62-3.

of securing a widespread support, numerous influential men
were appointed to the committee of the Congress.   Louis
Blanc rubbed elbows with John Ruskin and A. J. Mundella.
William Allan of the engineers' union, George Odgers of
the London Trades Council, and other labor leaders found
themselves in close proximity to Christian Socialists and
churchmen.   The clergy named were Charles Kingsley, the
Honorable J. W. Leigh, Septimus Hansard, W. N. Molesworth, and J. H. Sandy.[1]

Apparently this committee was simply an honorary one,
but the Christian Socialists secured strategic positions in the
management of the Congress.   Thomas Hughes was its first
president and Ludlow edited the first Report and wrote its
preface.   Along with Neale he was elected to the Central
Board.[2]   In 1875 Neale became the salaried general secretary
and legal adviser of the Congress with the duty of editing
the Report.   He held this position until his retirement in
1891.   Although for some time he was " treated ' with a
studied disrespect,' long before he resigned the secretaryship
he had completely won the confidence of the working classes,
who regarded him with reverence and affection." [3]   Ludlow
took a prominent part in the affairs of the Congress until
1875 when he resigned from the Central Board to take up
his official duties as Registrar of Friendly Societies.[4]

Neale, Hughes, and Ludlow sought to infuse the policy of
the Congress with two guiding principles: the necessity of a
religious basis for co-operation and the importance of co-
operative production.

From the religious point of view, therefore, it was no

[1] *Report of the Co-operative Congress,* 1869, p. 6.   The committee
consisted of 107 persons.

[2] *Ibid.,* 1870, p. 51.

[3] *Dictionary of National Biography,* vol. 40, p. 139.

[4] *Report of the Co-operative Congress,* 1875, p. 23.

doubt gratifying to have churchmen outside the movement take an interest in co-operation.   As the offices of the Central Board and the warehouses of the Wholesale Society were located in Manchester, it was natural that Bishop Fraser should come in contact with the movement.   Hughes said that he was "the first person of any influence outside the co-operative body to draw public attention" to it.   When admonished by the Grocers' Defense Association that a "dignified neutrality" in such matters was proper to a bishop he rejected their advice with some asperity.   Presiding at the Manchester Congress of 1878 he took the attitude of a friendly critic and admitted that although a believer in their principles "he had never spent sixpence in a co-operative store, and didn't mean to so long as his tradesmen served him well."   "From this time he was hand in glove with the co-operators, coming whenever he could to all great gatherings, and always telling them of any weak spot in their armour or backslidings in their doings." [1]   Bishop Lightfoot of Durham addressed the Newcastle Congress of 1880.   He took the opportunity of refuting "the claims of Communism (meaning thereby State Socialism)", which he was sure Englishmen must condemn, and in a piece of reasoning no doubt true and certainly satisfactory to himself brought co-operation within the limits of orthodox economics.   "If competition be, as some men seem to think, an unmixed evil, then even productive co-operation cannot, I fear, altogether escape blame.   But it is competition where competition inflicts the least hardship.   It is competition with the great capitalist." [2]

The religious implications of co-operation, clear enough to Christian Socialists, were less apparent to some of their

[1] Thomas Hughes, *James Fraser, Second Bishop of Manchester*, pp. 231-3; *Report of the Co-operative Congress*, 1878, pp. 15-18.

[2] *Report of the Co-operative Congress*, 1880, pp. 3 *et seq.*

allies.   This divergence of views was plainly defined in 1881. Hughes and Neale had been commissioned to prepare a " Manual for Co-operators " which should contain a statement of principles as well as provide information and a set of rules for adherents.   They devoted a somewhat lengthy section to the claims of Christianity.   Pointing to the fact that even men like Owen and Fourier had had some theory of man and his place in the universe behind their systems,

we ought [they said] to find in the religious faiths subsisting among men some one at least, and that not an insignificant uninfluential faith which will supply, in conceptions proper to itself, a solid basis for the modes of action through which we think that co-operation may effect the social reforms sought for by its means.

Looking about them they discovered that Christianity exactly met this requirement, and launched into a fervid justification of their choice.

What Christianity has done in the past, those who regard it as the mighty agent provided by God to redeem men from that slavery out of which the slavery of the body springs—the slavery to selfishness—may fittingly ask it to do for the present and the future.   We who appeal to Christianity to evolve co-operative industry and associated life are, in truth, asking it to tame into obedience to the law of brotherhood, which is the law of reason, those energies that, left to the law of nature, can produce only " the struggle for existence ", known to modern political economy under the name of free competition.[1]

When the Manual was presented to the Congress, G. J. Holyoake took pronounced exception to including such material in a text-book.   The object, he thought, should be confined to teaching men to carry on the ordinary business of

---

[1] *A Manual for Co-operators*, pp. 4, 10.

life, not to meddle with religious questions.   Hughes upheld the viewpoint of the authors.   Neale replied in the preface to the Report of the Congress that Holyoake " would have the rules for human conduct be their own foundation."   There must be a confusion in his mind between theology and religion.   " To give co-operation a religious basis is to ask religion to come out from the churches and chapels, which Mr. Holyoake regards as their proper home, into the busy haunts of industry and trade, to deal with the practical affairs of mankind." [1]   But Holyoake had the last word, for he outlived his adversaries.   A generation later he recalled the dispute in his memoirs.   " I objected to this as violating the principle on which we had long agreed, namely of Co-operative neutrality in religion and politics, as their introduction was the signal of disputation which diverted the attention of members from the advancement of Co-operation in life, trade, and labour." [2]   It was a conflict between idealism and hard-headed practicality.   The Congress, however, on the motion of Benjamin Jones, accepted the Manual with thanks.[3]

However much Holyoake and the Christian Socialists fell out over religion, both were ardent supporters of producers' co-operation.   Hughes and Neale in the Manual pointed out the difference between co-operators and socialists.   " The essential distinction is that co-operators are those social reformers who approach the great problems of social reform with their eyes open and their hands free.   Admitting the greatness of the end which the prophets of socialism have set before their disciples, they claim for the end to be greater than the insight of the prophets; and, refusing to be bound by the words of any master, investigate their social systems

[1] *Report of the Co-operative Congress*, 1881, preface, pp. iv-v.

[2] *Bygones Worth Remembering*, vol. ii, p. 112.

[3] *Report of the Co-operative Congress*, 1881, p. 2.

in the free spirit of scientific inquiry, not blindly adopting, nor having any prejudices against them." [1]   The sentiment is unexceptionable—might well, indeed, be adopted as a motto by any reasonable reformer—but the constancy with which the Christian Socialists adhered to the doctrine of co-operative production seems to have been of the essence of faith rather than science.   For societies of this type continually decreased in numbers, relatively to the consumers' organizations.

It must have been largely due to the influence of the Christian Socialists that the Co-operative Congress steadily inclined to the productive principle.   In 1876 the Central Board " wish it were possible to announce . . . a real progress in the application of co-operation to that important sphere of production, on which the permanent well-being of mankind must depend." [2]   A similar resolution was carried by a large majority in 1877.[3]   Christian Socialists had always tried to interest trade unions in this phase of co-operation.   Hughes renewed the appeal in 1869, quoting a favorable statement of the Trades Union Congress.[4]   In periods of extraordinary trade-union activity the productive idea always had a certain amount of fascination for unionists. This was true in 1833-4, 1852, and 1871-5.   But in the last period they looked upon it not as a revolutionary measure but as a means of providing temporary occupation for unemployed members.[5]

The distributive societies were urged, also unsuccessfully, to lend their surplus capital to producers' associations.[6]   But

---

[1] P. 24.

[2] *Report of the Co-operative Congress*, 1876, p. 20.

[3] *Ibid.*, 1877, p. 50.

[4] *Ibid.*, 1869, p. 15.

[5] S. and B. Webb, *History of Trade Unionism*, p. 335.

[6] *Report of the Co-operative Congress*, 1869, p. 13.

when the Wholesale Society began to manufacture its own stock, Neale regarded the innovation as a travesty of his principle. " Mr. Neale held with Mr. Hughes and others that the Wholesale Societies should register separate societies for each productive department, nurse them, supply them with capital, and ultimately hand them over to the work-people, while still supplying them with the trade necessary to keep them fully and profitably employed." [1]

Christian Socialists supported producers' co-operation because they saw in it the only means by which the standard of living could be raised, class conflict avoided, and the interests of workers in particular industries protected. Neale assured the trade unions of his interest in their welfare,

but it is no part of the duty of co-operators to conceal from the the body of Trades Unionists the conviction . . . that, as a means of permanently raising the condition of the mass of the working population, the system of Trades Unionism must be pronounced, still more emphatically than the system of joint-stock competitive enterprise, to be " weighed and found wanting "—that the teachings of political economy as to the condition by which the wealth of mankind can be increased, are substantially founded in the nature of things . . . and that wages cannot . . . be raised in equal degree all around, without the effect of correspondingly raising prices, but that such a process must end by leaving every worker at last . . . where it found him.[2]

[1] Benjamin Jones, *Co-operative Production*, vol. ii, p. 758. The Christian Socialists and the Wholesale Society also crossed swords over the question of a bank. Ludlow in 1869 had suggested the establishment of a bank for the whole movement. The Wholesale Society set up a banking department of its own, a proceeding criticized by Neale who said that "the surest way to have injudicious lending was for a concern to lend money to itself." (*Reports of the Co-operative Congress*, 1869, p. 33; 1877, p. 12; 1878, p. 40.)

[2] *Report of the Co-operative Congress*, 1876, preface.

Hughes and Neale did not confine their co-operative activities to the Congress. In the face of past failures they now and again launched a producers' society with the most invulnerable optimism. In 1867 Hughes became a director and Ludlow a shareholder of the Framemakers' and Gilders' Association. Five years later Hughes established the London Company of Builders " to test the principle of co-operation as a preventive of strikes." [1] Neale helped to found the Cobden Mills in 1866.[2] America, which had been the proving ground for other European theorists, was the site of Hughes' model community of " Rugby ". The experiment was a dismal failure, however, and left its patron in serious financial difficulties.[3] Two propagandist organizations were also initiated—the Guild of Co-operators (1878) of which Hughes was chairman, and the Labour Association (1884) with which Neale allied himself.[4]

Before leaving this subject we must notice a curious aberration of Hughes as a co-operator. At the Congress of 1869 Mr. Archibald Briggs, a capitalist, read a paper in which he described a profit-sharing system in operation at his colliery. The scheme ran exactly counter to the most vital points of co-operation. In 1867 H. C. Briggs, his brother, had appeared before the Trades Union Commission of which Hughes was a member and with disarming candor had admitted that the plan was instituted for the purpose of avoiding strikes, that it " infinitely " strengthened the hands of employers, and that the addition to wages was more apparent than real.[5] Nevertheless Hughes did not hesitate to pro-

---

[1] Benjamin Jones, *op. cit.*, vol. ii, p. 549.

[2] *Dictionary of National Biography*, vol. 40, p. 139.

[3] *Economic Review*, vol. vi, p. 311.

[4] *Report of the Co-operative Congress*, 1879, p. 46; E. V. Neale, *The Principles, Objects, and Methods of the Labour Association.*

[5] *Reports of Commissioners*, 1867, vol. 39, pp. 200 *et seq.*

nounce this caricature " in my judgment, the most important development of Co-operation we have yet seen." It devolved upon Ludlow to take up the cudgels.

Mr. Ludlow said that the Messrs. Briggs' practice was better than their theory, or he would have a bad opinion of them. The plan of the paper seemed to be—to extract from the worker the largest possible amount of labor for the smallest possible bribe in the way of bonus. (" No," from Mr. Briggs.) It started with the idea that the capitalist was entitled to the full average rate of present profit; and that all the labourer was to get, beyond his average wages, was half the extra profits created by his own exertions.

Nor did he notice any provision for workers' participation in the management.[1] Hughes' attitude remains inexplicable. Whether it represented good humor, lack of comprehension, or disillusionment, he held tenaciously to the idea. All three are indicated in his epitaph to the benevolent intentions of Messrs. Briggs when they discontinued their practice in 1875.

I know that the company was never looked upon as a true co-operative society by many of our number. . . . But I have always held that if co-operation is to do what we believe it will do . . . there must be room in its ranks for every class—an acknowledged place for employers and capitalists as for artisans and labourers. Besides, I have always held, and never more strongly than now, that the conduct of any large productive industries, except the very simplest, requires an education which does not exist among workpeople.[2]

4. *Trade Unionism*

Profit-sharing had to wait upon the enlightenment of employers, a process which was slow and by no means sure.

---

[1] *Report of the Co-operative Congress*, 1869, pp. 10, 33.
[2] *Ibid.*, 1875, p. 22.

Trade unionism, on the other hand, was a present force and one of rapidly growing importance for the elevation of labor. It was divesting itself of the revolutionary eccentricities which had alarmed the upper classes, and becoming a cautious, perhaps too cautious, instrument of reform. Christian Socialists had looked kindly on it from the beginning, and while their hopes of bringing about its alliance with or transformation into producers' co-operation were disappointed, they continued to work for its recognition and legalization.

In 1860 Hughes and P. H. Rathbone became joint honorary secretaries of the new National Association for the Promotion of Social Science, a body which received a good deal of publicity and counted numerous well-known figures among its membership. The annual congress of the same year appointed a Committee on Trades Societies and Strikes, on which Ludlow, Maurice, and Godfrey Lushington held places. Ludlow and Hughes contributed important accounts of two recent strikes in the coal and engineering trades to the voluminous report published by the Committee. In concluding his statement Hughes said, " I believe that the present state of feeling between employers and employed can never be improved, will only become worse, while the unions remain unrecognized by the law, and misrepresented, hated, and feared by all classes of society except that great one of which they are exclusively composed, and whose ideas and wishes they do, on the whole, faithfully represent." When the report came up for debate he called attention to the radical difference of opinion between himself and the employers who had spoken to the conference the day before. " They treated the labor of their men, which was in fact the lives of their men, on the same principles on which they treated a dead commodity. They most rigorously applied to it the same law of supply and demand as they applied to any other com-

modity." Entirely different rules were in fact necessary.
Writing in 1896, Ludlow did not perhaps claim too much
when he said that "nearly the whole of modern political
economy in respect to labour questions is based upon the
distinction drawn by Hughes." [1]

The investigation of the Social Science Association coin-
cided with an important conflict in the London building trade.
In 1859 the men asked for a nine-hour day, the masters
retorted by requiring all their employes to sign an agreement
not to join trade unions, and a strike ensued which lasted
until the middle of 1860. A troubled peace came when both
sides gave up their demands. Agitation continued, however,
and the employers announced their intention of paying by
the hour instead of by the day. Again their workmen struck,
but the depleted finances of the unions were in no position to
stand a further drain. As the struggle therefore soon
appeared to be hopeless some of the unions withdrew. Meanwhile a volunteer committee undertook to bring about a
settlement. Hughes, Ludlow, R. H. Hutton, Godfrey Lushington, and Frederic Harrison met delegates of the trade
unions and conducted an independent inquiry into the strike.
They published their findings in letters to the newspapers,
pointing out the disadvantages of payment by the hour and
recommending that the matter be referred to arbitration.
The masters were in too strong a position to make concessions, however, and while the trade was paralyzed until 1862
by the stubborn resistance of the bricklayers and masons
even they had eventually to admit defeat.[2]

[1] *Trades Societies and Strikes*, pp. 187, 599; *Economic Review*, vol. vi,
p. 308.

[2] R. W. Postgate, *The Builders History*, pp. 169-73, 209-11; S. and B.
Webb, *History of Trade Unionism*, p. 245; Frederic Harrison, *op. cit.*,
vol. i, pp. 250-51; *Times*, 15, 18, 19, 22, 23 July, 1861, letters of the
committee and replies of the masters.

The trade-union interest was still poorly represented in Parliament—even perhaps worse than it had been in 1824-5. But several men now entered the House of Commons who helped in some degree to redress the balance. Holyoake takes credit for Hughes' successful candidacy in 1865, a step which he had suggested some three years before. He now drew up election bills, wrote letters to the newspapers, and even prepard Hughes' election address. Hughes received these offices with a chilliness which Holyoake attributed to their religious differences, but the campaign was successful and Hughes took his seat for Lambeth in 1866.[1]

His maiden effort, a ten-column speech on the reform bill of 1866, incidentally advocated a democratic suffrage, but it was mainly a plea for comprehensive social reform. Twitted with irrelevancy by some of his auditors, he proceeded to review the progress of the working class for the last twenty years. In the face of neglect by the legislature which had condoned crowded dwellings, adulterated food, "the poorest education of any free people on earth," and the absence of courts for the arbitration of labor disputes, they had accomplished results by mutual assistance " of which any class might be proud." He pointed to the bad condition of workhouses and infirmaries and to breaches in the factory acts. Adequate protection of trade unions was lacking and the Master and Workman Acts particularly needed amendment.

That was a flagrant case. If, in a case of contract between master and man, the workman was charged with breaking the agreement, the first step was personal, and the workman was put in prison; while if the master broke his part of the contract, the first process against the master was to make him pay his fine.[2]

---

[1] G. J. Holyoake, *Bygones Worth Remembering*, vol. ii, chap. 21.
[2] *Hansard*, 1866, vol. 182, col. 1700 *et seq.*

The admission of artisans to the electorate gave a remarkable fillip to Ministers' sympathy for the working class. In 1867 the use of violence in a strike at Sheffield had caused indiscriminate charges to be levelled at unionism. At the suggestion of Robert Applegarth, a labor leader, the government appointed a royal commission to lay before the public all the facts concerning trade unionism.[1]

No doubt the public needed enlightenment, but most of the commission had made up their minds before they sat down. Their task was to find some common ground upon which to base a report. Frederic Harrison and Hughes alone among the members of the commission represented the full trade-union viewpoint—and with no illusions as to the virtue of impartiality. According to Harrison the burden of supporting the union cause fell to himself, due to the pressure of Hughes' parliamentary duties.[2] Yet Hughes was a constant and vocal attendant at the commission.

Its sessions frequently reached the heights of a popular criminal trial. Leading questions by the prosecution and the defense helped to bring out the sterling sentiments of a friend or elicited damning admissions from an enemy. No matter was too private or personal to be without interest to the commission.[3] Such a thirst for details required a good

---

[1] S. and B. Webb, *History of Trade Unionism*, pp. 260 *et seq.*

[2] Frederick Harrison, *op. cit.*, vol. i, pp. 316 *et seq.*

[3] The following is an instance:

Roebuck: To what do you attribute your rise from being a working joiner to an employer of labor, is it to great diligence on your part?

A.: That is partly it, I suppose.

Hughes: Where did you get your capital, if I may ask the question?

A.: I married a wife.

Lichfield: Do you attribute your rise to an employer to hard work and constant attention to it?

A.: Yes, I do in the main.

(*Reports from Commissioners*, 1867, vol. 32, p. 42.)

deal of time for its satisfaction and a final report was not issued until 1869. In its recommendations, laissez-faire received the customary obeisance, but unionism benefited from a new exegesis of the gospel. "A fair field for the unrestricted exercise of industrial enterprise" was now found to be compatible with legal recognition of the right to combine even if the combination were in restraint of trade. Nor was there any objection to giving the unions a corporate standing. While they had abused their power in the past, the commissioners were hopeful of a more intelligent policy in the future. They saw no reason to change the law in regard to picketing—which "prevents the free exercise of the right to employment"— or in regard to the suability either of individuals for loss or damage during a strike, or of unions for interfering with contracts of labor or trying to enforce the closed shop.[1]

The earl of Lichfield, Hughes, and Harrison declined to sign the principal report and submitted a dissenting opinion. They held that the doctrine of the common law which made all combinations illegal and even conspiratorial should be "broadly and unequivocally rescinded." "Molestation" and "obstruction" should be dealt with under the criminal law rather than under the law of 1825. Trade unions should be granted registration under the Friendly Society Acts for the protection of their funds. Hughes and Harrison added an appendix in which they elaborated their defense of unionism and condoned most of the practices to which their colleagues had objected. Like the majority, they drew attention to the benefits of arbitration.

Before dealing with the legislation based on this inquiry, we must consider the growing popularity of arbitration and conciliation in the field of industrial relations, and the importance Christian Socialists were beginning to attach to

[1] *Reports from Commissioners*, 1868-9, vol. 31, pp. 252 *et seq.*

them. Arbitration as it was usually practised had been unduly cumbersome. A. J. Mundella is generally regarded as the inventor of a new and more effective means of settlement.[1] Impressed with the French *conseils de prud'hommes*, in 1860 he had succeeded in getting most of the other manufacturers of Nottingham to co-operate with representatives of trade unions in establishing a permanent board of conciliation for the hosiery industry.[2] In the same year Hughes, speaking before the Social Science Association, had voiced the hope that " the masters and men would come to a reasonable means of settling their disputes without strikes. He felt that there certainly might be tribunals in each trade in which masters and men might be fairly represented." [3] Nevertheless he looked upon boards of arbitration as makeshifts which " can never solve the labour question. They imply two camps, and what is needed is one only." [4]

Mundella's scheme had been so successful that the Trades Union Commission called on him to explain its method. The evidence showed that while boards of conciliation might work effectively under the tutelage of a diplomatist like Mundella, certain safeguards were needed to make them generally useful. For one thing the responsibility of the trade unions must be increased. " I do not see," said Mundella, " how you can establish a board without a union. A union seems to me to be necessary in order that there may be something like cohesion on the part of masters and men." [5] The commission agreed and recommended the legal recognition of trade unions. But while their responsibility for entering

[1] M. F. Robinson, *The Spirit of Association*, p. 304.
[2] *Reports of Commissioners*, 1867-8, vol. 39, p. 74.
[3] *Trades Societies and Strikes*, p. 600.
[4] M. le Comte de Paris, *The Trades Unions of England*, editor's preface (by Hughes) written in 1861, p. xi.
[5] *Reports of Commissioners*, 1867-8, vol. 39, p. 97.

into engagements might thus be increased there was no assurance that the agreement would be carried out.

Charles Le Cour Grandmaison, a friend of Mundella's, asserted many years after that the object of both Mundella and the Christian Socialists in working for the legalization of trade unions was to make arbitration effective by giving the unions greater responsibility and holding them accountable for agreements made by their leaders with employers.[1] It certainly appears that Hughes at least was willing to make engagements of this nature enforceable at law. In the joint statement appended to the commission's report, Harrison and Hughes considered that

the existence of associations of some kind is indispensable to the formation of either codes of rules or boards of arbitration. . . . On the one hand, whatever tends to give a permanent legal and public character to unionism tends, in our judgment, to improve the existing unions, and to fit them to co-operate on sound mutual agreements with employers. On the other hand, we think that some facilities might be given to the legal machinery required for enforcing agreements made *bona fide* under such courts, and to the awards of tribunals of arbitration regularly constituted, to which there had been a *bona fide* appeal.[2]

Mr. and Mrs. Webb have described in detail the legislation of 1871-5 which placed trade unionism in a position to test the predictions of its advocates. Here it is only necessary to refer to Hughes' part in the campaign. In 1867 he had sponsored an Associations of Workmen Bill for the protection of trade-union funds which had been jeopardized by a recent decision in the court of Queen's Bench. The bill failed, however, despite the authoritative support of John

[1] *Revue des Deux Mondes*, April, 1898, *Mundella et les Conseils d'arbitrage en Angleterre*, pp. 389-91.

[2] *Reports of Commissioners*, 1868-9, vol. 31, p. 284.

Stuart Mill.[1]   Two years later when the Trades Union Commission had finished its labors Hughes and Mundella introduced a bill which would have swept away all the combination laws and in addition protected the finances of the unions.
Hughes asked consideration for workingmen equal to that
already granted employers.

In 1844 [he said] Parliament repealed the Forestalling and
Regrating Acts, and enabled any combination to take place
among traders who dealt in the necessaries of life, without regard to the supposed interests of society; and he now asked it to
pass a similar measure for the working people of this country.

The bill was withdrawn, however, when the Government
refused to support it on the ground that the session was drawing to a close and there was insufficient time to consider it
properly.[2]

   In 1871 the Government offered a measure more suited to
its own tastes.   The bill legalized combination and granted
the desired protection to funds, but it adhered to the vague
phraseology of 1825 concerning the prohibition of " molestation " or " intimidation " of employers and non-union workmen.   The utmost concession that Hughes and Mundella
could secure was the separation of the offensive last part and
its submission as a second bill, called the Criminal Law
Amendment Bill.   They could not prevent its passage along
with the other and somewhat contradictory measure.[3]

   Matters rested in this unsatisfactory position until Gladstone's defeat in 1874.   The election also carried Hughes
into outer darkness.   His irregular opinions on trade had
aroused the embattled retailers of Frome to prevent his

---

[1] *Hansard*, 1867, vol. 186, col. 1451.

[2] *Ibid.*, 1869, vol. 197, col. 1356.

[3] *Ibid.*, 1871, vol. 204, cols. 207, 2035.

renomination as the Liberal candidate.   Named for Marylebone, he had retired the day before the poll.[1]   Nevertheless Disraeli placed him on the royal commission to examine the Criminal Law Amendment Act of 1871, the Master and Servant Act of 1867, and the law of conspiracy.

The final report of this commission was liberal enough for Hughes to sign but he submitted a memorandum calling for more drastic reformation of the law than his colleagues (except the trade-union representative, Alexander MacDonald) deemed advisable.   He did not ask for the total repeal of the Criminal Law Amendment Act which MacDonald demanded.   But he objected to any criminal action under the Master and Servant Act except in cases of culpable negligence resulting in injury to persons.   Breaches of contract and damage to property [2] should be dealt with as civil causes.   Imprisonment in consequence of inability to pay damages was analogous to imprisonment for debt.

I may remark [he said] that the leading principle of recent legislation in England has been, that men shall not be imprisoned because they cannot pay their debts, but only if they can and will not.   Solvency (or at any rate supposed solvency) is ground for imprisonment in all other cases, but in the case of trade offences, insolvency.[3]

But the Government outstripped its commission in the desire to conciliate workingmen.   In 1875 the Criminal Law Amendment Act was entirely repealed, " definite and reasonable limits were set to the application of the law of conspiracy to trade disputes," and a more liberal Employers and

[1] *Guardian*, 19 August, 1874, p. 1061 ; *Dictionary of National Biography*, supplement, vol. viii, p. 3.

[2] Except wilful damage, which was punishable under the Malicious Injuries to Property Act.

[3] *Reports of Commissioners*, 1875, vol. 30, pp. 37-8.

Workmen Act replaced the old law of Master and Servant.[1]

The Christian Socialists can not be dismissed without a final word of comment. Probably Hughes was intellectually the least gifted among the group of leaders. His estimate of profit-sharing is a little disheartening. In Parliament his success as a speaker was decidedly moderate. But whatever his failings as an orator, his breadth of interest is not open to question. Anyone who examines his parliamentary career finds him vindicating the Reform League, supporting legislation against false weights and adulteration, attacking gambling on horse-races, advocating sanitary reform. He demanded the trial of Governor Eyre for cruelties in Jamaica, so becoming, in spite of his proverbial good-humor, one of that " Knot of rabid Nigger-Philanthropists, barking furiously in the gutter "—the particular aversion of Thomas Carlyle.[2]

The Working Men's College alone would have served to keep alive the memory of Christian Socialism and perpetuate its influence. But every cause its leaders promoted, whether it was co-operation, trade unionism, or the Friendly-Society movement, brought Christian Socialist ideas to bear upon men who were neither Christians nor socialists. In addition to this they possessed the unintentional advantage of picturesqueness and romantic interest. The author of *Tom Brown* and "muscular Christianity" found himself a transatlantic hero. Maurice's ejection from King's College created a sensation which was more than temporary.[3] The spectacle of Neale sacrificing a fortune to an idea—and that an unconventional one—was not without its elements of

[1] S. and B. Webb, *History of Trade Unionism*, p. 291.

[2] Frederic Harrison, *op. cit.*, vol. i, p. 342.

[3] The present Dean points with pride to a portrait of Maurice which hangs conspicuously in his office.

drama; it was besides a convincing proof of his sincerity. "I believe," says Mrs. Webb, "that in all the annals of British Philanthropy no more honorable example can be found of a life devoted from first to last to the disinterested and self-denying service of the wage-earning class." [1]

It appears that Mr. and Mrs. Hammond take a very restricted view of two early Victorian enterprises when they regard Christian Socialism as "little more than a phase; it had more body and more passion than 'Young England' but not a very much longer life." [2] "Young England" was merged but not extinguished in the tide of Tory Democracy; Christian Socialism lost neither its name nor its power to attract. It became identified with a different school of theology and its modes of action were altered, but its spirit and intention still persist.

The years between 1854 and 1877 witnessed an attempt on the part of socially-minded churchmen to cure the ills of society by voluntary action. Reform was to be accomplished by stimulating either the benevolent sentiments of the powerful, or the disposition of the poor to help themselves. Indiscriminate charity tended to fall into disrepute. Comfortable ignorance was being superseded by the desire to examine conditions at first hand. Organized action also came to be more appreciated. It invaded the field of purely philanthropic enterprise, in the form of housing associations, conventual bodies, and a Charity Organization Society. This tended to corrupt the abiding principle of self-help. But the purity of that Spartan discipline was already rapidly fading in the presence of adult education, Friendly Societies, co-operation, and trade unionism.

[1] Beatrice Webb, *My Apprenticeship*, p. 349 (footnote).
[2] J. L. and B. Hammond, *Life of Lord Shaftesbury*, p. 271.

For while churchmen fashioned voluntaryism into a social philosophy which was a kind of emasculated laissez-faire, they often accommodated their actions to a much more lenient standard—the principle of opportunism. State action as a method of reform was virtuously waved aside when it presented itself in the shape of a theory, only to be welcomed as an expedient when all other means had failed. Logic of this kind underwent frequent strains during the period just treated. In the hands of a more adventurous and realistic generation it was destined to burst violently asunder.

CHAPTER IV

"Bos Loquitur"

The years 1872-1874 present themselves to Mr. and Mrs. Webb as the second of three high-points in trade-union history.[1] For the first time since 1834 a widespread militant organization of rural labor for definitely economic objects came into being.[2] The "lumps of living flesh", pityingly contrasted with the keen, independent factory operatives by a reviewer of *The Christian Observer,* acquired minds of their own, and "the cringing, beaten plaint of our half-fed agricultural labourers" turned to a blunt though temperate demand for justice.[3] The phenomenon was no less important to the Church than to labor. In 1867 a crisis appeared to be at hand.

We seem to be approaching the destructive epoch of English history [said James Fraser] and revolution with no principles of reconstruction is the order of the day. I want to see a great effort made to popularize the Church and education. The masses are hostile to the one and indifferent to the other. Why is this? and why are we clergy so misrepresented and misunderstood?[4]

---

[1] S. and B. Webb, *History of Trade Unionism,* p. 328.

[2] Other issues were involved as appears below.

[3] *Christian Observer,* 1858, pp. 125, 511. The second quotation is from a pamphlet by the Rev. E. Munro.

[4] Thomas Hughes, *James Fraser, Second Bishop of Manchester,* p. 142.

142

THE CLERGY AND TRADE UNIONS

The answer, so far as the country clergy were concerned, revolved about the unique and apparently anomalous position they occupied in local affairs. The economic and numerical strength of the Establishment was still concentrated in the rural districts, where it touched the laborer as landlord, spiritual director, and agent of government. Possessing the appearance if not the fact of unity, the Church lay peculiarly open to denunciation or approval as a whole by any group which came in contact with its representatives in any of their capacities.

Until 1872 it had maintained an attitude of aloofness in industrial disputes. With the exception of the Christian Socialists, few churchmen concerned themselves with trade unions or the warfare between labor and capital. A conference arranged by the Rev. Edward White in 1867 between trade-union officials, other workingmen, and ministers and laymen of various denominations to consider the relation of workingmen to religious institutions marked the limit of inspiration.[1] *The Guardian,* it is true, as an organ of general information felt impelled to comment on strikes, and the tradition of editorial omniscience led it to formulate a theory of trade-union action. But its opinions were derived from popular sources, changing, but on the whole distrustful of labor. In 1855 it pronounced all strikes wasteful and suggested arbitration as an alternative. Some years later it had abandoned arbitration as a possibility too remote for consideration, recognizing the strike as the only weapon of labor but claiming for employers the equivalent right of lock-out. The nine-hour day ridiculed in 1859 was accepted in 1871 as an escape from " the sordid routine of existence in which

[1] *Working Men and Religious Institutions, Full and Extended Report of the Speeches at the Conference at the London Coffee House ... Monday, Jan. 21, 1867.*

the lives of most working men " were spent.   But *The
Guardian* considered the demand itself an evidence of the
well-being of laborers.[1]

This attitude of detachment could not well be preserved
when the question of organized rural labor thrust itself before the country.   Trade unionism in the towns appealed for
support to other and more powerful interests than the
Church, whose favor or antipathy, not being critically important, was easily overlooked or under-valued.   In the
village, on the other hand, the clergyman ruled as one of the
twin magnates of the community, and however earnestly he
wished the apron and gaiters to remain badges of peace they
were certain to be discovered fluttering on the battle-grounds
of economic strife.

PEACEFUL REMEDIES FOR RURAL ILLS

Long before the events of 1872, the condition of the agricultural laborer had been a subject of more or less serious
concern to churchmen.   Clergymen, it is true, were accused
of timidity in attacking the delinquency of the rich.

It appears to me [said one of them in 1844] that we are mor-
bidly apprehensive of plain speaking in the pulpit. We state
abstract duties and such statements people are quite content to
hear. Might not some detailed statements of the special duties
of farmers, manufacturers, shopkeepers, etc., be so made as,
without undue siding with the employed classes, might bring
what influence the Church still has, to bear upon their wretched
condition?—might promote cottage allotments in the country
—might shorten the hours of open shops in towns . . . ?[2]

Nevertheless, something, no matter how tentative or narrow in conception, was being done.   The prejudices of

---

[1] *Guardian*, 21 Nov., 1855, p. 857; 10, 31 Aug., 5 Oct., 1859; 24 Apr.,
28 Aug., 1867; 27 Sept., 29 Nov., 1871.

[2] *British Magazine*, 1844, vol. 26, p. 54.

clergymen and country gentlemen, even in an age of political economy, bound them to a tradition of charity to the lower orders.

If they had closed their purses and opened their mouths, their course would have been more sound in principle, but would have been thought least hopeful by those best acquainted with the tone of mind prevailing among the farmer class notoriously wedded to routine and intolerant of every kind of external interference.[1]

Charity might blunt the sharpest edge of poverty, but it did not touch the causes of distress. Real improvement would come only as a result of more fundamental measures. These arrived slowly. The clergy lightened the burdens of labor by abandoning their right to personal tithe during the agitation of the 1830's, but their most important contribution to rural progress before 1870 was probably their encouragement of thrift through the promotion of Friendly Societies, and the support they gave to education. The latter, in fact, depended largely on their efforts. As an assistant commissioner on children's employment, the Rev. James Freser, said in 1867, " But for the great zeal and activity of the clergy, and their large sacrifices, not only of money, but of labour and of time, in three-fourths of the rural parishes of England there would either be no school, or at best only the semblance of a school." [2] Aside from these matters, however, the clergy often aided if they did not lead other attempts to better rural conditions.

Before 1870 much had been said and written about housing conditions in the country, but there was still little to choose between the warrens of city artisans and the kennels of village laborers. Professor Bowden has pointed out that

[1] *Guardian*, 18 Dec., 1872, p. 1569.

[2] *Reports of Commissioners*, 1867-8, vol. xvii, p. 19.

the sensibilities of migrants to the towns during the latter part of the eighteenth century were not likely to be shocked at the quarters provided for them, considering the dwellings they had left behind.[1]   There was probably no great difference a century later.   The rose-covered cottage presented a romantic outward appearance; unfortunately the laborers had to live inside.   Some proprietors, like Shaftesbury, felt a responsibility for their tenants' decency and even comfort, and the Society for Improving the Condition of the Laboring Classes built a few model dwellings, but the reform was meager enough.   The Rev. James Fraser, whose observations extended over ninety-six parishes, remarked in 1867 that

the majority of the cottages . . . are deficient in almost every requisite that should constitute a home for a Christian family in a civilized community. . . . Modesty must be an unknown virtue, decency an unimaginable thing, when in one small chamber . . . two and sometimes three generations are herded promiscuously . . . where the whole atmosphere is sensual, and human nature is degraded into something below the level of swine.[2]

Allotments were a favorite mode of relief for the laborer. They represented, in part, a reaction against enclosure, which had deprived him of a proprietary interest in the land.   A series of acts beginning in 1819 placed it in the power of churchwardens and poor-law authorities to distribute in small plots land acquired by enclosure operations.[3]   But in 1843 a select committee of the House of Commons which included Lord Shaftesbury and Lord John Manners admitted that

[1] Witt Bowden, *English Industrial Society*, pp. 264-5.

[2] *Reports of Commissioners*, 1867-8, vol. 17, p. 35.

[3] W. Hasbach, *A History of the English Agricultural Labourer*, pp. 211 *et seq.*

legislative intervention had so far been unavailing.[1] Private efforts were measurably successful. Numerous landholders granted space for gardens to their tenants, the management usually falling to the magistrates, the clergy, and " the most respectable of the shop-keepers and farmers " of the locality. The practice by 1843 was in no sense universal but some three thousand families in Kent thus eked out their wages and the system existed in all the agricultural counties.[2] An agent of the Labourers' Friendly Society acknowledged the aid he had received from the clergy in promoting allotments. " During my last journeys in the counties of Berkshire, Oxford, Gloucester and Buckingham, which occupied six months, and during which I held twelve public meetings, and formed ten local associations, of 170 subscribers, who enrolled themselves as members of the Parent Society . . . 48 were clergymen." [3] The scheme could be defended on quite other grounds than charity—it cut down poor relief, and improved the relations between landlord and tenants, " increasing his acquaintance and interest in their circumstances, and exciting in them more thankfulness and respect." [4]

The rural phase of producers' co-operation, popular as a theory, was seldom practised. The outstanding example was a farm at Assington, Suffolk, to which reformers often pointed as an evidence of the soundness of their views.[5] In the process of time, however, this undertaking, which had been inaugurated before the Rochdale Society, became con-

[1] *Report from the Select Committee on Labouring Poor (Allotments of Land)*, 1843, p. vi.

[2] *Ibid.*, p. iii; " Minutes of Evidence," pp. 5, 10.

[3] *British Magazine*, vol. 5, p. 61.

[4] *Report on Allotments*, 1843, p. v.

[5] See Fraser's description of this experiment, *Reports of Commissioners*, 1868, vol. 17, pp. 46 *et seq.*

verted into an ordinary capitalistic enterprise, for by 1892 only one of the shareholders was actually employed on the farm.[1]

Factory legislation was quite extensive before the necessities of agricultural labor received any consideration. In 1867, however, in consequence of a motion by Shaftesbury in the House of Lords, the Royal Commission on the Employment of Children, Young Persons, and Women in Agriculture examined the situation of this class of labor. The Rev. James Fraser, whose ability as an investigator had been tested by the Education Commission in 1858 and again in 1865 as an agent to survey the elementary school system of the United States, was appointed an assistant commissioner. He collected a mass of extremely valuable evidence, 100 of the 216 pages of his report consisting of personally noted minutes of 96 ad hoc parish meetings, a very early instance of the " mass interview " so highly praised as a sociological method by Mrs. Webb when it was used many years later in Charles Booth's investigation of poverty in London.

The government was slow to act upon the evidence presented by its commission, the only immediate effect being a considerably watered-down version of a very moderate bill presented by Shaftesbury restricting the employment of agricultural gangs. As far back as 1843 special commissioners of the Poor Law had reported on the evil effects of migrant gang labor. Farmers contracted with gang-masters for the labor of men, women, and children as a cheap means of getting their field work done.[2] The unconventional habits prevalent among the members of these gangs shocked the clergy perhaps as much as did the exploitation to which they were subjected and the reduced wages which native labor was

[1] B. Jones, *Co-operative Production*, vol. ii, p. 617.

[2] E. Selley, *Village Trade Unions*, pp. 26-7; J. W. Bready, *Lord Shaftesbury and Social-Industrial Progress*, pp. 321-2.

forced to accept through gang competition. Even *The Guardian,* which had been singularly uncritical before 1867, was electrified by Shaftesbury's proposals and placed the responsibility for immediate action on the landed classes.[1]

Any considerable amelioration of the laborer's position depended upon the generosity of his betters unless he could strengthen his bargaining power. To do this the agricultural population must either be reduced in numbers to the point where the burden of competition was thrown upon the employer, or the example of urban trade unionism must be imitated. Orthodox political economy sanctioned the first alternative. Malthus's positive checks operated, it is true, but the situation required a more powerful cathartic than the Crimean War or the diplomatic militarism of Lord John Russell. Famine as distinguished from chronic hunger was a remote possibility only to be tolerated in Ireland. Lord Shaftesbury, to be sure, admitted that the government were doing their best with pestilence, but this solitary ray of hope was dimmed by the total failure of the preventive check, for the doctrine of continence missed the rural districts completely and agricultural labor continued to be inveterately fecund.

By the law of supply and demand laborers should have voluntarily deserted the low-wage country districts and sought employment elsewhere. But the agrarian population was notoriously immobile and conservative. Not only did a vast gap exist between town and village wages but even between the rates of pay in different rural areas.

The Rev. E. D. Girdlestone was perhaps the first reformer to make extensive use of this elementary fact. From modest beginnings he advanced as we shall see to more alarming positions and so, as a neutral observer declared at the time, " may fairly be considered as the pioneer of the agricultural

[1] 1867, pp. 445, 767, 853.

labourer's movement." [1]   When he removed from Lancashire to Halberton in North Devon in 1866, the situation of local labor struck him with all the force of its unfamiliarity.   Seven or eight shillings a week wages, and a diet of "tea-kettle broth" and occasional microscropic pieces of bacon were native customs which he did not intend to countenance without a struggle.   Private appeals to the farmers' conscience brought no response.   Nor did a sermon in which he linked the cattle plague with injustice to labor as a manifestation of the hand of Providence add to his popularity.   But a letter to the *Times* was his crowning iniquity.   Even the clergy of the district took sides against the interloper.   At an Easter vestry meeting the more respectable members of his parish evinced the spirit of the season by howling him down and refusing a church rate. But Halberton had caught a Tartar.   The parishioners carried the rate case to the Queen's Bench and lost it, whereupon they withdrew from the church in a body.   When, as a supreme reproof, the distracted farmers presented themselves at the Wesleyan chapel they met with the minister's cold advice to return whence they came.   Meanwhile the letter to the *Times* brought numerous offers of better situations for laborers in other parts of England and Ireland as well as money contributions from philanthropists.   This was Girdlestone's opportunity.   He set on foot a regular system of migration, which involved an immense burden of personal work, not lightened by the petty annoyances which the farmers were able to throw in his way—such as their reluctance to give letters of recommendation to departing laborers.   In the six years of his ministry at Halberton he sent between four and five hundred laborers, two-thirds of them with families, into other counties, where their circumstances were

---

[1] F. G. Heath, *The English Peasantry*, p. 138. Heath was field correspondent of the London *Morning Advertiser* during the laborers' strikes which began in 1872.

greatly improved.[1] Speaking before the British Association in 1868 he reported that the men then received wages " varying from twelve shillings a week the lowest, to twenty shillings a week, house and garden rent free, and in some cases there has been fuel and potato ground, one or more, given in addition."[2] The movement affected neighboring counties as well as Devon, and a tide of emigration set in toward the north from Dorset, Wiltshire, and Somerset.[3] Halberton and its neighborhood felt the repercussion in the form of a rising wage scale. The seven or eight shillings of 1866 became seventeen shillings in 1872.[4]

THE NEW AGRICULTURAL UNIONISM

Girdlestone had modesty enough to recognize that migration was no cure-all even though he had made a reputation by it. No available remedy ought to be neglected. A suggestion he let fall in 1868 gained perhaps more publicity when it was recalled a few years afterward than when he delivered it. In 1872 it sounded prophetic.

Agricultural Labourers' Unions [he said in the address referred to above] of a strictly protective character, and well guarded against intimidation to either employers or fellow workmen, might be formed with advantage. The whole system of unions is not to be condemned because of the outrages of a few. All professions, all trades, even landowners and farmers, in their Chambers of Agriculture, have their unions. Why are agricultural labourers alone left to struggle hopelessly, because singly, while all others are combined?[5]

[1] Heath, *op. cit.*, pp. 139-153.

[2] British Association for the Advancement of Science, *Report*, 1868, p. 165.

[3] F. G. Heath, *op. cit.*, p. 156.

[4] *Reports of Commissioners*, 1884-5, vol. 30, " Evidence," p. 635; Girdlestone's testimony before the Royal Commission on Housing.

[5] British Association, *Report*, 1868, p. 166.

The statement was no random effusion. He firmly believed, as he repeated publicly on many succeeding occasions, "that it was very doubtful whether the labourers would be able to raise themselves to an independent position, except they were united." [1]

The wilderness in which Girdlestone cried was not so completely deserted as perhaps he fancied. An Agricultural Laborers' Protective Association, formed in Kent in 1866 "with a view to the amelioration of their social condition and moral elevation, and to endeavour to mitigate the evils of their serfdom," succeeded in temporarily raising wages due to a scarcity of labor. But the improvement checked the normal emigration and a reduction followed.[2] The next year portentous rumblings were heard in Buckinghamshire and Oxfordshire. "A novel strike—a strike among the agricultural labourers", achieved two or three minute paragraphs in *The Times* and *The Guardian*. The strikers at Gawcott, Buckinghamshire, assisted some hundred laborers to emigrate and with the aid of contributions held out for several weeks until they gained an increase of 1s. 5d. These tactics were copied in Oxfordshire. "In the latter county the initiative has been taken by the females, many of whom go out into the fields to work. The price had been 6d. per diem for picking ' couch ' from the ground and the women have obtained a rise to 8d. by threatening a strike." [3]

More far-reaching than these early isolated protests and of greater importance for our purpose was the West of England Labourers' Improvement Association, known as the Herefordshire Union, which was initiated toward the end of

---

[1] *Macmillan's Magazine*, 1873, vol. 28, p. 436, his article " The National Agricultural Labourers' Union ".

[2] E. Selley, *op. cit.*, p. 36.

[3] *Times*, 18, 25 March, 6 May, 1867; *Guardian*, 27 March, 17 April, 8 May, 1867.

1870. This association originated in the village of Leint-wardine where a favorably disposed vicar [1] gave it his sup-port. It opened its ranks to farmers as well as laborers and depended more on persuasion than threats. The secretary of the Union was a Dissenter but the president and twenty vice-presidents were clergymen.[2] The motto of the Union was "Emigration, Migration, but not Strikes", and the language of its manifestoes had a plaintive, almost a servile, note. A letter "to the Landlords, Clergy, and Farmers of West England, and Others," signed by the honorary presi-dent, the Rev. D. Rodney Murray, rector of Crampton Bryan, is surprisingly humble for the year of strikes, 1872. The laborers (it said) ought to have wages equal to those paid by the best employers—fifteen shillings a week with extras, better cottages, contributions to assist emigration, and garden allotments. " Besides this we respectfully ask landlords to let some of us, under certain conditions, one of their farms (should a favourable vacancy occur), to be worked on the Co-operative principle." The letter carried a slight sting in its tail.

If you, our natural leaders and allies, turn from us, can you wonder if we seek other guides? And we pray you not to mis-interpret our moderation; weakness and ignorance sometimes maintain themselves by violence: it is our strength in the truth and justice of our cause that makes us moderate and makes us firm.[3]

The Herefordshire Union was the most extensive agrarian movement that had occurred since 1834. Successfully pro-

[1] The Rev. Edward Jonathan Green was the *vicar* according to *Crock-ford's Clerical Directory*, 1883, p. 466. He had been given the place in 1853. E. Selley, *op. cit.*, pp. 36 *et seq.*, gives credit to the *rector*.

[2] *Transactions of the National Association for the Promotion of Social Science*, 1872, p. 410.

[3] E. Selley, *op. cit.*, p. 36; *Guardian*, 11 Sept., 1872.

moted by its secretary, T. H. Strange of Leintwardine, it spread within a year to six counties and claimed a membership of thirty thousand.[1]   Whatever may be thought of the tactics employed, they resulted in a two-shilling increase in wages.   Beyond that the Union unquestionably helped to pave the way for a more independent and less pacific effort.

At this juncture appeared a man who from almost complete obscurity leaped into national fame within a few months.   Not since the time of Orator Hunt, William Cobbett, or Robert Owen had a popular leader so captured the imagination of the working classes.   At the beginning of 1872 Joseph Arch was a laborer in Barford, Warwickshire, where his ancestors had occupied the same free-hold cottage for a hundred and fifty years.   He took a good deal of naïve pride in having raised himself above the intellectual and economic level of his class.   At forty-six his past experiences well fitted him for leadership.   As an itinerant hedger he had traversed a considerable part of England and Wales, constantly impressed with the evil circumstances of agricultural labor; and being a Primitive Methodist preacher in his spare time he had acquired confidence and ability as a speaker.   His independent, self-assertive nature, tested in conflicts with his parson and his employers, marked him off from the generality of long-suffering workers who surrounded him.[2]

For some time Joseph Arch had been a convert to the gospel of trade unionism, but he determined to take no action among the agricultural laborers until, as he said, their misery should become unbearable.   The train of events which brought him into the field as an agitator began with the publication of a letter by several laborers in a nearby village stating the low wages and hardships of their position.   The

---

[1] Joseph Arch, *The Story of His Life, Told by Himself*, p. 110.
[2] *Ibid.*, chs. 1, 2; F. G. Heath, *The English Peasantry*, ch. 7.

letter inspired a group of workmen at Wellesbourne [1] with the idea of a local union and Arch was called upon to start it. He immediately fell in with the request and at a meeting on February 7, 1872, at Wellesbourne induced two or three hundred men to form a union and sign a strike agreement. They asked for sixteen shillings a week, a rise of about four shillings, and struck work when the demand was refused. [2]

The small flame kindled at Wellesbourne spread with phenomenal speed to the central and eastern counties, in some of which unions already existed. Joseph Arch travelled about encouraging the strikers, several London newspapers sent down sympathetic correspondents, and a tide of contributions began to flow in. The moderation of Arch had much to do with the generous support he received. Calling himself " a peaceable Wat Tyler of the fields ", he continually impressed on his followers the necessity of abstaining from rioting or other violence which might alarm the persons in authority to whom they looked for aid. His schemes kept pace with the popular enthusiasm. Six weeks after the first outbreak a union embracing all Warwickshire was formed, and at the end of May a National Agricultural Laborers' Union to federate the existing county organizations was created. Several clergymen were present on the platform of the Congress which initiated the Union. [3]

The employers, however, did not look on these proceedings with the benevolent detachment characteristic of many townspeople. Some compromises were offered and some

---

[1] G. Howell, *Labour Legislation, Labour Movements, and Labour Leaders*, p. 256, says the men lived at Charlecote; Arch gives Wellesbourne as the place from which the original request came. (Joseph Arch, *op. cit.*, p. 67.)

[2] Joseph Arch, *op. cit.*, pp. 68 76.

[3] *Ibid.*, pp. 83-104.

concessions made, but stubborn resistance and counter-offensive were the rule. Joseph Arch had not originally favored emigration as an alternative to battle, but after a trip to Canada in 1873 to look over the prospects for settlers he returned with the conviction that it was a " disagreeable necessity." [1]

In 1874 the affairs of the Union, which now had a membership of one hundred thousand, reached a crisis. By concerted action among the employers a lock-out of members of the N. A. L. U. in the eastern counties threw their men simultaneously on the funds of the Union. The offensive was met with increased exertions. At a great meeting in Exeter Hall Samuel Morley donated five hundred pounds and Archbishop Manning dignified the proceedings with his presence. Thomas Hughes appeared on the platform, but clergymen of the Established Church were conspicuously absent.[2]

The lock-out rubbed at least one prelate the wrong way. Bishop Fraser of Manchester had never failed to speak his mind; he did not hesitate now. An indignant letter, crackling with italics and interrogation points, burst into the somber columns of *The Times*.

Are the farmers of England going mad? . . . And what can they hope to gain by this ill-advised procedure? They may drive their best labourers either to the other side of the Atlantic or into some new employment; they may fill the workhouses with able-bodied men and women, stripped of their homes and all that has made life, amid their many hardships, still dear to them. But will they have settled the wage question, will they have improved their own condition or prospects? *Will they have conquered?* . . . And if farmers say they cannot afford

---

[1] Arch, *op. cit.*, p. 204; S. and B. Webb, *History of Trade Unionism*, pp. 322 *et seq.*

[2] *Times*, 2, 14 Apr., 1874; Joseph Arch, *op. cit.*, p. 123.

to pay this rate of wages with their present rentals, *and can prove the truth of this statement*, then rents must come down—an unpleasant thing even to contemplate for those who will spend the rent of a three hundred-acre farm on a single ball or upon a pair of high-stepping carriage-horses. . . . I am no lover of the principles of Trade-Unionism but they have been forced upon the working classes by the inequitable use of the power of capital.[1]

Not for nothing had the Bishop drudged on the Education and the Children's Employment Commission; for once a clergyman spoke with authority and his words bit deep. Thinly veiled injunctions for bishops to mind their prayers appeared. Lady Stradbrooke murmured significantly of tithes. His salty language shocked the maidenly ear of *The Times,* and *The Guardian* politely accused him of levity. But *The Spectator* welcomed him to the select company of the saved, gleefully reminding him that he had " quietly pitched his almost inevitable reversion of London into the sea." His portrait (done in lithograph) with the inscription " A Friend of the People " was borne aloft in a procession of laborers at Manchester while a horse-drawn printing machine ran off copies of the letter.[2]

THE CLERGY AND THE N. A. L. U.

But Fraser's epistle to the farmers did something more than rebuke sin in high places. It revived a controversy, intermittent since 1872, as to the actual and proper attitude of the Church toward the union and the strike.

Labor sympathizers charged the clergy with indifference and opposition to the movement. The *Spectator* did not mince words.

[1] *Times*, 2 Apr., 1874, p. 7.

[2] *Ibid.*, 11 Apr., p. 5; 16 Apr., p. 10; 23 Apr., p. 10; 8 Apr., p. 9; 22 June, p. 12; *Guardian*, 8 Apr., p. 416; *Spectator*, 4 Apr., p. 424.

There never was in the whole history of the Church of England anything so unfortunate as the attitude the Clergy as a body seem to be adopting towards the Labourers and their Union. . . . From Dr. Ellicott, whose five-minute speech will within five years turn the bishops out of the House of Lords to the last new curate who is congratulated on "smashing Tyndall" the Clerical Order seems determined to regard the Labourers' uprising as hostile.[1]

While the Union was in process of formation,

there was a parson here and there [said Arch] who went with us openly; but the majority were against us; and others blew hot now cold, and flew around like weather-cocks as squire or farmer or villager grew strongest at the moment. These shining lights of the Church as by Law Established were but poor farthing rushlights to the agricultural labourer.

As to the parsons generally, I never expected them to have much sympathy with us.

Bishop Fraser acknowledged that the assumption was general.[2]

Two incidents helped to strengthen this conviction.

During the lock-out at Ascot in Oxfordshire a number of strike-breakers were called in from outside. A mob of women—wives of the strikers—assailed the intruders with much verbal if not physical violence. Arraigned before the magistrates at Chipping Norton the women were charged with intimidation, and sixteen of them, some with nursing children, sentenced to seven or ten days at hard labor.[3] *The Church Herald* congratulated the justices, who happened to

---

[1] 6 Sept., 1873, p. 1118.

[2] Joseph Arch, *op. cit.*, p. 102; *Church Congress*, 1872, p. 365.

[3] Joseph Arch, *op. cit.*, p. 139; A. Clayden, *Revolt of the Field*, pp. 31-44.

be clergymen, *The Christian Observer* cautiously remarked that no doubt they acted conscientiously, while *The Guardian* refused to commit itself on the justice of the decision.[1] Others reprobated what they considered unnecessary harshness. Lord Chancellor Selborne was " unable to conceive any state of circumstances which would make it necessary, or calculated to promote the real ends of justice, to send so large a number of persons to prison in a case of this nature. . . . Such excessive and indiscriminate severity " creates " sympathy with the law breakers, rather than with the law." [2] To Joseph Arch it was only another evidence that clerical justices were harder than laymen.[3] In fact one of the magistrates partially recanted, stating that he had been inclined to leniency, but that since his associate prosecuted the case so vigorously he was constrained to support him, believing that the sentence was legally mandatory.[4]

In 1872, Dr. Ellicott, whom Dean Wellesley later referred to as " an amiable, insignificant man, talking constantly and irrelevantly, with some book learning", was bishop of Gloucester and Bristol.[5] Early in the strike he delivered a sulphurous apothegm on outside agitators and Joseph Arch in particular: " There is an old saying, ' Don't nail their ears to the pump, and don't duck them in the horse pond,' " a treatment which he nevertheless seemed to favor.[6] The sentiment was too picturesque to go unnoticed and the bishop was roundly criticized not only by the person immediately concerned but by some of the clergy themselves. Yet accord-

---

[1] E. Selley, *op. cit.*, p. 60; *Christian Observer*, July, 1873, p. 563; *Guardian*, 11 June, 1873, p. 764.

[2] *Accounts and Papers*, 1873, vol. 54, p. 21.

[3] Joseph Arch, *op. cit.*, p. 144.

[4] *Accounts and Papers*, 1873, vol. 54, p. 21.

[5] *Letters of Queen Victoria*, second series, vol. i, p. 545.

[6] Joseph Arch, *op. cit.*, p. 121.

ing to his lights Ellicott did try to promote an understanding between the workers and employers of his diocese. In the autumn of 1872 he arranged a meeting of laborers, agriculturists, a leader of the N. A. L. U., a magistrate, and a member of parliament to hear the complaints of local workers. Various suggestions were offered; Ellicott acknowledged that the situation of the men was very hard and suggested allotments as one means of improving it. His admonition to the laborers in the presence of their employers on the sin of drunkenness and the necessity of improving their moral tone was perhaps not so fatuous then as it would be now.[1]

In addition to these two widely advertised cases, other instances of ecclesiastical opposition occur. *The Christian Observer* devoted little space to the strike but that little was used to discredit it.[2] *The Labourer's Chronicle*, organ of the N. A. L. U., enthusiastically collected unpleasant specimens of clerical reaction.[3]

On the other hand, one might, without great difficulty, draw up a rather impressive list of churchmen who welcomed the Laborers' Union and cordially supported its policies. Near the top would stand the bishop of Manchester, whom we have so often met before. As he is the precursor of a type of prelate which is now more in favor and therefore more frequently met with it may be well to sketch briefly his careei and opinions particularly as they bore on agricultural problems.

James Fraser was raised to the see of Manchester in 1870 at the age of fifty-two. No other of Gladstone's episcopal appointments, says Lord Morley, proved to be so popular

---

[1] *Times*, 1 Oct., 1872, p. 8.

[2] Jan., 1874, p. 62 *et seq.*; May, p. 399; Sept., p. 720.

[3] E. Selley, *op. cit.*, p. 57.

and successful. The son of an India merchant, he had won —more through industry than brilliance—a fellowship at Oriel College, Oxford. But a love of horses kept alive his instincts of humanity: he " owned one of the best hacks which stood at Simmonds ". Taking priest's orders in 1847, he began his ministry at Cholderton, a country living near Salisbury and " the poorest in the gift of Oriel ". There and at Upton Nerfet, Berkshire, whither he removed in 1860, he gained an insight into rural problems which fitted him for more important duties later on. Advancement in the Church followed a successful parish administration; he became bishop's chaplain and chancellor of the diocese, and as the parochial schools had always been his particular care, he was appointed, at the bishop of Salisbury's suggestion, to the Education Commission with the result we have seen. Gladstone selected him for promotion to Manchester on the basis of his record as an educator. While many of his contemporaries were busily dissecting theological doctrines and belaboring each other with weapons from the armory of Cranmer or Laud, Fraser kept out of such disputes except when he was shouldered into them as head of a diocese. " If the law requires me to wear a cope, though I don't like the notion of making a guy of myself, I will wear it." This tranquillity of mind in ecclesiastical matters left him more time and inclination to follow his social predilections.

With me social questions have always taken rank, not only far above political, but even far above ecclesiastical questions. By this remember I mean . . . that without relaxing my hold on what I believe to be the great truths of Christianity, I still feel that the great function of Christianity is to elevate man in his social condition.

In this respect Fraser may be considered a worthy successor of Bishop Wilberforce, although the latter used his political influence to more advantage.   Fraser was almost unknown in the House of Lords.[1]

It must not be supposed that Bishop Fraser in championing the cause of rural unionism did so in an unqualified manner. He constantly pointed out the necessity of moderation in language, action, and demands.   Far from admitting that laborers were entitled to all they could force employers to allow, he had definite ideas of what constituted a " fair " wage.   Eighteen shillings a week desired by the Lincolnshire laborers were "immoderate and unreasonable, and indicative of a purpose to go on enlarging their claims till they have reached a point far beyond the limits of what I ventured to call ' equitable ' remuneration." [2]   The same not too exact standard entered the calculation when he arbitrated a painters' dispute in Manchester.   Differences in income springing from social rank were phenomena which he never questioned : " I heartily wish that every working man in England were in possession of every comfort which his station will reasonably allow him to procure." [3]

Girdlestone, who had accepted a canonry at Bristol in 1872, throughout the period of agitation defended the cause of labor, justifying the right to strike and attacking the lockout as vigorously as Fraser.   Early in 1872 he appeared at a meeting of union sympathizers which included Mundella, Auberon Herbert, J. W. Leigh, vicar of Stoneleigh, Joseph Arch, and others.   At the Church Congress of 1873 he strongly upheld the labor point of view and warned the clergy not to forfeit the regard of the workers by continuing to oppose the union.   It is true that he felt it necessary to sever his connection with the N. A. L. U. for reasons which

---

[1] Thomas Hughes, *James Fraser, Second Bishop of Manchester*; Morley, *Life of Gladstone*, vol. ii, p. 432.

[2] *Times*, 14 Apr., 1874, p. 10; 17 Apr., p. 12.

[3] Thomas Hughes, *James Fraser*, pp. 225 *et seq.*

will shortly appear, but he remained in full agreement with its economic policies. Like Fraser he believed that the lower wage districts should be relieved first, and advised laborers who received as much as fifteen shillings a week to let well enough alone and send aid to the Devon workers.[1]

A group of city churchmen also supported the strike. Naturally Christian Socialists felt called upon to raise their voices. Hughes was one of the signers of a letter approving the organization of the N. A. L. U., and J. Ll. Davies unreservedly sanctioned the objects of the strike in letters to *The Times* and a speech before the Church Congress. "Bishop Ellicott," he said, "might learn a lesson in moderation and courtesy if not also of sympathy with the weak, from Mr. Auberon Herbert." The popular objections to stirring up conflict between classes he brushed lightly aside —"I doubt whether, as a rule, there has been hitherto much mutual love lost between the farmers and the labourers." "We do not want to look on at a fair fight, we want to see a depressed class elevated."[2] Harry Jones, rector of St. George's in the East, hailed the new-found independence of the laborers and tossed a jibe at their masters who "locked them out of Suffolk, with only the rest of the world to go to."[3] Thorold Rogers, although he had recently resigned his cure, may perhaps be classed with this group. Joseph Arch acknowledged his assistance in the affairs of the N. A. L. U.[4]

Country clergymen added their voices to the chorus. "A Leicestershire Clergyman", without disclosing his identity,

[1] *Times*, 27 March, 2 May, 1872; 5 Apr., 1874; *Church Congress*, 1873, pp. 33-5.

[2] *Times*, 30 March, 14, 21 August, 1872; *Church Congress*, 1873, pp. 29-31.

[3] *Times*, 29 Apr., 1874, p. 14.

[4] Joseph Arch, *op. cit.*, p. 237.

warmly approved the sentiments of J. Ll. Davies.[1] More important is the evidence of Henry Burgess, vicar of Whittlesey, who showed how much influence a sympathetic priest might have on the conduct of a union. He had " not the slightest apprehension of the terrible consequences " associated with strikes and lock-outs. " I have been a friend of the Labourer's Union in this neighborhood since its commencement, contributing to its funds, presiding at its annual dinner, and preaching four times on topics suggested by it." Taking some credit for the absence of discontent in his district, he attributed the good understanding between masters and men to his keeping them informed of each other's difficulties and hardships. A reasonable wage he defined as one " sufficient to keep a labourer's wife and children out of the fields, and to pay for his children's schooling." [2] In Nottinghamshire we find the Rev. C. E. T. Roberts, agent of the Littleport branch of the N. A. L. U., presenting moderate demands to the employers, only to be refused. " It speaks well for the men," he said, " but badly for the farmers." [3] The Hon. J. W. Leigh, vicar of Stoneleigh, countenanced the Union by his presence at sympathetic meetings, using the opportunity to advocate co-operative farming as it was practiced in his parish. It is true that a correspondent of the London *Daily News,* while referring to him as " at once the brother of the Lord of the Manor and the father of his parish," criticized his lavish charity and paternalism: " In Stoneleigh Hodge indeed wears the collar of villeinship, but it is padded inside and nicely gilt." [4] At the Church Congress of 1873 H. B. Smith, vicar of Houghton Regis, con-

---

[1] *Guardian,* 28 August, 1872, p. 1088; 4 Sept., p. 1127.

[2] *Times,* 15 Apr., 1874, p. 12; 6 Apr., p. 8.

[3] *Ibid.,* 15 Apr., 1874, p. 12.

[4] *Ibid.,* 2 May, 1872, Leigh at the Conference at Willis's Rooms; 5 June, 1872, meeting at Leamington to form the N. A. L. U.

demned the aloofness of clergymen. It is true, he said, that
the Church is the Church of all, "but I also hold that the
Church and the clergy may take part in any struggle to con-
fer a benefit on a particular part of society."[1] W. H.
Lyttelton, rector of Hagley, inveighed against the Quaker
doctrine of passive obedience and believed that the Herefordshire Union might learn "manly self-dependence"
from the N. A. L. U which in turn would be wise in adopting, *"wherever it is possible,"* the conciliatory attitude of
the former. As for the clergy, those who favored the movement should say so. They might profitably follow Sir
Robert Peel's maxim: "If you see a move coming . . . *head
it.*"[2] The Rev. Brooke Lambert refused to be alarmed at
the prediction that laborers would lose their independence
if they combined, and sought to prove that unions were de-
fensible even on economic grounds.[3]

Numerous other clergymen preferred to maintain what
they called a neutral position. Sometimes this consisted in
ignoring as far as possible the transactions which were taking place, sometimes it meant admitting enough of the claims
of both parties to neutralize each other. An example of the
latter attitude is the manifesto of a south Warwickshire
clerical meeting which recognized the right to combine, but
deprecated strikes and lock-outs both of which were equally
justifiable and equally useless.[4] Whatever its own opinions
on the strike, *The Guardian* preached neutrality joined with
a willingness to mediate as the best policy for clergymen.[5]
The Ely diocesan conference pronounced in favor of non-

---

[1] *Church Congress*, 1873, p. 38. Also *cf. ibid.*, p. 41, the remarks of
the Rev. R. M. Grier, who opened his school-room to union meetings.

[2] *Guardian*, 27 Nov., 1872, p. 1491.

[3] *Ibid.*, 28 Aug., 1872, p. 1127; 11 Sept., p. 1157.

[4] *Ibid.*, 24 Apr., 1872, p. 550; 4 Sept., p. 1128, letter of Rev. W. Wood.

[5] *Ibid.*, 11 June, 1873, p. 764; 26 Aug., 1874, p. 1093.

interference.[1]   In the agitation for barring clergymen from commissions of the peace, intensified by the Chipping Norton affair mentioned above,[2] and favored by many churchmen, may be seen the desire to keep the clergy out of public positions where their actions might bring odium upon the Church.   No legislation to this end resulted but it is significant that the number of clerical justices of the peace sank from 1,187 in 1873 to about 30 in 1906.[3]

Without pausing here to consider whether the sweeping accusations of indifference or hostility levelled against the Church were accurate, we may examine some of the motives which probably actuated those clergymen who did remain neutral or opposed to the laborers' movement.

So far as the advocates of non-intervention possessed a theory it rested partly on an idea of the Church's exclusively spiritual mission.   By nature Christianity was independent of secular arrangements.   As a reviewer in *The Christian Observer* had phrased it many years before, " It is one of the glorious features of Christianity, that it is adapted to any social state and to any form of temporal government." [4] Moreover, the Church was pledged to peace by its founder— it must not " stir up class against class." Partisanship would alienate one of the parties and prevent the clergy from acting as mediators.   The injured party might even leave the Church.   This, as a speaker at the Church Congress said, actually happened in two cases where clergymen favorable to the employers tried to reach a settlement and the laborers

---

[1] *Guardian*, 29 July, 1874, p. 979.

[2] P. 158.

[3] *Hansard*, 1872, vol. 210, cols. 1074-9; *Guardian*, 11 June, 1873, p. 764; *Accounts and Papers*, 1873, vol. 54, pp. 35 *et seq.*; 1906, vol. 99, pp. 623 *et seq.*

[4] 1859, p. 732; also *cf.* the bishop of Oxford's remarks on the Church's duty in regard to strikes, *Church Congress*, 1873.

withdrew.[1]   Girdlestone's experience at Halberton illustrated the effect of too much zeal in the opposite direction.[2]

Constant reference to "strife between classes" perhaps also indicates an exaggerated fear of the subversive character of unionism.   Country priests, without personal experience of such matters, and accustomed to invariable docility on the part of laborers, were likely to be excessively alarmed.   The state of mind of even the *Christian Observer* was almost psychopathic: "If such an organization were to prevail, it would be little short of a social revolution."[3]

Clergymen asked themselves if violence was after all necessary.   The opinion prevailed that the condition of the laborer had during past years shown a constant tendency to improve, and a union leader of those days has recently confirmed this impression.[4]   The Gang Act of 1867 and the Education Act of 1870 might be interpreted as a growing tenderness for the worker's welfare.   *The Guardian,* it is true, confessed that the laborer had a right to complain of the failure of wages to keep pace with rents.[5]   But might he not reasonably expect that the agencies already in existence would continue to raise his position without recourse to strikes?   The extension of allotments, the sense of justice of employers like Shaftesbury and Lord Nelson seemed to be encouraging promises of a brighter future.[6]   The laborer already possessed means to improve his condition, and the

[1] *Guardian,* 28 Aug., 1872, p. 1087, letter of Rev. J. H. Snowden; *Church Congress,* 1873, p. 39.

[2] *Supra,* p. 150.

[3] 1872, p. 399.

[4] George Edwards, *From Crow-scaring to Westminster,* p. 37; *cf.* R. E. Prothero (Lord Ernle), *English Farming Past and Present* (1912 ed.), p. 468, who notes a steady rise in wages from 1851 to 1870.

[5] *Guardian,* 4 Sept., 1872, p. 1117.

[6] *Ibid.,* 13 Nov., 1872, p. 1427, Lord Nelson's address to his laborers; 25 Sept., 1872, p. 1213, letter of Rev. W. Lea.

duty of a parish clergyman therefore resolved itself into the simple problem of schooling him in " habits of cheerfulness, obedience, truth and industry." [1]

Current economic doctrines adverse to unionism also fascinated clergymen. The " law of supply and demand " as applied to wages was almost as popular as that other stereotyped means of avoiding thought, the phrase " setting class against class ".   At a workers' meeting O. W. Davys, rector of Wheathamstead, "reminded the labourers that their labour was a marketable article, and   . . . would receive its price if they made it worth it."   A clerical conference in Warwickshire was " persuaded that the price of labour should be regulated by the natural law of supply and demand."   In any event, it was said, wages could fluctuate within only a narrow margin, and the advantage of a union lay simply in its ability to gain the benefit of these minute changes more rapidly.[2]

Social ties and economic interest may be supposed to have caused some clergymen to take sides against the laborer.

I am hardly in a position to tell [said the Rev. Henry Burgess] how I should feel . . . if I were a frequent guest with a resident lord of the manor, or my humble vicarage were overlooked by a Ducal mansion, or if I depended upon voluntary gifts in the form of pew-rents for the support of my family or the payment of church expenses.

Furthermore, the leadership of the union movement was in the hands of Nonconformists who as a class demanded the disendowment of the Church and so helped to discredit the movement so far as churchmen were concerned.   Lastly, many clergymen were landholders, a fact which might pre-

---

[1] *Guardian*, 4 Feb., 1874, p. 127, letter of a Devonshire rector.

[2] *Times*, 24 Apr., 1872, p. 550; 11 June, p. 5; 13 Apr., 1874, p. 8, letter from a Dorsetshire clergyman.

dispose them against the union. But if it did, pecuniary motives were not always the reason. In fact sometimes they did not enter the situation directly at all, for the landlord often received his entire income from rents, and if these were not affected by higher wages he might be perfectly willing to see the laborer get as much as he could from the farmer. Thus the Rev. Mr. Jones of Fakenham advised a farmers' meeting at Bury to negotiate with the union instead of fighting it. But the farmers demurred. " It appeared that though he is the owner of 300 or 400 acres of land in the county, Mr. Jones does not farm his land, and is not, therefore, an employer, and the farmers seem to think that the difficulties of the situation did not come home to him." [1]

Paradoxical though it may sound, more than one clergyman was alienated from the labor movement because it was partly religious, or rather because it was religious after the Nonconformist fashion. Thorold Rogers believed that the peasants could not have been aroused at all except for the Primitive Methodists. [2] The chief agitator himself was a preacher in his spare time, and the sect had a good deal of strength in the country districts. [3] The Primitive Methodists addressed themselves particularly to the working classes— their organization in fact dates from a schism in the Wesleyan Methodist body over the question of the revival of field-preaching. In 1853 they numbered some 260,000. [4]

[1] *Times,* 15 Apr., 1874, p. 12; 23 Apr., p. 10; Hasbach, *op. cit.,* p. 282.

[2] *Six Centuries of Work and Wages,* p. 514.

[3] F. G. Heath, *The English Peasantry,* chap. 7 (" Joseph Arch "); G. Edwards, *op. cit.,* chap. 3. Edwards was an " exhorter ". According to the religious census of 1853 the majority of the Wesleyan Methodists (among whom the Primitive Methodists were included) were to be found in the rural districts. Their greatest strength lay in Cornwall, Yorkshire, Derbyshire, Durham, and Nottinghamshire; they were weakest in Middlesex, Sussex, Surrey, Essex, Warwickshire, and Hertfordshire. (*Accounts and Papers,* 1852-3, vol. 89, p. cxliv.)

[4] *Accounts and Papers,* 1852-3, vol. 89, pp. lxxxi-ii.

The reasons for antipathy between the clergy and the Methodist leaders are not far to seek. Dissenters were of course normally suspect because they attacked the privileges of the Church and criticized its doctrine and forms of worship. Class hatred embittered the feelings of the Methodists.

After all, [said *The Quarterly Review*] Joseph Arch is not a labourer; he is a dissenting minister of a rustic type, influenced by the jealousies and prejudices of his class. From the Rev. Baldwin Brown and Mr. Spurgeon, down to the humblest Primitive Methodist minister, there is an abiding sense of inferiority to the clergy.[1]

The early experiences of Arch did not tend to make him forget this inferiority. The petty tyranny of a village parson and his wife who cut off the allowance of soup and coal because Joseph's mother was not properly humble and who made his father wait for communion until the gentry and tradesmen had been served etched itself deeply on his mind.[2]
The very amenities which soften the hard features of class warfare have always been a provoking obstacle to reformers. Charity dispensed by the parson no doubt closed the ears of many laborers to the tidings of liberty and thus became an additional grievance to the union leaders.[3]
If the acts of certain clergymen had not been singled out for contempt because they were supposed to represent the attitude of the Church, or if sweeping charges had been avoided, there is little doubt that clergymen would have looked upon the laborers' movement with greater indulgence. Joseph Arch himself tried to do justice to the enemy but he was convinced of their fundamental iniquity. The strikers'

[1] Vol. 137, p. 503.
[2] Joseph Arch, *op. cit.*, pp. 20-21, 53-4.
[3] Arthur Clayden, *op. cit.*, pp. 124 *et seq.*

journal bore at its mast-head a challenge to combat: " *The Labourers' Union Chronicle,* An Independent Advocate of the British Toilers' Rights to Free Land, Freedom from Priestcraft, and from the Tyranny of Capital ". Its editors did not neglect the second person of their trinity. After the period of stress had passed, the Rev. J. Oakley, a strong advocate of the Union, declared that

the old management of the *Chronicle,* never exactly devoted to the side of the Church, was not long ago deliberately superseded with a view to get rid of all hesitancy about attacking her in season and out of season; and that the Labourers' Union and its organ in the press is [sic] being almost avowedly *worked* as an engine of the Liberation Society.[1]

Bishop Mackarness plaintively asked why the clergy were attacked at this time—in other strikes they had never been abused. The criticism, he said, came not from the laborers themselves but from " preachers of that new kind of religion which seems, above all things, to make its professors good haters of religionists more wealthy or more educated than themselves." [2] Words like these did not always cover a basic opposition to labor. Canon Girdlestone broke with the Union in 1873 because of the " dangerous turn the agitation was taking," and denounced " their meddling with the resources of our clergy and any political tinkering of theirs with the connection of Church and State." [3]

At least one truth emerges from an analysis of contemporary opinion on the attitude of the Church during the strike: general statements must be received with caution. Frequently they emit more heat than light. The common

[1] *Church Congress,* 1877, p. 77.

[2] *Ibid.,* 1873, p. 23; also *cf. Guardian,* 12 March, 1873, p. 339; 19 March, p. 371. Letters accusing the strikers of injustice to the clergy.

[3] E. Selley, *op. cit.,* p. 88.

vehicles of sentiment within the Church adopted a negative attitude which may be interpreted in various ways. It is true that in the Church Congress of 1873 which devoted part of its agenda to considering " the Church's duty in regard to strikes " clergymen who spoke favored the labor point of view almost without exception—in rather forcible contrast to lay speakers. How the silent majority felt does not appear. *The Guardian* may be considered as representing a certain body of opinion. From the first it recognized the essential justice of the laborers' demands. A leader headed " Bos Loquitur " asserted that wages had not kept pace with rising prices. " The strike of the Warwickshire labourers was therefore no more than a demand for a share in the national prosperity. It has been conducted with very creditable freedom from disturbance." [1] Nevertheless the paper advocated a hands-off policy for the clergy during the strike. Convocation and bishops in the House of Lords entirely, and diocesan conferences almost completely, ignored the question. Thus nothing which might be construed as an official pronouncement by the Church as a whole appeared.

Certainly the Church as compared with the Primitive Methodists did not attempt to direct the movement. A later writer has said that none of the agitators came from the Establishment.[2] The Church failed indeed to come up to the expectations of even the milder advocates of labor among the clergy. If a generalization were possible it might be given in the words of Canon Girdlestone:

It is quite true that the clergy have not taken the part which they ought to have taken in assisting the labourer to improve his position. It is true, also, that almost all have stood aloof from this movement; that some have openly opposed it; and

---

[1] 5 June, 1872, p. 737.

[2] Joseph Arch, *op. cit.*, preface by the countess of Warwick, pp. xi-xii.

many more invariably and instinctively sided with landowners and farmers.[1]

This is quite unlike dismissing the matter with a reference to Bishop Ellicott and the Chipping Norton magistrates as do Mr. and Mrs. Webb.[2] One observer in fact believed that ministers of all sects were equally indifferent, but he ascribed it to " timidity " and in 1873 noticed " already an improved state of feeling " in the Church of England.[3]

The lock-out of 1874 achieved all the employers expected of it. After a bitter struggle which lasted several months the N. A. L. U. admitted defeat, discontinued strike relief, and turned its attention to emigration.[4] The membership declined from 100,000 in 1874 to 40,000 in 1876.[5] One or two flare-ups occurred within the next twenty years but by 1900 agricultural unionism had in effect disappeared. But the impression of its early vigor was not erased. Rural labor henceforward could not be left outside the calculations of statesmen, and the suffrage act of 1884 was no doubt an echo of the strife of 1872-4. Joseph Arch, a Napoleon without an empire, entered Parliament for northwest Norfolk in 1892. His retirement in 1901 closed a chapter—but not the last one—in agricultural unionism.[6]

[1] *Macmillan's Magazine*, vol. 28, p. 439.

[2] *History of Trade Unionism*, p. 332.

[3] F. G. Heath, *op. cit.*, p. 235.

[4] *Times*, 28 July, 1874, p. 8.

[5] G. Howell, *op. cit.*, pp. 260-61; *Accounts and Papers*, 1877, vol. 77, p. 144.

[6] Joseph Arch, *op. cit.*, pp. 386 *et seq.*; E. Selley, *op. cit.*, p. 93. Arch lived in retirement until his death in 1919 at the age of 93.

CHAPTER V

The Reformers Organize
1877-1895

A HISTORIAN in search of labels would not greatly violate
the facts if he called the last quarter of the nineteenth century in England " the Age of Reform Societies ". Every-
one who took the least interest in social matters seemed suddenly to discover the value of group action. Within the
space of a few years appeared the Social Democratic Federation, the Land Reform Union, the Fabian Society, the
early labor parties, and many other less heralded organizations. The designation applies equally well to the same
period in the social history of the Church, for here interest
plainly centers in the three new reform movements whose
rise and progress are the subject of this chapter.

THE SPRINGS OF ACTION

From one point of view the University Settlements, the
Guild of St. Matthew, and the Christian Social Union were
simply the evidence of a keener interest in social reform on
the part of churchpeople, and of a growing dissatisfaction
with existing conditions. The factors which produced this
state of mind not only brought the reform organizations
into existence, but continued to win them adherents and to
direct their principles. But during the whole period new
forces were perpetually making their appearance, reshaping
or driving out the old, and leaving their impress on the
movements we are about to consider. One example of this
is the sudden popularity of the doctrines of Henry George.

174

Another is the action of reform societies upon each other. A complete list of " influences " at this point would therefore be perhaps somewhat confusing. We may observe their general character, however, and consider the details as it becomes expedient.

First of all, industrial conflict and the energy of labor sympathizers kept the grievances of the working class continually before the country. The revolt of agricultural labor was only an episode in a drama which the Church must sooner or later pass judgment upon. Other clergymen were no doubt as poignantly moved as Charles Gore, one of the founders of the Christian Social Union.

The only time in his life [he said] when he was very strongly driven to desert the Church was at the outbreak of the agitation against Joseph Arch. The attitude of the Church toward Joseph Arch's movement was lamentable; the clergy and the well-to-do laity were deaf towards the almost inconceivable record of injustice which that movement voiced.[1]

Then too, as we have seen, not a few of the older Christian Socialists survived to transmit the gospel to a younger generation. From a chair at Cambridge Maurice, until his death in 1872, expounded his system of liberal theology and his theory of social obligation. These teachings were reinforced and continued in a more secular vein by the doctrine of civic responsibility set forth at Oxford by such great preceptors as T. H. Green and Benjamin Jowett. Hughes, Neale, and Ludlow continued to work through the force of example. For some years Ludlow took an active interest in the affairs of the Christian Social Union, attending its meetings and writing articles for *The Economic Review.* He could remember things antediluvian, so that, in spite of his own disappointments, the future still held promise.

[1] *Convocation of Canterbury,* 1918, p. 275.

When at a meeting of the Union " some youthful, cheerful, Pessimist such as 'Mr. Masterman " bewailed the present times and mores, Ludlow would gently remind him of the " hungry forties ".[1]

In the decade of the 1880's new forces gained prominence which deepened popular interest in social questions yet brought with them the confusion of ideas characteristic of a renaissance. Auberon Herbert called it " an age of sloppiness." " The reaction against the theory and practice of empirical socialism," says Mrs. Webb, " came to a head under Mr. Gladstone's administration of 1880-1885, an administration which may fitly be termed the ' no man's land ' between the old Radicalism and the new Socialism." [2] Continental ideas were gaining a rather tardy popularity in England through the belated discovery of Karl Marx and Auguste Comte. Moreover, a new school of economists, who for many years had been tilting obscurely at the dogmas of their classical forbears, suddenly received the gift of tongues. As we shall see, churchmen had a finger in all these transactions. Their distinctive contribution, however, was a restatement in much more definite terms of the social ethics of Christianity.

THE SETTLEMENT MOVEMENT

So far as churchmen were concerned, this intellectual ferment might have passed away like froth if they had not combined it with a direct knowledge of working-class problems. From the union of theory with personal experience were bound to spring more effective and lasting efforts at social amelioration. In an earlier chapter [3] we have noticed the thin stream of clergy and prosperous laity who were

[1] H. S. Holland, *A Bundle of Memories*, p. 281.

[2] *My Apprenticeship*, p. 178.

[3] Chapter iii, pp. 98-103.

finding their way somewhat haphazardly into the slums for the purpose of reclaiming the masses and enlightening themselves. This movement was now to assume a more systematic form.

In 1860 John Richard Green came out to East London where he remained for nine years, latterly as vicar of Stepney, acquiring, among other things, the social point of view which dominates his *Short History of the English People*. For a short time one of his parish visitors was Edward Denison. Both Denison and Edmund Hollond (who was also in East London at the time) were so struck with the value of the experience that they believed the opportunity should be extended in a more methodical way to others. It so happened that John Ruskin's thought tended in the same direction. In 1868, therefore, Ruskin, Denison, and Green discussed the possibility of some new effort among the poor. They concluded that a permanent colony of young men who would follow Denison's and Hollond's example of life and work in East London ought to be established. Denison seems to have been the moving spirit in the project, for when his health failed shortly afterward and he removed from East London the plan was given up. Hollond, however, found some kind of substitute in the Charity Organization Society, which he helped to found.[1]

It will be remembered that Samuel and Henrietta Barnett were attracted to Whitechapel through Hollond's representations.[2] From the time of his arrival in 1873 Barnett visited Oxford frequently enough to keep in touch with the

---

[1] Werner Picht, "Toynbee Hall und die Englische Settlementbewegung" (*Archiv für Socialwissenschaft und Socialpolitik*, IX, 1913), p. 8 and footnote. Dr. Picht's book was translated into English in 1914. R. A. Woods and A. J. Kennedy, *The Settlement Movement, a National Estimate*, pp. 18-21.

[2] *Supra*, p. 101.

rising generation of students. His purpose was to interest them in social work by inducing as many as possible to come and see the condition of East London for themselves. A number responded; among these embryonic reformers were several whom we shall meet hereafter. Charles Marson, Henry Scott Holland, and Sidney Ball spent a novitiate in the slums.[1] There they lived during the vacation, "working as Charity Organization Agents, becoming members of clubs, and teaching in classes or school."[2] So far as his own future was concerned, however, Barnett's most important disciple was Arnold Toynbee. Toynbee's residence (in 1879) was short but he returned to Oxford an effective propagandist. Largely through his efforts, meetings in support of Barnett's work were held at the University, and the procession of Oxonians to East London continued. About the same time the cause profited—as did social reform generally—by the publication of an anonymous pamphlet called " The Bitter Cry of Outcast London," which greatly shook the complacency of Victorian England.

In 1883 at the beginning of a career filled with promise, Arnold Toynbee died, but his influence on the settlement movement was increased rather than lessened by his death. The best memorial to a loved friend seemed to be a continuation of the work which had consumed almost his last energies. Accordingly, on 17 November, 1883, a historic meeting took place at Oxford. Among the undergraduates who gathered in the rooms of Cosmo Gordon Lang (the present archbishop of Canterbury) were Bolton King, F. S. Marvin and J. A. Spender. Barnett explained to the group his idea of a university settlement, and the plan was received with enthusiasm. Barnett himself was of course the inevitable

---

[1] H. Barnett, op. cit., vol. i, p. 302. Mrs. Barnett names twelve in all.

[2] S. A. and H. Barnett, Practicable Socialism (new series), pp. 96-7.

choice for warden or head of the new establishment, which was to be known as " Toynbee Hall." [1]

Toynbee Hall is in a very real sense a monument to the social power of the Church of England as well as to Arnold Toynbee, and all its activities might reasonably be included in our account. Fortunately, however, the whole story, if not as well known as it should be, is easily available elsewhere.[2] Only its general outline and relation to the Church need be considered here.

Samuel Barnett dominated the enterprise and his social principles are worthy of attention not only because they determined its activities but because they helped to guide and animate the conscience of the Church as a whole. He believed that the principal mission of Toynbee Hall was to promote understanding and sympathy between classes. There had been many previous attempts on the part of churchmen to " improve " the poor but few efforts to understand them. Evangelism had been tried in which a certain amount of social work had been mingled with the chief business of preaching the gospel. One example of this was the Church Army, which, founded in 1882 on the model of the Salvation Army, was gradually being drawn into charitable and rescue work.[3] Furthermore, the interest and generosity of college men had already been enlisted in missions such as those established in London by Eton and Christ Church in 1881.[4] But Barnett perceived serious defects in the latter.

The clergyman [to whom is entrusted the adopted district] begins with a hall into which he gathers a congregation, and

[1] H. Barnett, *op. cit.*, vol. i, pp. 308-10.

[2] Especially in the work just cited and in W. Picht's *Toynbee Hall and the English Settlement Movement.*

[3] Montague Chamberlain, *The Church Army*, pp. 14-26.

[4] James Adderley, *Looking Upward*, pp. 3-4.

which he uses as a center for "mission" work. He himself is the only link between the college and the poor. He gives frequent reports of his progress, and enlists such personal help as he can, always keeping it in mind that the "district" is destined to become a "parish". Many districts thus created in London now take their places among the regular parishes and the income of the clergy is paid by the Ecclesiastical Commissioners, the patronage of the living is probably with the Bishop, and the old connexion has become simply a matter of history. . . . A college mission excludes Nonconformists. . . . It is not . . . the form best fitted to receive the spirit which is at present moving the Universities. [But] a Settlement enables men *to live within sight of the poor.* . . . He who has even for a month, shared in the life of the poor can never again rest in his old thoughts.[1]

What direction, one might ask, would the new thoughts take? In Barnett they inspired a profound dissatisfaction with the existing order. "The fact that the wealth of England means only wealth *in* England, and that the mass of the people live without knowledge, without hope, and often without health, has come home to open minds and consciences."[2] The end of settlements was thus something more than mere "fellowship", which at worst might have meant a sentimental acquiescence in things as they are and at best a little charity dispensed to the unfortunate. The sentiment must eventuate in a readiness to accept and to initiate reform. It is true that from the point of view of a Fabian Socialist Barnett's views were "chaotic".[3] By his own account Maurice, Comte, and the study of history had most influenced him intellectually. He was, in fact, what Mrs. Webb would call an "empirical Socialist." "Social

---

[1] *Practicable Socialism* (now series), pp. 98, 103.

[2] *Ibid.*, p. 97.

[3] Beatrice Webb, *My Apprenticeship*, p. 202.

reform," he said, " is the necessity of our time which all recognize. Whether it is by voluntary or by State action that the life of the majority is to be raised and ' equality of opportunity ' opened to all, none can say." [1] This empiricism at least saved him the pain of periodically recasting his philosophy (a soul-trying process not unknown even to Fabians). It certainly did not prevent him from adopting new, even if unpopular, ideas as they arose.

This attitude is well illustrated by his relations with the Charity Organization Society. In 1868 this organization had been adumbrated in a paper read before the Society of Arts by the Rev. Henry Solly, a Unitarian minister already known as the originator of workingmen's clubs. Upon its inauguration the next year Solly became its first secretary. Samuel Barnett was an early and enthusiastic member.[2] Among its wider objects were the improvement of education, the encouragement of provident societies, better sanitation and housing, and emigration. More and more, however, it limited itself to the discouragement of indiscriminate charity and sought to provide a rational method of distribution. Cases were investigated before relief was granted, and the society attempted to make itself a clearing house for information as well as a central collection agency.[3] At first Barnett was in complete accord with the society's principles. As early as 1880, it is true, he had objected to a lack of sympathy in its operations, and a too rigid classification of cases into " deserving " and " undeserving." [4] Nevertheless C. O. S. business occupied much of his attention and that of his friends both before and after the establishment of

[1] Albert Gray and W. H. Fremantle (editors), *Church Reform*, p. 176.
[2] Helen Bosanquet, *Social Work in London, a History of the Charity Organization Society*, pp. 13-22.
[3] *Ibid.*, pp. 28, 72.
[4] H. Barnett, *op. cit.*, vol. ii, p. 59.

Toynbee Hall. But in 1895 a definite break occurred. Barnett inclined toward wider state action while the C. O. S. somewhat inconsistently objected to such things as old-age pensions and the municipalizing of hospitals. According to Barnett the Society had become enslaved to a set of shibboleths. Its attachment to "Independence of State Relief" and "Saving" he placed in that category.[1] The Barnetts' breach with the C. O. S. (for in this, although not in some other things, Mrs. Barnett followed her husband) "sent a thrill through the philanthropic world of London," says Mrs. Webb. "They discovered for themselves that there was a deeper and more continuous evil than unrestricted and unregulated charity, namely, unrestricted and unregulated landlordism."[2]

Samuel Barnett's theory is to be discovered in his practice, and this for many years centered in Toynbee Hall. The settlement movement did not always proceed along the lines he could have wished; nevertheless he remained a constant believer in its efficacy. He saw to it that a permanent connection was maintained with the universities. Groups of supporters were organized at Oxford and Cambridge, and a body of "associates" formed—the list including such influential names as W. J. Ashley, James Bryce, Canon Fremantle, Alfred Marshall, R. L. Poole, and J. R. Seeley.[3]

At the end of 1884, then, a group of university men took up their residence in a house erected for that purpose near St. Jude's Church. The quarters were comfortable, even commodious, so as not to violate needlessly the sensibilities of the pioneers. As Barnett said many years later, they "must live their own life. There must be no affecta-

---

[1] Helen Bosanquet, *op. cit.*, pp. 142-3.

[2] B. Webb, *My Apprenticeship*, pp. 200-201.

[3] Toynbee Hall, *Annual Report*, 1886; H. Barnett, *op. cit.*, vol. ii, p. 37.

tion of asceticism and no consciousness of superiority. . . .
They have not come as ' missioners,' they have come to settle,
that is, to learn as much as to teach." [1]   Yet sometimes a
prig appeared.

Not so much among the inmates and other members themselves [says Mr. H. W. Nevinson] as among the solemn people
who came down to encourage our " noble enterprise," there was
a lot of pompous chatter about " shedding the light of University teaching among the dark places of the world." Even
young graduates from Oxford and Cambridge were inclined
to regard themselves as slightly superior to " the uneducated,"
forgetting that " the workers " were always incalculably ahead
of them in the true education which is the knowledge of life.[2]

In the leisure time which members could spare from their
own vocations they were expected to carry out in East London the first object of the association: " to provide education and a means of recreation and enjoyment for the people
of the poorer districts of London and other great cities; to
enquire into the condition of the poor and to consider and
advance plans calculated to promote their welfare." [3]   Barnett succeeded in obtaining a public library for Whitechapel
in 1891 together with a small natural history museum.   For
her part Mrs. Barnett not only applied her practical abilities
to the administration of Toynbee Hall but also carried on
extensive work among women.   Many girls were assisted in
finding places, clubs were formed, and a gymnasium provided.   Much rescue work was done.   By 1889, 2,350 girls
had received aid and counsel.   Another, what might be
called " extra-mural," venture was the " Toynbee Commission " on unemployment which published its findings in The

[1] S. and H. Barnett, *Practicable Socialism* (new series), p. 127.
[2] *Changes and Chances*, p. 79.
[3] Toynbee Hall, *Annual Report*, 1886, p. 3.

Times in 1892. The report was signed by (among others) W. J. Benn, Sidney Buxton, H. S. Holland, the Rev. Edwyn Hoskyns (now bishop of Southwell), George Shipton of the London Trades Council, and Sidney and Beatrice Webb.[1]

The manifold educational enterprises of Toynbee Hall need only be indicated here. They were, however, the distinguishing feature of the Settlement's work. Numerous clubs and guilds organized by the residents helped to cajole many along the path of learning. The inmates also discovered unsuspected talent as teachers in dealing with subjects running the gamut of the alphabet from " Ambulance " to "Zoölogy". Well-known personages came to expound their views—Bernard Shaw, for example, told why " The Working Classes are Useless and Ought to be Abolished." [2] The Settlement also became a center of University Extension. Barnett, in fact, hoped that Toynbee Hall might expand into a " great democratic University." To that end residential houses for students were opened in 1887 and 1890. The parent house threw off missionary centers giving courses in Limehouse and Poplar. University Extension had since its beginning taken the form of lecture courses. In 1887 Barnett suggested that tutorial courses were preferable, and the idea was adopted in 1900. Always interested in improving the standard of teaching in schools, he placed the resources of Toynbee Hall at the disposal of the School Board as a means of providing a broader cultural background for pupil-teachers, and raised a scholarship fund to assist prospective teachers in securing a university education.[3]

Some asked whether Toynbee Hall was reaching the class for which it was originally designed. The Annual Report

[1] H. Barnett, *op. cit.*, chs. 17, 18; vol. ii, p. 39.

[2] *Ibid.*, vol. i, pp. 330-31, 370-71.

[3] *Ibid.*, vol. i, pp. 338 *et seq.*, vol. ii, p. 13.

for 1898 was not wholly reassuring. " A reproach sometimes leveled at Toynbee Hall, that it caters for the ' middle '
rather than for the ' working ' class, does not apply, at least,
to the Debates. It is, of course, true that the ' middle ' class
is predisposed to swallow with avidity whatever it believes
to represent the culture of the upper ten thousand, while the
workingman affects rather a distant independence that is
easily mistaken for hostility. At any rate, it is certain that
in our debates we meet the genuine British working man
(not merely those of the poorer class), and perhaps a large
enough selection (for the weekly audience averages 200 to
250) to enable us to judge of his views and ideals, his
knowledge and his prejudices." [1]

A more serious defect of Toynbee Hall in the eyes of
some churchmen was the minor (or unobtrusive) place religion occupied in its régime. Out of this dissatisfaction
arose a second venture in settlement work—Oxford House in
Bethnal Green. Among those who planned the new foundation were E. S. Talbot, Warden of Keble College, the Rev.
W. O. Burrows (later bishop of Truro), the Rev. W. J. H.
Campion, Mr. Douglas Eyre, and the Hon. J. G. Adderley.
In many essential features Oxford House imitated Toynbee
Hall, but the residents of the former were all professed
churchmen and the Settlement made a point of its co-operation with the parish churches of the neighborhood. Much
of its educational work was carried on through specially
organized clubs for boys, young men, and older men. Oxford House came within the orbit of University Extension,
but this was a strictly minor activity in comparison with its
importance at Toynbee Hall.[2]

In labor politics Oxford House was less venturesome than

---

[1] H. Barnett, *op. cit.*, vol. i, p. 368.

[2] *Ibid.*, vol. ii, p. 29; J. G. Adderley, *In Slums and Society*, p. 47;
Oxford House, *Annual Report*, 1894, " Ten Years' Retrospect."

Toynbee Hall. In one year, says Mrs. Barnett, Canon Barnett "interfered" in no less than fourteen trade disputes. During the great Dock Strike of 1889 he entertained the trade-union leaders at supper at Toynbee Hall. For the benefit of timid friends at the University, however, he disclaimed any intention of identifying the Settlement with the union cause. At Oxford House

it was thought [said W. R. Anson] that to take the part of one or other belligerent in a trade war was a breach of neutrality, and an act of political partisanship in which we might not indulge. In the result we were saved from any share in the headlong, hateful scramble after popularity for a party, sect, or institution to which that unhappy dispute gave rise.

As organizing secretary and then Head of the Settlement from 1885 to 1887 J. G. Adderley had helped to put Oxford House on a firm basis. It is possible that if he had still been in authority in 1889 its policy would have been more active and less pacific, for, as we shall see, he was one of the group who tried to stir the Church to effective action during the strike. But his successors were men of a different temper. The Rev. H. H. Henson (now bishop of Durham), who presided over the destinies of Oxford House during 1888, had vivid opinions of his own, but they were in general quite the reverse of Adderley's. From 1889 to 1897, under the Rev. A. F. Winnington Ingram (at present bishop of London), Oxford House made steady progress along the lines originally marked out for it—these did not include positive action in trade disputes.[1]

The settlement movement achieved wider recognition and won more followers than any other movement we shall chronicle in this book. It fathered the American phase of

[1] H. Barnett, *op. cit.*, vol. ii, p. 66; *Economic Review*, vol. iii, p. 21; Oxford House, *Annual Report*, 1888; J. G. Adderley, *op. cit.*, p. 97.

settlement work—Jane Addams, for example, visited Toynbee Hall in 1887 and 1889, and Stanton Coit, founder of the
Neighborhood Guild of New York, resided there in 1886—
while a host of imitators sprang up in Great Britain itself.
The idea has now become the property of the European
world.[1]

THE GUILD OF ST. MATTHEW

The settlement movement did not commit itself to any particular theory of social reform.   Nor did philosophizing
occupy a very large place in its program.   If their activities
are an index, settlements could have lived quite happily without being sustained by the contemplation of Utopias.   Certain
beneficial results were expected to flow from association with
the working classes, contingencies being met as they arose
on the basis of practical experience and the dictates of common humanity.   Members must look elsewhere for the definition of ultimate ends.   Two organizations connected with
the Church helped to supply this need.   More sensitive than
the settlements to movements of social theory, they owed a
large share of their prestige to the growing popular interest
in such matters.

According to Mr. Bruce Glasier, an associate of William
Morris in the Social Democratic Federation, " the Guild of
St. Matthew . . . . may rightly claim to have sounded the
note of the forthcoming Socialist movement." [2]   Such a
heroic rôle was not contemplated for it by the founders of
the Guild.   It originated, in fact, with the younger parishioners of Bethnal Green as an expression of regard for the
Rev. Stewart Headlam.   Broader objects were in a sense
thrust upon it.

[1] R. A. Woods and A. J. Kennedy, *op. cit.*, pp. 41, 46; H. Barnett,
op. cit., vol. i, p. 30.

[2] J. Bruce Glasier, *William Morris and the Early Days of the Socialist
Movement*, p. 12.

The career of Stewart Headlam would merit attention even if the Guild of St. Matthew had never appeared. He was one of the most remarkable and colorful — unfriendly critics said erratic—social reformers that the Church of England has produced. The son of a Liverpool business man, he was born at Wavertree in 1847. He came honestly by an argumentative disposition—nothing delighted his father more than to uphold the Evangelical dispensation in a well-fought debate. But a father's natural pride was somewhat tempered by the fact that controversy threatened to disrupt the family peace. During his Eton years Stewart came under the influence of F. D. Maurice through one of his teachers, William Johnson — an influence which the elder Headlam tried vainly to eradicate. The prepossession was increased when Stewart went to Cambridge and sat at the feet of the master himself.[1]

Headlam was drawn to Maurice at first more by the latter's theology than by his social opinions—if the first can be separated from the second. Either one would have brought tribulation to a prospective clergyman of Headlam's undiplomatic nature; when he disclosed a Ritualistic bias they became insurmountable obstacles to his progress in the Church. The first warning came when Bishop Jackson delayed his ordination to the priesthood. The Bishop anticipated a melancholy but orthodox end of man's career—at the Day of Judgment exactly half would be numbered among the goats; Headlam, on the other hand, was incurably hopeful. It looked for a time as if, whatever man's destiny, Headlam's career as a clergyman would end before it began. The difficulty, however, was finally overcome and his ordination took place in 1872. But the peace was only an armistice. During the next ten years he held four curacies, all but one of which

---

[1] F. G. Bettany, *op. cit.*, chs. i, ii.

he was forced to vacate after disagreement with the authorities. But the time was not misspent. If his superiors could
teach him nothing, he learned willingly of the poor. Visiting the wretched, examining schools, teaching classes in his
rooms, going swimming with small boys, and piloting little
girls on sight-seeing trips he acquired a fund of practical
knowledge which gave vitality to his opinions on social reform for the rest of his life.[1]

It was while Headlam served at St. Matthew's, Bethnal
Green, that the Guild of St. Matthew began. Parish guilds
were becoming popular at that time and a group of young
people decided to form one for their own church. Frederick
Verinder, who from that time forward was perhaps Headlam's closest associate in social work, was its chief organizer.
At the inaugural service on St. Matthew's day, 1877, the
society had forty members.

Very shortly the Guild found it necessary to follow its
pastor into the wilderness. Headlam, who had conceived a
fondness for the theater and the dance, especially since his
curacy in Drury Lane (1870-1873), delivered a lecture before the local Radical Club on "Theaters and Music Halls"
in which he indiscreetly advised young ladies "whose name
was Dull to see these young women who are so full of life
and mirth." Perhaps Bishop Jackson and Headlam's rector
perceived a connection between dullness and virtue. At any
rate they were sure that the stage was disreputable and Headlam found himself temporarily "at liberty" at the beginning of 1878.[2]

Two results came of his dismissal. Far from being dis-
heartened by the frowns of authority, he determined to
restore the reputation of stage people with members of the
Church. Accordingly in 1879 he appeared as head of the

[1] F. G. Bettany, *op. cit.*, chs. iii-viii.
[2] *Ibid.*, pp. 41-4, 79-80.

Church and Stage Guild, which was made up largely of actors, leavened by a few audacious clergymen. Headlam's first care was the state of ballet-dancers, who particularly suffered from the puritan conscience. Soon after the appointment of Frederick Temple to the see of London in 1885 Headlam and a party of friends stormed the episcopal fastnesses of Fulham in the interest of this class of performers. But Temple, who had witnessed the ravages of the ballet at Rugby and Oxford, was an impossible nut to crack. The bishop found himself enmeshed in a debate on the moral, symbolic, esthetic, and mythological value of legs, but he could not be seduced, and the only result was to show how far these members had to go before they reached their present position of authority.

On the grounds of his defense of dancing—at least ostensibly—Temple withheld for many years Headlam's license to preach. The latter therefore spoke from bitter experience when, commenting on a recent clerical appointment, he wrote, " It is a terrible slur on a man's reputation to have pleased both Lord Salisbury and Dr. Temple." Nevertheless the Church and Stage Guild before its disappearance about 1900 did much to remove the prejudice of churchpeople against the theater. Sir Johnston Forbes-Robertson gratefully recognized its educational value. Sir Henry Irving, who was fully conscious of the immense chasm between himself and the plebeian members of his profession and therefore not much in sympathy with the democratic tendencies of the Guild, also paid it tribute: " People sometimes maintain that the stage is indebted to me for the great esteem in which it is now held, but really, did they but know it, actors owe far more to that man Headlam." [1]

The other result of Headlam's departure from Bethnal

---

[1] F. G. Bettany, *op. cit.*, pp. 64-9, ch. x; *Church Reformer*, vol. vii, p. 28.

Green involved the fate of the Guild of St. Matthew. It had been a purely local society; but when Headlam left, its leaders determined to extend their appeal to the Church as a whole. The original objects of the Guild had been to popularize the Church and its services, combat secularism (Headlam had already broken a lance with the arch-skeptic Bradlaugh), and promote education, social intercourse, and recreation among its members. Very shortly the latter point was so modified as to become the keynote of the Guild: "To promote the study of social and political questions in the light of the Incarnation." "Those last six words," said Headlam, "were the *raison d'être* of all our Christian Socialism and efforts toward social and religious reform."[1]

The Guild was primarily a propagandist organization—it devoted itself to indoctrinating its own members and converting the philistines. Lectures, conferences, and occasional mass-meetings were the means ordinarily used. Branches were established in various parts of England— H. C. Shuttleworth and F. Lewis Donaldson (now canon of Westminster) conducted a very efficient one at Oxford. In 1883 Headlam purchased *The Church Reformer,* which became the unofficial organ of the Guild as well as an untrammelled medium of expression for himself. But in spite of its success with a limited public—John Morley " said . . . . that there was enough matter in it to stock five ordinary newspapers "—the paper never became self-supporting and had to be abandoned in 1895.[2]

From the standpoint of numbers the Guild was almost insignificant. Headlam considered that its most successful period was about 1884, but at that time the membership cannot have been much over a hundred, perhaps a third of whom were priests. The membership increased somewhat

[1] F. G. Bettany, *op. cit.,* pp. 79-81.

[2] *Ibid.,* pp. 82-3, ch. xi.

thereafter, but never rose above four hundred.[1] It would of course be as unreasonable to estimate the influence of the Guild simply by counting heads as it would be to judge the Fabian Society in the same way. The Guild was only a goad which pricked forward the opinions of average people. Headlam possessed a genius for advertising and kept the public informed of the Guild's activities through letters to the newspapers, pronouncements on current affairs, and addresses to public bodies. Thus it reached a much wider group than its own membership. H. W. Massingham and Bernard Shaw, for instance, attended Headlam's assemblies although they never joined the Guild. "'Shaw used our meetings,' says an old member of the Guild, 'as a training ground for public speaking and debate.'"[2]

It has already been intimated that Headlam pretty thoroughly dominated the policy of the Guild. This he did not only by reason of his position as Warden but by the vigor and charm of his own personality. Yet he was about as immune to criticism as he was to fear. While this attitude, as we shall see, alienated many who would not have a program thrust upon them, it certainly clarified the position of the Guild. Headlam knew what he wanted, and when he fastened on a principle it was never repudiated.

Land reform held a leading position in this hierarchy of ideas. In an address to the Guild in 1884 he made it clear that " A Priest's Political Program " must include " such measures as will tend — (a) To restore to the people such values as they bring to the land; (b) To bring about a better distribution of the wealth created by labour; (c) To give the whole people a voice in their own government; (d) To abolish false standards of worth and dignity." " Person-

---

[1] F. G. Bettany, *op. cit.*, pp. 81, 83. *The Church Reformer* in 1885 (vol. iv, p. 210) put the membership at 126 including 40 priests.

[2] F. G. Bettany, *op. cit.*, pp. 87-9.

ally," he said, " I am inclined to believe that if the first part
of our resolution were carried out, the second would follow
as a matter of course." [1]   Elsewhere, by easy transitions, he
connected prostitution and drunkenness with the absence of
a tax on land values.[2]

Unlike some reformers, Headlam never sheltered himself
from criticism by dealing only in generalities.   It was a gesture of humility rather than a statement of policy when on
one occasion he said, " It is not for me to discuss special
measures ; "—he had just suggested a twenty per cent tax
on land values!   To those whose interest in the land question was anemic his proposed list of questions to candidates
at the election of 1885 offered a sufficiently varied and
specific menu :

Will you support (1) Free Education, (2) The rating of un-
occupied land in towns, (3) An increase in the land tax, (4)
The conferring on municipalities the power to rate land-values
exclusive of house-values, (5) The expenditure of public money
in improving the dwellings of the poor, (6) An eight-hours bill,
(7) A bill shortening the hours in shops, (8) Increased power
for municipalities to undertake industrial work for the purpose
of relieving distress? [3]

NEW TRENDS IN SOCIAL THEORY

The Guild of St. Matthew moved across a stage crowded
with other actors, each of whom tried to draw the eye of a
somewhat torpid audience.   To a casual or hostile onlooker
the performers seemed to possess hardly more than one idea
in common : a dissatisfaction with things as they were.   Actually, the drama was threaded with certain new economic
and ethical-theological motives.   Their general purport, what

---

[1] *Church Reformer*, vol. iii, p. 217.

[2] *Ibid.*, vol. iv, pp. 76, 175, 197.

[3] *Ibid.*, vol. iv, p. 220.

Headlam and the Guild of St. Matthew made of them, how they ushered in a new enterprise of churchmen—the Christian Social Union—must now be explained.

Laymen inferred (and very often still infer) from the teaching of classical economists that man's material prosperity or lack of it depended on the operation of certain superhuman forces working in a medium of free competition. The competition was furnished by men who, it was assumed, acted from selfish motives expressed in terms of pounds, shillings, and pence. Since the condition of free competition was supposed to be already in effect secured, nothing remained but to let the cosmic forces operate. This may have been a misconception of the scientific viewpoint, but the two resembled each other closely enough to prevent serious conflict for many years. Social reforms, especially when they involved legislation, stood little chance of success unless they could be translated into the terms of this popular philosophy, for mere human laws could hardly be expected to compete with a divine system. Subsequent events showed that these ideas would stand a good deal of uprooting.

The reign of natural law was a little too despotic to go long unchallenged. " The ethical progress of society depends," said Huxley, " not on imitating the cosmic process, still less on running away from it, but on combating it." [1] But had the classical school even correctly transcribed its indefeasible laws? Very early John Stuart Mill was moved to redefine his categories: " Unlike the Laws of Production, those of Distribution are partly of human origin, since the manner in which wealth is distributed in any given society depends on the statutes and usages therein obtaining." [2] Other economists pointed out the bearing of non-competing

---

[1] Quoted by H. S. Holland in *Our Neighbors*, p. 5.

[2] *Principles of Economics*, vol. i, pp. 41-2; also pp. 258-9.

groups of workmen on value, the existence of reserved prices, and the limitations of the wage-fund theory. Moralists watched these changes with approval. " Mr. Thornton, Professor Cairnes, and Professor Walker," said Arnold Toynbee, " restored observation to its place." [1] So it happened that while the multitude admired the stern simplicity of the temple from without, the priests inside were busily grubbing at its foundations. Now and again sounds of conflict in which cabalistic words flew back and forth came from the interior, but the laity were uncertain whether to be alarmed at a revolution or to rejoice at the progress of science. Cliffe Leslie, writing in 1874, remarked that " the English market for economic publications is extremely limited, the works on the subject are necessarily few, but it is notorious that various doctrines to be met with in the English text-books have often been questioned in lectures, articles, discussions, and private conversation." [2]

Out of the welter of criticism rose a new school of economics which has been called the Neo-Classical. Foreshadowed by Stanley Jevons and brought to a commanding position by Alfred Marshall, it regarded economic phenomena as, within limits, susceptible of treatment by mathematical and diagrammatic methods similar to those of physical science.[3] But a new humanitarian strain was audible in the theory of this group. Marshall by 1883 had formulated the system which from then on he expounded at Oxford and later at Cambridge, and which he introduced in 1890 to a wider public with these words:

Political Economy or Economics is a study of mankind in the

[1] *Lectures on the Industrial Revolution in England*, p. 10.

[2] T. E. Cliffe Leslie, *Essays on Political and Moral Philosophy*, pp. 179 *et seq.*

[3] A. C. Pigou, *Memorials of Alfred Marshall*, p. 24.

ordinary business of life; it examines that part of individual and social action which is most clearly connected with the attainment and the use of the material requisites of well-being. Thus it is on the one side a study of wealth, and on the other, and more important side, a part of the study of man.[1]

Even Mr. J. A. Hobson, who rails at " economic bookkeeping," is forced to admit that "doubtless the sense that human well-being is the end of economic activities may be said to pervade his work." [2] Indeed, from the viewpoint of social reformers any change in doctrine whatever could not help being for the better.

There was another group of economists no less dissatisfied with Ricardian principles and more closely identified with the social movement in the Church. This was the historical or Realist school, which imported much of its method from Germany. T. E. Cliffe Leslie was one of the first English exponents. We find him in 1870 agreeing with Buckle's criticism of the deductive methods employed by the classical school.

Political Economy [he goes on to say] is not a body of natural laws in the true sense, . . . but an assemblage of speculations and doctrines which are the result of a particular history, colored even by the history and character of their chief writers.

In a later essay he pays his respects to Wilhelm Roscher and Karl Knies.[3]

Arnold Toynbee carried on the succession. As an Oxford undergraduate he had studied both economics and history to good purpose. As we have seen, one branch of his social interest led up to Toynbee Hall. Another flourished at Ox-

[1] *Principles of Political Economy*, p. 1.

[2] *Political Science Quarterly*, vol. 40, pp. 341 *et seq.*

[3] T. E. Cliffe Leslie, *op. cit.*, pp. 148-50, 167 *et seq.*

ford. On continuing his residence as a tutor, he lectured to
working men on economics and free trade. He also founded
a society for political education whose members were to
write and lecture on social subjects. In 1881 he became a
member of the Oxford Board of Guardians of the Poor.
But his *Lectures on the Industrial Revolution,* published
posthumously in 1884, gave him an enduring reputation.
F. W. Maitland said that Henry Spelman invented the feudal
system. In the same sense Toynbee created the Industrial
Revolution.[1]

Two men whose careers were less romantic but whose
contributions were more substantial (at least in bulk) supplemented Toynbee's work. William Cunningham's *Growth
of English Industry and Commerce* appeared modestly as a
single volume in 1882. William Ashley published the first
part of his *Introduction to English Economic History and
Theory* in 1888. Both owed much to the Germans; Cunningham, in fact, had studied at Tübingen; Ashley, at Hei-
delberg.[2]

Like the neo-classicists, the historical school helped to
emancipate Englishmen from the tyranny of economic law.
More than that, they drew attention to another set of standards by which contemporary society might be judged.
Merely to recall industrial organizations and economic
moralities of the past was enough to cast doubt upon the
cheerful assumption that English history was a tale of un-
broken progress from barbarism to civilization. But the
historians were more specific. They evinced a positive sympathy with medieval conditions and a corresponding distaste
for the brutalities which had accompanied the emergence of

[1] Blanqui had used the term as early as 1837.

[2] A brief account of Ashley's career is given in *The Economic History
Review,* 1928, pp. 319-21; of Cunningham's, in *Proceedings of the British
Academy,* 1919-1920, pp. 466-73.

the present order.   Thorold Rogers is usually placed with
the Ricardians, but spiritually he was a Realist, and he could
not contemplate a history of prices without emotion.

It may well be [he wrote] that the progress of some has been
more than counterbalanced by the distress of the many, that
the opulence and strength of modern times mocks the poverty
and misery which are bound up with and surround them, and
that there is an uneasy and increasing consciousness that the
other side hates and threatens.[1]

Ashley, Cunningham, and Toynbee were neither so explicit
nor perhaps so pessimistic, yet their works if properly used
are a series of case-books for reformers.   Medieval guilds
and sumptuary legislation, the canonist doctrine of the just
price, even mercantilism, receive from them a considerate
hearing.   In Ashley's opinion,

History seems to be proving that no great institution has been
without its use for a time, and its relative justification.
Similarly it is beginning to appear that no great conception, no
great body of doctrines which really influenced society for a
long period, was without a certain truth and value, having regard to contemporary circumstances.[2]

"It was the labour question," said Toynbee, ". . . that
revived the method of observation.   Political Economy was
transformed by the working classes."   Science repaid the
debt.

Those . . . who have applied the historical method to political
economy and the science of society, have shown an unmistakable disposition to lay bare the injustice to which the humbler
classes of the community have been exposed, and to defend
methods and institutions adopted for their protection which

[1] *Six Centuries of Work and Wages*, p. 186.

[2] *An Introduction to English Economic History and Theory*, vol. i, p. xi.

have never received scientific defence before. . . . For while the modern historical school of economists appear to be only exploring monuments of the past, they are really shaping the foundations of many of our institutions of the present.[1]

With some notable exceptions, such as Mr. and Mrs. Sidney Webb and Charles Booth, the historical school, at least before 1900, was virtually confined to churchmen. Toynbee and Ashley, though laymen, took their religion with uncommon seriousness.[2] Thorold Rogers had been a clergyman. Cunningham was a parish priest before he became archdeacon of Ely. H. de B. Gibbins, author of *The Industrial History of England* (1890) and *Industry in England* (1897), was also a clergyman. Ashley, Cunningham, Gibbins, and also W. A. S. Hewins, contributed articles to the *Economic Review* of the Christian Social Union.

Still another group of writers on economic subjects must be referred to in any history of the Church reform organizations. Ideally, an economist, as a scientist, submerges his personal bias in an objective description of facts. Actually, the socialists fail to attain the dignity of economists not only because they use propaganda but because they take no pains to conceal it. To place them with economists, therefore, perhaps requires an apology.

Karl Marx died relatively unknown in England, in 1883. H. M. Hyndman had interpreted some of his philosophy for the benefit of the Social Democratic Federation, but neither then nor later was it accepted as a compulsive system by any great body of Englishmen. Yet, as a Christian Socialist has said, the writings of Marx did help to strengthen the general concept of social duty.[3] Henry George, if not a socialist in

[1] *Op. cit.*, ch. v.

[2] *Cf.* Ashley's *The Christian Outlook, being the Sermons of an Economist.*

[3] H. S. Holland, *Our Neighbors*, p. 7.

the orthodox sense, was at least socialistic.   His *Progress and Poverty* appeared in 1879.   According to Hyndman, " Marx looked it through and spoke of it with a sort of friendly contempt; ' The capitalists' last ditch,' he said." [1] Nevertheless it had a lasting influence on English social reformers.   " To Henry George," says the historian of the Fabian Society, " belongs the extraordinary merit of recognizing the right way of social salvation," namely, political action.[2]

Henry George advertised his existence to Englishmen by a rather kaleidoscopic lecture tour of Ireland in 1881 just when it was in a state of agitation over the land question. Most of 1882 he spent in England, returning for a short visit at the instance of the Land Reform Union in 1884.[3] Enumerating the causes which led to the formation of the Christian Social Union, Scott Holland says:

Into this disturbance of outlook already at work there flared suddenly the flaming portent of Henry George. . . . No one who had once read *Progress and Poverty* could remain the same man that he had been. . . . I remember the rough energy of the man, baited by smart Oxford undergraduates in the Clarendon rooms, and giving them back the taunt that stung: " What is the use of arguing with you, you well-fed men ! " [4]

Readers will already have guessed that Stewart Headlam drew most of his ideas on land reform from Henry George. The absorption was perhaps aided by George's markedly religious though heterodox bent, a trait which suddenly struck Hyndman in the midst of a debate : " Then his arched bald

[1] H. M. Hyndman, *The Record of an Adventurous Life*, pp. 257-8.

[2] E. R. Pease, *A History of the Fabian Society*, p. 19.

[3] Henry George [Jr.], *Life of Henry George*, vol. ii, pp. 345 *et seq.*, 415 *et seq.*

[4] H. S. Holland, *Our Neighbors*, p. 5.

head rose up like an apse on the other side of the table, and I saw that his bump of reverence was of cathedral proportions." One admirer called him a Christian Socialist.[1] At a farewell banquet to George, Headlam, who presided over the meeting of "three hundred ladies and gentlemen," pointed a moral:

The people, after hearing Mr. George, had come to the conclusion that private property in land was not justified by morality or religion and it was plain that such private property in land was utterly against the Ten Commandments, and was altogether opposed to the teachings of the life and character of Jesus Christ.[2]

Economists created an economic man, and deduced a set of laws from his assumed egotism. At first they conceded that he had no real existence. Then they began to fear he had. Hastily abdicating their somewhat fortuitous position as priests in a cult of selfishness they now dwelt on the value as well as the power of altruism. As social duty had again become popular men cast about for a philosophy suitable to the occasion. Many found it in the writings of Auguste Comte. "It is difficult," says a Fabian Socialist, "for the present generation to realize how large a space in the minds of the young men of the 'eighties was occupied by the religion invented by Auguste Comte."[3] Men like Frederic Harrison, Godfrey and Vernon Lushington, E. S. Beesly, and F. S. Marvin, all of whom had joined the Christian Socialists in numerous philanthropic enterprises, adopted the "religion of humanity." "How marvelous," exclaimed a future president of the Christian Social Union, "that it

[1] Hyndman, *op. cit.*, p. 267; Henry Rose, *Henry George, a Biographical, Anecdotal, and Critical Sketch*, pp. 77, 82.

[2] *Times*, 7 April, 1884, p. 6.

[3] E. R. Pease, *op. cit.*, p. 14.

should be left for them [the Positivists] to rediscover some of the simplest teachings of Christianity." In a volume of sermons which Westcott later wrote on " Social Aspects of Christianity " he acknowledged his debt to Comte.[1] Less picturesquely, at Oxford, another philosopher was fitting out his disciples with a system of social ethics.

T. H. Green [said his friend Scott Holland] had taught us the obligations which bound the Universities to the larger life outside. . . . It was Green who identified the interests of this ideal imagination with the common affairs of men and women; who charged us with the ardour which made him always the active champion of the poor and the preacher of the obligations of citizenship.[2]

Much as churchmen owed to the newer economics and to secular philosophy they could scarcely regard these merely human products as the final justification of a social policy. Christian Socialism still found its best apology in the teachings of the Church, interpreted according to Evangelical, Ritualist, or Broad Church tenets. As we have seen, these three traditions had been useful to the social reformer during the first half of the century.[3] Now, working upon each other, constantly changing as one generation of churchmen handed them on to the next, they were still indispensable to those who needed the assurance that in working for man's temporal improvement one served God according to the Church of England.

Few Evangelicals are to be found among the leaders of movements described in this chapter. Perhaps Samuel Barnett may be counted as one. Like the advocates of temper-

---

[1] Arthur Westcott, *Life and Letters of Brooke Foss Westcott*, vol. i, p. 291; B. F. Westcott, *Social Aspects of Christianity*, preface, p. xii.

[2] *A Bundle of Memories*, pp. 89, 145.

[3] *Supra*, pp. 21-36.

ance, the city missionaries and the Church Army, all of
whom were strongly Evangelical, he found it necessary to
remove certain barriers of poverty and ignorance before a
purely spiritual message could be preached with much prospect of success. For many years churchmen argued the
futile question whether the pig made the sty or the sty made
the pig. Evangelicals never submitted to the sty but they
learned from bitter experience that it was quite as stubborn
a fact as the pig.

After the death of Dean Stanley, Brooke Foss Westcott
became perhaps the leading figure in the Broad Church party.
Born in 1825, he came of a midland family whose fortune
descended from an Indian nabob and a Birmingham manufacturer. His father was an amateur scientist of severe
tastes, little given to sentimental outpourings even in the
privacy of family life. " As a rule, Mr. F. B. Westcott's
letters to his son were, save for a few geological passages,
almost exclusively of a botanical character." An equal restraint, verging sometimes on puritanism, marked the personal habits of his son. " To live is not to be gay or idle
or restless," he said as a youth of twenty-four. " Frivolity,
inactivity, and aimlessness seem equally remote from the
true idea of living." He even felt called upon to apologize
for attending a concert.[1]

But religion and human service gave him the emotional
outlet which he denied himself in other ways: " The aim of
living is the good of men. The motive of living, the love
of God." Westcott's writings convey the warmth and color
of his faith. He had early fallen under the chill influence of
R. D. Hampden but the balance was somewhat restored by a
reading of Newman's *Tracts.* So when that manifesto
of the Broad Church, *Essays and Reviews,* appeared he
wished it to be " seriously and reasonably assailed." His

[1] Arthur Westcott, *op. cit.,* vol. i, pp. 1 *et seq.,* 93, 114, 145.

via media was far removed from that of the Tractarians yet near enough to feel its glow. Of *Ecce Homo* he says:

I cannot think that any estimate of our Lord's work and person which starts from its ethical aspect can be other than fatally deceptive. . . . I feel more strongly than I dare express that it is this so-called Christian morality as "the sum of the Gospel", which makes Christianity so powerless now.[1]

As a lad Westcott had been deeply stirred by the Chartist movement. But his academic career, first as a Harrow master, then as divinity professor at Cambridge, secluded him from direct contact with social problems. Yet the friendships he formed at the University kept him in the main current of ideas. From undergraduate days he had been on intimate terms with J. Ll. Davies, the Christian Socialist. Alfred Marshall was one of a group called the Eranus Club, founded by Westcott, which discussed questions arising out of the special studies of its members. Twenty years later when Westcott suddenly became a man of large affairs as bishop of Durham his correspondence with Marshall, now the famous economist, shows that each gained something from the other. "Everything you say," said Marshall, " draws me toward forms of belief which are not altogether my own, but the substance of which I am in some measure able to hold fast, strengthened by holy influences such as yours."[2]

Beliefs which had been private opinions unfolded themselves in public when, in 1883, Westcott came to London as canon of Westminster. The call to bear witness of a gospel which he saw daily violated was indeed irresistible. A course of sermons on " Social Aspects of Christianity " delivered in 1886 made it clear that his belief rested on a very

---

[1] Arthur Westcott, *op. cit.*, vol. i, pp. 212, 223, 289.

[2] *Ibid.*, vol. i, pp. 7, 43, 385; A. C. Pigou, *op. cit.*, p. 383.

simple reading of that gospel aided by a close study of F. D. Maurice.

I do not think [he said] that our real controversies in the immediate future are likely to be speculative; they threaten to be terribly practical. Behind the disputes of words, the abstract reasonings about the Being of God or the constitution of men . . . lie the fundamental questionings of social duty: What . . . is the foundation on which a kingdom of God can be built, and how can we do our part in hastening its establishment?

This kingdom was of the present as much as of the future.

It places its members in a social and personal relationship to a divine Head, as citizens to a King, as children to a father. . . . It is the social incorporation of a spirit, which penetrates and hallows every region of human activity, . . . which combines in a harmonious union the manifold energies of enterprise.

Three propositions epitomized the contribution of Christianity to the settlement of all modern difficulties:

If the Word became flesh, the brotherhood of man is a reality for us.

If the Son of God was crucified, the fall, and with it the redemption, are realities for us.

If the Son of Man rose again from the dead, the eternal significance of our short space of labour is a reality for us.[1]

The Tractarian tradition gained both in strength and variety of expression as the period of Newman and Pusey was left behind. Under the name of Ritualism it meant to opponents merely sacramentalism and a too friendly disposition toward the Church of Rome, thus having a unity thrust upon it which it did not possess. One group, to be sure, did give these sentiments a special prominence. The English Church Union (founded in 1860) was prepared " to

[1] B. F. Westcott, *Social Aspects of Christianity*, pp. xii, 4-5, 8, 88.

defend and maintain unimpaired the Doctrine, Discipline, and position of the Church of England as an integral part of the whole Catholic Church of Christ." Hampered by self-respect or an imperfect vision of the truth, it has worked ineffectually for reunion with Rome ever since.

But one did not have to be a reunionist to discover social values in Ritualism. When Charles Booth made his religious survey of London he found that High Church parsons " bring to their work in the slums a greater force of religious enthusiasm " than Evangelicals or Broad Churchmen.[1] A favorite phrase of Stewart Headlam's was "It is the Mass that matters." He felt that the sacrament confirmed in an act of common worship at once the democratic and altruistic sentiments of the partakers and the social meaning of Christ's life, work, and death. All that conspired to make it impressive—candles, genuflections, the sign of the cross, a belief in the Real Presence—were therefore valuable. Appearances moved him intensely. He was a Ritualist because of his artistic sensitiveness to form just as he was a reformer because of his sensitiveness to the outward facts of human suffering. But all Church doctrine, as he understood it, was a treasury of texts for reformers, constantly misinterpreted by the clergy though it was. " Truly the Church catechism seems to be a revolutionary levelling document. No wonder that many of the clergy have ceased to teach it, and put their own pious little manuals in its place." Another member of the Guild of St. Matthew, the Rev. Thomas Hancock, called the Magnificat " the hymn of the universal social revolution." [2]

Headlam was a sacramentalist by emotional conviction.

---

[1] *Life and Labour of the People in London*, third series, vol. vii, p. 46.

[2] F. G. Bettany, *op. cit.*, pp. 210-14; *Church Reformer*, August, 1883, p. 3; vol. i, p. 244; S. D. Headlam, *The Guild of St. Matthew* (a pamphlet published in 1890).

But there were others of a more analytic turn who believed that the attitude of mystical acceptance needed buttressing. The young High Church party, as they were sometimes called, published a reasoned statement of their views in 1889. *Lux Mundi* stands with the *Tracts* and *Essays and Reviews* as a landmark in nineteenth-century Anglican theology. In essence it was a reinterpretation of Christian doctrine to fit modern intellectual and social needs. The tone of the book was reasonable rather than dogmatic. The authors, among whom were Charles Gore, Scott Holland, Arthur Lyttelton, E. S. Talbot, W. J. H. Campion, and Aubrey Moore, addressed themselves not to the converted but to those who found the way of faith hard to travel in face of historical criticism and the certitudes of modern science. They met rationalism with proposals of conciliation instead of condemning it root and branch. Gore conceded that if the Old Testament contained primitive myths it might be interpreted dramatically or idealistically. Lyttelton claimed a pragmatic value for belief in the Atonement—it had, he said, a moral fitness: "the human heart accepts it, and by the cross is assured of forgiveness." According to Talbot, the advent of Christ was in a sense not miraculous; history had prepared the way; the time was ripe. So, too, the moral content of Christianity was a historical fact, temporarily obscured by Lutheranism and Calvinism, but now merely reassuming its earlier importance. "The conscience of to-day . . . . refuses to believe that the imprimatur of religion can be given to that which is not good, or that God would put us to moral confusion," said Aubrey Moore. How this moral urge was to realize itself the authors did not state—they implied that suitable programs would flow spontaneously from an aroused social conscience. Christianity, said Campion, is not pledged to uphold any particular form of property as such. But where Christian ethics steps in is, firstly, to show that property is secondary not primary, a means and not an end. Thus in so far as Socialism looks to a moral regeneration of society by a merely mechanical alteration of the distribution of the products of industry, or of the mode of holding property, it has to be reminded that a change of heart and will is the only true starting-point of moral improvement.

On sacraments Gore took much the same stand as Headlam. " They are the ordained instruments of grace, and . . . are in one of their aspects *social* ceremonies." [1]

Thus *Lux Mundi* was distinctly in the Broad Church tradition although even Westcott found it rather strong fare—too strong, in fact, to read. While the book touched upon social reform only in a vague way, most of its contributors belonged to movements treated in this chapter and so were closely linked with the Broad Church on its social side, especially through F. D. Maurice. As C. F. G. Masterman said, " His [Maurice's] influence has been almost entirely in the strengthening of a movement whose leaders he fought unwearyingly for nearly half a century; and . . . . the bulk of his ' honey ' passed into the ' Ritualistic hive.' " Yet that hive was well stocked with its own honey. From our point of view the corporate sense which Ritualists sought to instill by raising the sacraments to a new importance was just as significant as the intellectual catholicism of Broad Churchmen. [2]

But it ought to be obvious that a churchman's party label did not tell the measure of his social interest. It depended largely on himself what use he was to make of Evangelical, Broad, or High Church doctrine. Indeed it sometimes seems

---

[1] *Lux Mundi*, fifth edition, pp. 78-9, 130, 322-3, 440, 510-11.

[2] Arthur Westcott, *op. cit.*, vol. ii, p. 68; C. F. G. Masterman, *Frederick Denison Maurice*, p. 5.

as though each, if properly interpreted, would sanctify almost any course of social action he might choose to follow. And if one body of doctrine failed him he could always borrow from another.

THE CHRISTIAN SOCIAL UNION

While *Lux Mundi* was enlightening the more philosophic part of the British world, its authors were launching a new enterprise for the benefit of the working classes—the Christian Social Union. The time was exceptionally favorable. First of all a bolder habit of thought prevailed which was the natural result of earlier experiments in social reform, a better knowledge of the conditions under which most of the population lived, and the movements in economics and theology which we have just described. As Bishop Gore has put it,

The makers of the movement were people of very different experiences, though they were at one in being churchmen. There were students of theology, of the New Testament, and of the Christian Fathers, and students of economics who were conscious of the trend of economic doctrine away from the old "orthodox" standpoint represented by Ricardo. There were readers, who would hardly have accounted themselves professed students, who had been fired or inspired by the works of Maurice and Kingsley or by *Ecce Homo*. There were those, both men and women, who had plunged into the Settlement movement, then at its height, under the passionate impulse of sympathy for the masses of men and women and children in the slums of great cities who were being exploited in the interests of the possessors and accumulators of wealth. There were workers like Miss Gertrude Tuckwell and Miss Constance Smith for the uplift of women. There were clergy or church workers who found their whole spiritual work blocked by the gross injustice of social conditions.[1]

[1] Stephen Paget, editor, *Henry Scott Holland*, p. 241; *cf.* also H. S. Holland, *Our Neighbors*, p. 1.

Then, too, certain events occurred in 1888 and 1889 which may be called the precipitating causes of the Christian Social Union. The Lambeth Conference of 1888 allotted a moderate share of its time to a discussion of Socialism. It has been surmised that Scott Holland had a good deal to do with this novel departure. From the standpoint of reformers, the opinion of the Conference in regard to social action would not have been remarkable except for the fact that it carried the authority of 145 bishops. " Excessive inequality in the distribution of this world's goods : " ran the encyclical,

vast accumulation and desperate poverty side by side: these suggest many anxious considerations to any thoughtful person, who is penetrated with the mind of Christ. . . . To study any schemes proposed for redressing the social balance, to welcome the good which may be found in the aims or aspirations of any, and to devise methods, or in any other way, for a peaceful solution of the problems without violence or injustice, is one of the noblest pursuits which can engage the thought of those who strive to follow in the footsteps of Christ.

The pronouncement gave reformers a new ground of appeal.[1]

In 1888 also a definite project began to take shape in the minds of the *Lux Mundi* group. Scott Holland " talked the matter over long and carefully with such men as Mr. Aubrey Moore, Mr. Gore, Dr. Talbot, Mr. Illingworth and Mr. Richmond," but the final steps were not taken until 1889. Wilfrid Richmond helped materially in bringing the matter to a satisfactory conclusion. Although not a contributor to *Lux Mundi,* he had been associated with Holland and Arthur Lyttelton in a society formed at Oxford in 1879 for the discussion of social questions; " Pesek ", as the group called itself (from the initial letters of politics, economics,

[1] R. T. Davidson, *The Lambeth Conferences,* p. 265.

socialism, ethics, Christianity), foreshadowed the Christian Social Union.[1]   In 1888 Richmond published *Christian Economics*.   While admitting his debt to Ruskin, Walker (the economist), Cunningham, and Toynbee, he rejected not only classical economy as a guide to conduct but, what was more surprising, historical economy as well.   The latter, he said, teaches us what to do " provided that what we want is to pursue our own interest, as men have generally, and with progressive wisdom, more wisely and cunningly pursued it." He, on the other hand, insisted on " the principle that economic conduct is matter of duty, and therefore part of the province of conscience and morals."   This, he carefully pointed out, did not imply state socialism.

As a matter of fact, the principle maintained in this book, that economics are within the sphere of conscience, might be made a ground of argument either for forwarding or for resisting the modern tendency towards state interference in economic life.   The object I should wish to secure would be that it should become the grand argument for both sides. . . . The moral basis is in either case essential.[2]

In March and April, 1889, Richmond gave a series of lectures at Sion College, London, which he later published under the title *Economic Morals*. They were attended mainly by clergy; Westcott, Canon Furse, the bishop of Marlborough, and Holland sat as chairmen of the meetings. Scott Holland was not slow to make use of the interest created by the lectures. He began to turn it into a Movement. On June 14th, 1889, the first step toward organization was taken at a meeting in the chapter house of St. Paul's. Holland, of course, presided, and a committee was appointed to

[1] Percy Dearmer, *The Beginnings of the Christian Social Union*, p. 4 and footnote; Stephen Paget, *op. cit.*, p. 100.

[2] *Christian Economics*, preface, pp. v, viii; pp. 24-5.

form a society for which the name "Christian Social Union" was proposed. Meanwhile Holland kept in touch with his Oxford friends. He learned from John Carter, a member of the Guild of St. Matthew, that the Oxford branch of the Guild had decided to disband and would be amiably disposed toward a new society. The center of interest remained in London, however. Evidently the committee of June 14th had done its work, for a circular appeared, early in October perhaps, which announced the objects of the union. They were:

1. To claim for the Christian Law the ultimate authority to rule Christian practice.

2. To study in common how to apply the moral truths and principles of Christianity to the social and economic difficulties of the present time.

3. To present Christ in practical life as the living Master and King, the Enemy of wrong and selfishness, the Power of righteousness and love.

The organization was further elaborated at a meeting in St. Paul's chapter house on November 22d, 1889. Those present elected Westcott president with an executive committee consisting of Holland (chairman), Canon Furse, R. Eyton, H. C. Shuttleworth, J. G. Adderley, A. W. Jephson, and G. C. Fletcher (secretary), all being clergymen. Oxford responded in February, 1890, by choosing a separate body of officers. The list read: President, Scott Holland; Vice Presidents, Rev. W. J. H. Chavasse (later bishop of Liverpool), Rev. Charles Gore, Rev. Prof. Sanday, T. C. Snow, and J. Wells. John Carter was secretary of the executive committee.[1]

---

[1] P. Dearmer, *op. cit.*, pp. 2-8. There is some uncertainty as to whether the London or the Oxford group came into existence first. After the publication of Dr. Dearmer's account in 1912, Mr. Carter produced

The relations between the London and Oxford groups may as well be disposed of here. They were not, it appears, very cordial. Each established branches of its own in other towns without, however, trenching on one another's ground. In 1893, to be sure, a Central Council consisting of delegates from all the groups was set up, and this body elected a Central Executive with Westcott as president. London, " embued with the modest spirit of its Chairman [Scott Holland], dropped gracefully into the London Branch of the Union." But it did not relinquish its virtual independence or sever the tie with its branches. Neither did Oxford.[1] The schism was due primarily to a difference in policy. The Rev. John Carter, secretary of the Oxford Branch, directed the local activities of the Union, and his rather positive attitude was resented by some of the London members, more particularly because they looked upon him as a conservative. Recently, however, one of the left-wing group, the Rev. J. G. Adderley, has generously acknowledged his services: " It should be recognized how large a debt we owe to Rev. John Carter. By patient work he formed an intellectual basis on which the whole fabric of the C. S. U. rested, or perhaps we should call it the fortress from which it fired its guns." [2] No doubt also there were questions of prestige involved in the relations between Oxford and London. The Central Council was instituted " that there might be no jealousy between London and Oxford." [3]

Similar difficulties of personality and principle marked the

evidence of a meeting to organize the Oxford group some months before similar proceedings can be shown to have taken place in London. This evidence appeared conclusive to Canon Holland. (*Commonwealth*, 1912, p. 180.)

[1] P. Dearmer, *op. cit.*, pp. 10-13.

[2] *Commonwealth*, 1927, p. 13.

[3] Private information; also A. V. Woodworth, *Christian Socialism in England*, p. 145; Stephen Paget, *op. cit.*, p. 204.

relations between the Christian Social Union as a whole and the Guild of St. Matthew. Professor Shuttleworth, a mainstay of the Guild, welcomed the Union in a tone of disappointment. At a preliminary meeting " it was urged," he said,

. . . that a Society such as that proposed had been in existence for many years—the Guild, namely, of St. Matthew; and Canon Scott Holland bore willing testimony to the excellency of the aims of this Guild, and to the good work it had done and was still doing. No doubt the members of the Guild of St. Matthew do not see quite clearly why these good people, who are now at last interesting themselves in Christian economics, would not come into their ranks, and help on the work, of which, for so long a time, and under many discouragements and misrepresentations, they have been the pioneers.

" I can well understand," wrote Headlam caustically a few months later, " that it would be perhaps for many reasons a little difficult for some of these dignified gentlemen to come and join our little Society." [1]   Headlam there placed his finger on one main obstacle. No one questioned his goodness of heart, but the intellectual preëminence of the C. S. U. leaders was indisputable. It would have been asking too much of them, perhaps, to become the mere followers of Headlam, who notoriously ran the Guild pretty much to suit himself.

So far as the reputation of its leaders was concerned, the Christian Social Union felt well able to stand upon its own feet. The early career of its president, Westcott, has already been sketched. In 1889 he still held the regius professorship of divinity at Cambridge and was regarded as one of the foremost theologians and biblical scholars of his time. In 1890 Lord Salisbury nominated him to the bishopric of Durham,

---

[1] P. Dearmer, *op. cit.*, pp. 6, 7.

the fourth ranking see of the Church. So far his life had been cloistered but he speedily proved himself equal to the secular opportunities of his new office, as the services which he rendered to the northern miners will show.[1]   At the same time, Scott Holland doubted whether Westcott ever fully appreciated the evil conditions of society.   Always an ascetic—he had cherished the idea of a monastic community of clerical families at Westminster—he could not bring himself to contemplate steadily the disheartening realities of modern life. That was why, perhaps, he was able to retain the optimism which Holland regarded as his chief contribution to the Christian Social Union.   Even as bishop of Durham, he was in the world but not of it.   " When his Archdeacons presented to him the carefully collected case of an Incumbent who had broken every Commandment, he dismissed it on the ground (so it was reported) that his category of humanity refused to admit the existence of such a sinner." [2]

On the other hand, Henry Scott Holland, chairman of the London Branch, had long felt at home among the problems of the working class.   He was not only a popular figure at Oxford among the younger churchmen who hoped to renew the bond between the Establishment and the masses, but he had served an apprenticeship in the London slums.   Like those of most other Christian Socialists, Holland's family circumstances were such that he could have lived comfortably remote from such matters.   His father inherited a fortune made in trade, and his mother was a daughter of Baron Gifford of St. Leonards, Chief Justice of the Common Pleas. Parental hopes pointed toward a diplomatic career for the son.   When he entered Balliol College in 1866, however, he was swept away on the full tide of the Oxford Movement.

Holland might have followed the more dogmatic line of

---

[1] *Infra*, pp. 259-61.

[2] H. S. Holland, *Brooke Foss Westcott*, pp. 22-3.

the older Tractarians but for the friendships he made at
Oxford. Of this circle were the rising group of young
churchmen who later collaborated in *Lux Mundi*. He also
formed a strong personal attachment for T. H. Green, ab-
sorbing the latter's social idealism without, however, adopting his liberal philosophy in its extremer forms. "The
dividing line," said Wilfrid Richmond, "was that between
the man to whom philosophy was a religion and the man to
whom religion was a philosophy." Another Oxonian of the
elder generation won Holland's allegiance—friendship with
Gladstone colored his theological as well as his political
views. "Holland had been brought up by Tories," says
Mr. G. W. E. Russell, "but in all the great controversies of
1866-94 he followed the Gladstonian flag with the loyalty of
a good soldier and the faith of a loving son." It was Gladstone who made him a canon of St. Paul's in 1886.[1]

But outwardly at least Holland's ruling trait was not one
of passive acceptance. His immense energy and what some
called his "rhetoric" or his "journalism" often deceived
them as to his intellectual depth. "Speed, impetuosity, a
mighty rushing wind—those are the ideas that his name still
calls up to my mind," says Mr. H. M. Nevinson. "Body
and soul seemed always to be going at full gallop as though
the Holy Grail were just in sight." He saw no reason why
vital religious and social principles should be limited to an
exclusive group of Oxford men. Therefore he became an
Apostle—at Oxford, as a mission preacher in the slums of
Hoxton in 1873 and 1874, and still later when he became
the motive force of the Christian Social Union. Yet to a
certain extent the offices he held in the Church cut him off
from the class which as a social reformer he should have
known most intimately. Such at least is the opinion of

---

[1] *Commonwealth*, 1918, p. 165.

Canon F. Lewis Donaldson.   "I find it difficult," says Canon Donaldson,

to present any adequate account of his relation to Labour.   For that relation was not direct.   He did not move in Labour circles; he had little contact with the masses of the people.   His name and fame were great, yet I could not say that even his name was one to conjure with among the people.   He could not be described as a labour man. . . . Sometimes in committee or on platform, sometimes privately, he met some of the Labour leaders; he was well informed about their movements.   But he was never in and of those movements.   His work as a leader of the C. S. U. occasionally brought him into investigations, and often into close touch with individuals; but yet broadly considered, it is true to say that he viewed Labour rather from outside than from inside.[1]

The name of Westcott gave weight and dignity to the Christian Social Union, and Scott Holland was its prophet, but Charles Gore became more and more the acknowledged intellectual leader of the society.   Born in 1853, Bishop Gore (as he now is) descends from two noble families, his father having been a brother of the fourth Earl of Arran and his mother, a daughter of the fourth Earl of Bessborough.   He was at Harrow during Westcott's mastership and thence entered Oxford as a member of Balliol College.   A fellowship of Trinity, the focus of the Oxford Movement, followed.

When I became on " Oxford don " in 1875 [he says] I found myself drawn, partly as a disciple, partly as a colleague, into a circle of rather older men who were already at work at the urgent task of seeking to conciliate the claims of reason and revelation and so to interpret the ancient, catholic faith as not to lay an intolerable strain upon the free action of the intellect.[2]

---

[1] *Commonwealth*, 1918, p. 304; H. M. Nevinson, *op. cit.*, p. 44.

[2] A. L. Illingworth, *The Life of John Richardson Illingworth*, preface (by Bishop Gore), p. xi.

It is this respect for the individual which has conditioned both his socialism and his theology and which has sometimes brought him into conflict with authority in defense of his own views. Thus while Librarian of Pusey Library, the very center of the older Tractarian tradition, he put forward in *Lux Mundi* and the Bampton Lectures of 1891 an interpretation of the Incarnation which outraged the "orthodox" school. As a consequence he resigned his office in 1893, becoming vicar of Radley. The next year he received a canonry of Westminster. But meanwhile he was deep in the affairs of the Christian Social Union. He appears as a delegate from Oxford to draw up the new constitution in 1893, is elected a vice-president (with Canon Holland), and writes pamphlets for the society. More successful than Westcott in promoting the monastic idea, he set on foot the Community of the Resurrection, which, as we shall see, also has its place in the social history of the Church.[1]

In the Christian Social Union there was room for three leaders; in the Guild of St. Matthew, Stewart Headlam usually had his way. Unfortunately Headlam possessed certain personal idiosyncracies which no doubt further limited his following. Strict moralists could no more comprehend his enthusiasm for the ballet than his lack of discretion in going bail for Oscar Wilde although he did it with the phrase of a good authority on his lips: " Nec ego te condemnabo: vade, et iam amplius noli peccare"—the sentiment was doubtless misapplied. With sublime disregard for the conventions he even took a destitute ballet dancer and her brother into his home.[2]

While the Christian Social Union built up its following at

---

[1] P. Dearmer, *op. cit.*, p. 18; *Encyclopedia Britannica*, eleventh edition, art. "Gore, Charles"; *Who's Who* (British), 1928, art. "Gore, Charles". *Burke's Peerage*, 1929, p. 145.

[2] F. G. Bettany, *op. cit.*, p. 131; private information.

the expense—so Headlam felt—of his own organization, the Guild of St. Matthew nevertheless exerted a very direct influence upon the younger society. Without in all cases quitting the Guild, many of its members joined the Christian Social Union. A list of the more active members of the London Branch reads, in fact, almost like a roster of the Guild. The Rev. J. G. Adderley, A. W. Jephson, J. Cartmell-Robinson, W. E. Moll, and Professor Shuttleworth; and Mrs. F. Lewis Donaldson and Mr. (later Rev.) Percy Dearmer were numbered among the converts. This no doubt partly accounts for the left-wing tendencies of the London Branch. The views of Percy Dearmer, for example, who as secretary aided Canon Holland in getting the London Branch under way, were regarded a little apprehensively by the latter.[1] Certainly the writings Dr. Dearmer contributed to the cause have a vigor that much of its literature lacks.

Stewart Headlam little doubted that the "dignified gentlemen" at the head of the Union objected to the Guild because of its militant policy and the drastic reforms it advocated. It was said that Holland referred to two mainstays of the Guild, Headlam and Shuttleworth, as Headlong and Shuttlecock. From Holland's point of view this was no doubt a true description. "The mildness of the social doctrines of the Christian Social Union," said Headlam, "was what helped it to its larger numbers. The more academic and less revolutionary Socialists in the Church could embrace it, and so mild was it that Bishop Westcott could act as its President."[2]

In the sense that a larger number of persons could be induced to listen to them, the principles of the Christian Social Union were undoubtedly milder than those of the Guild. The great object of the Union during its early years (until

[1] P. Dearmer, *op. cit.*, p. 12; S. Paget, *op. cit.*, p. 204.
[2] F. G. Bettany, *op. cit.*, p. 90.

about 1897) was to reaffirm the idea of social obligation inherent in the Christian tradition. The Church, said Gore, could properly claim obedience in matters of social morality—a right which it had unfortunately almost abdicated.

The fact that a wide acceptance of this principle was regarded as necessarily antecedent to further action conditioned the whole earlier policy of the Union. It meant that the development of a comprehensive and detailed plan of reform must be relegated to the uncertain future.[1] Of course there were certain features of the industrial régime which obviously conflicted with Christian ideals, and certain adjustments which could be made without committing anyone to a particular scheme of social reorganization. But broadly speaking, the application of general truths was left to the individual conscience. A statement of Dr. Gore is perhaps as specific as any other early official pronouncement of the Union. Co-operation, he said, must take the place of competition. " This means . . . a stern discouragement of the accumulation of wealth, except as held consciously in trust for the public good; a strenuous opposition to the development of luxury, as distinct from knowledge and beauty; a constant practical realization of the temper of contentment, with sufficient and wholesome food and lodgment, air and clothing, work and leisure, and the greater blessing of giving as compared to receiving." [2]

While the doctrines of the Christian Social Union were in process of formulation, a document appeared which many regard as a landmark in Roman Catholic social thought. The encyclical " Rerum Novarum " of Leo XIII was received with mixed feelings by Scott Holland. The pope had stated some unmistakable truths, he said, but the general

[1] *Economic Review*, vol. v, p. 161, Westcott, Presidential Address.

[2] *Ibid.*, vol. ii, p. 153, " The Social Doctrine of the Sermon on the Mount."

effect of the pronouncement was disappointing. It was evident that Leo did not appreciate the extreme complexity of modern problems. He justified the possession of private property to those who had worked for it. But most commodities were social products, and this implied a mutuality of obligation.

There is a patriarchal simplicity assumed throughout. And this gives a far-away, old-fashioned, dreamy tone to all that is said. It reads like some old tale: we enjoy the quiet continuity with which it moves from point to point; it is so clear, so precise, so dignified. . . . But it has all nothing to do with the world in which we live: it is the voice of some old-world life, faint and ghostly, speaking in some antique tongue of things long ago.[1]

Reasons, some of which still appear to be valid, were not lacking as to why the Christian Social Union hesitated to put forward a systematic program of reform. There was an apocalyptic belief that human problems would be greatly simplified if men were truly converted to the idea of Christian fellowship. " The real obstacle to social advance," said Gore, " is selfishness or sin. No external reform will remove this. Nothing but the conversion of souls from self to God. Real social reform, then, will proceed, not by the method of majorities, but from small groups of sanctified men, like the apostles." [2]   Furthermore, none of the existing platforms exactly fitted the requirements of the Union. By attacking *laissez-faire* it had identified itself with socialism, but the doctrines of the latter were by no means satisfactory—at least to the leaders. Bishop Westcott even feared the title of the Union might suggest that members were pledged to Christian Socialism—" a most vague phrase." [3]

---

[1] *Economic Review*, vol. i, pp. 455 *et seq.*

[2] *Ibid.*, p. 152.

[3] Arthur Westcott, *op. cit.*, vol. ii, pp. 260-61.

Gore objected to the leveling tendencies of current socialism and to the undue emphasis it laid upon state action.   There were

vast inequalities of faculty, and considerable inequalities of need. . . . The manager, the organizer, the thinker, the teacher. the high official, have needs in the way of leisure, house-room, etc., which the ordinary worker has not.   And the well-being of society depends on the exceptional man being given the opportunity to realize his exceptional faculty.

With the general idea " that the society and the interest of the society, and all its members, is supreme over the individual," he agreed.   But " I may . . . confess myself to be among those who would somewhat jealously set limits to the paternal supervision of the democratic state."   He opposed not merely the socialism which would destroy marriage and the family but that which refused " liberty for the development of religion, or art, or science, or knowledge, except so far as the state recognizes its usefulness and supports its votaries." [1]   According to Westcott,

to expect stable progress from legislation alone, is like expecting human perfection from the conquests of science.   Legislation is often a mere appeal to force under the influence of some season of excitement. . . . Legislation is the last and not the first thing in social reform.   Its particular function is to register each successive advance in the popular conception of the just conditions of life.[2]

At this time the advanced High Church party was vigorously assailing state intervention in the affairs of the Church.

[1] *Christianity and Socialism* (C. S. U. pamphlet, 1908), p. 24; *The Incarnation of the Son of God* (Bampton Lectures, 1891), p. 228.

[2] *Economic Review*, vol. v, p. 162, Presidential Address, 1894.

One may conjecture that Gore's dislike of statism in secular matters partly reflected this sentiment.

A further reason why the Christian Social Union did not attempt to shepherd its members along a particular road to reform was its commendable modesty. " It cannot be said off-hand, without deliberate discipline," wrote Holland, " what exactly the lordship of Christ does demand of human society." There must be a thorough familiarity with the actual situation before remedies were applied.

We cannot all of us undertake such a study as this involves; we have not the leisure or the brains. . . . The knowledge and experience amassed by the few must be absorbed and utilized by the many. . . . They will spread the news; they will convey abroad the warmth that is generated by living contact with the realities of the social problem. . . . They will thus serve to make social despair more and more impossible.[1]

Essentially, then, the Christian Social Union was a body of churchmen and -women who pledged themselves to investigate social problems in the light of Christian morality. There the duty of the society as a whole ended. It was expected that practical reform proposals would ensue, but they were to emanate from individual members or from the branches acting on their own responsibility. Naturally, therefore, only the more significant or popular of these unofficial proposals can be touched upon here. But greater uniformity characterized the methods of study employed by the Union, and we shall look into these first.

Group discussion was a main feature of early C. S. U. activity. For convenience the great London Branch divided itself into eleven local groups. The Oxford Branch issued leaflets outlining the book or subject considered, sometimes with references to other sources of information, and fre-

---

[1] *The Ground of Our Appeal*, pp. 2-4.

quently including a summary of conclusions. Lectures and sermons figured largely in the London programs. Daily sermons in Lent attracted " crowded congregations " in the City and when published had a further wide circulation.[1] Prominent men not connected with the Union lectured monthly at the Shuttleworth Club. Many lectures were given in other parts of London. A series of addresses by Mr. J. A. Hobson on " Work and Life ", later printed in syllabus form, sold to the extent of 6,000 copies. The London Branch also established a lending library for the use of members.[2]

For publicity and educational purposes the Christian Social Union not only built up a fairly large pamphlet literature but also invaded the periodical field. In 1891 the Oxford Branch founded *The Economic Review,* a quarterly of considerable merit, which endured until 1914. " The *Review,*" said the editors,

will give a fair field and no favours to Socialists and Individualists alike. No project of social reform, however radical, will be excluded, provided it is supported by reasoned arguments: no defense of the existing order, however conservative, but will be admitted, if its logic is sound, and its point of view scientific.

The list of contributors to the first number included W. J. Ashley, W. Cunningham, W. A. S. Hewins, T. Kirkup, Hastings Rashdall, Wilfrid Richmond, and Thomas Hughes —a standard of pretentiousness which was not, of course, maintained.[3] At first the London Branch was represented by

---

[1] Titles of the volumes published were *Lombard Street in Lent, The Gospels of the Kingdom* and *A Lent in London.*

[2] A C. S. U. pamphlet by T. C. Fry, published about 1897; *Memoranda* of the Oxford Branch, 1898; C. S. U. (London Branch) *Annual Report,* 1896, p. 7.

[3] *Economic Review,* vol. i, p. 1.

Goodwill, which appeared in 1894 under the editorship of Holland and Adderley. In 1896 Holland launched a monthly magazine, *The Commonwealth,* which aimed at a broader public. Although it did the work of the Union, *The Commonwealth* was not responsible to it, and Holland could speak as vigorously as he pleased in its columns.[1] The magazine became self-supporting within a few years and has survived the Christian Social Union itself.

During the first six or seven years of its existence the Christian Social Union was occupied chiefly in educating itself. Otherwise its contributions to the settlement of social problems were rather meager, a condition which led to a change of policy about 1897. We reserve these later developments for the next chapter. But it should be mentioned that the Research Committee, which proved to be one of the most fruitful agencies of the London Branch, originated in 1895. Realists who demanded " practical " results could point to other achievements during the earlier period. The actions of individuals cannot, however, always be credited to the Union. In some of the following cases they would probably have occurred even if the Union had never come into existence. The Rev. J. W. Horsley conducted a campaign for the enforcement of the housing laws in Woolwich, incidentally testifying before a Royal Commission on the relation between slums and " sin, despair, and low morals." He pointed with pride to the fact that the death rate had been reduced from a scandalously high figure to a level better than the average of London. " To be the people's tribune," he said, " you must be the landlord's ' bogey '. Property owners will develop theological grievances and leave the church to join a chapel, where they will find an independent congregation with a dependent minister." [2] At

[1] S. Paget, *op. cit.,* p. 206.
[2] *Economic Review,* vol. iii, p. 51.

a Newcastle diocesan conference the Rev. W. E. Moll, a lecturer for the Union, secured the passage of a resolution that a decent wage " should be the first charge upon products." [1] Here is an early statement of a principle to which the Union gave great prominence later on. (It is worth noting that Horsley and Moll were old and active members of the Guild of St. Matthew.) We find the Rev. J. E. Hand attending " two deputations to Cabinet Ministers: one to the Secretary of State for War, to urge the adoption of the Eight Hours Day at Woolwich (since granted), and also to the Secretary of the Local Government Board respecting the boarding-out of pauper children." A conference of masters and workmen in the baking trade assisted by members of the Christian Social Union presented a memorial to the Home Secretary (Asquith) asking for legislation, but action was deferred until the completion of the factory measures. [2]

Group action on the part of the branches was usually cautious. The London Executive Committee in 1895 " arranged a conference between Miss [Gertrude] Tuckwell [a member of the Union], Mrs. Sidney Webb, and other representatives of women's labour, and certain of the Bishops, with a view to securing the Overtime Clause, Clause 26, and the Laundry Clause, in the House of Lords." Oxford invented the so-called white list which, before its limitations were perceived, became a favorite mode of procedure with the Union. The Rev. John Carter originated the idea. A trade was investigated, and shops conforming to a standard set by the local trade union or trade council were placed on an approved list. The humane public was then expected to transfer its custom to the fair shops, thus forcing recalcitrant tradesmen to reform. The idea was first applied in the tailoring trade. Where no standard conditions had been

---

[1] C. S. U. (London Branch), *Annual Report*, 1895, p. 15.
[2] *Ibid.*

worked out, another method was employed. The Oxford
Branch " has dealt with the unorganized bakery trade: a
code of rules has been unanimously accepted at a joint meeting of representatives of the master bakers, the journeymen,
and the consumers, and a union has been founded among
the journeymen." [1] But sometimes the efforts of a branch
to be helpful met with a rather distressing reception. In a
boot and shoe trade dispute the Leicester Branch " did its
best to take a useful part . . . but could not prevail upon
representative men from either side to render any help in
deciding what line to take; in fact, our applications were
resolutely ignored." [2]

Meanwhile the Christian Social Union gathered a membership whose numbers compared with the multiplicity of
opinions represented. In 1897 the 27 branches counted some
2,600 members. Of the London group, 42 per cent were
clergy, 32 per cent women, and 26 per cent laymen. The
figures for Oxford and its affiliated branches in 1898 were—
excluding Oxford and Durham and St. Aidan's College—
clergy, 50 per cent; laymen, 27 per cent; women, 23 per
cent.[3] Professor R. T. Ely was secretary of the American
organization of 1,000 members which had been established
in 1892. In 1897 the Union reported branches in Australia
and South Africa.[4] Quantitatively the Christian Social
Union had far outstripped the Guild of St. Matthew. That
it had surpassed it in influence is not so certain.

[1] C. S. U. leaflet, *Preferential Dealing* (published c. 1897) ; *Economic
Review*, vol. v, p. 105; C. S. U. (London Branch), *Annual Report,*
1896, p. 19.

[2] C. S. U. (London Branch), *Annual Report*, 1896, p. 17.

[3] *Ibid.*, p. 25; S. Paget, *op. cit.*, p. 204; C. S. U. (Oxford University
Branch), List of Members, 1898.

[4] *Year Book of the Church of England*, 1898, ch. xiii; C. S. U., *List of
Branches and Officers*, 1897.

EXTERNAL RELATIONS OF CHURCH REFORMERS

It remains to consider what may be called the extra-mural activities of churchmen connected with organizations described in this chapter. First of all, there was some overlapping of membership as concerned the Church bodies. For example, the Rev. J. G. Adderley and A. F. W. Ingram, successive heads of Oxford House, joined the Christian Social Union. Adderley was a member of the Guild of St. Matthew. The numerous other recruits of the Union from the Guild have already been mentioned.

Reformers were also able to make a direct impression on local administration. Canon Barnett and the residents of Toynbee Hall moved the Government to compel the privately owned water companies to furnish an adequate supply to East London. Oxford House and Toynbee Hall had representatives on the London School Board, the Board of Guardians of the Poor, and the London County Council.[1]

Perhaps the most colorful participant in local administration, however, was Stewart Headlam. Elected in 1888 to the London School Board, he was present at its demise in 1904. The functions of the Board were then absorbed by the London County Council, to which Headlam was elected in 1907. At the beginning his reputation as an " enfant terrible " caused some misgiving among his colleagues, and the Board attempted to limit his destructive possibilities by making him chairman of the Evening Schools Sub-Committee. But Headlam could not thus easily be suppressed. He proceeded to make evening and continuation schools an important part of London's educational policy. As the valedictorian of the School Board said, Headlam "has stamped his individuality to a remarkable degree upon this

---

[1] H. Barnett, *op. cit.*, vol. ii, pp. 59-61; Will Reason, *University and Social Settlements*, pp. 32, 39; Oxford House, *Annual Report*, 1894.

part of the Board's work." [1]   He was somewhat suspicious
of technical education and favored a broad rather than a
specialized curriculum.   The so-called Headlam Course embodied physical education, handicraft, and talks on travel,
invention, and the lives of great men.   Headlam was further
determined that school children should know Shakespeare as
a dramatist rather than as a literary exercise.   In collaboration with Mr. Ben Greet (a friend since Church and Stage
Guild days) he arranged for children's matinees at the Old
Vic. and at houses in the suburbs, some of the expense being
met by grants from the Council.   It was estimated that from
1918 to 1922, 100,000 children attended these performances.
Nor did Headlam fail to use his position to promote the interest of labor.   At his instigation, with the support of Mrs.
Annie Besant, the School Board agreed to pay the full union
rate of wages for work done by its authority.   It was the
first time that a public body had adopted such a principle.[2]

As we turn to the participation of churchmen in secular
reform societies, the ubiquitous Headlam again confronts us.
With his chief supporter in the Guild of St. Matthew, Mr.
Verinder, Headlam in 1883 helped to set on foot the Land
Reform Union.   " It was the publication of *Progress and
Poverty* which led to the formation of the society, now
known as the English Land Restoration League," wrote Mr.
Verinder.   " A few friends were meeting during the winter
of 1882-3 for the study of George's great Book.   In the following spring their study resulted in action.   They formed
a ' Land Reform Union,' ' to advance the principles laid
down by Henry George for the restoration of the Land to
the People.' " [3]   Propaganda was carried on chiefly by the

---

[1] H. B. Philpott, *London at School*, p. 139.

[2] F. G. Bettany, *op. cit.*, chs. 14-18.

[3] *Land for the Landless, Spence and Spence's Plan (1775) with Neo-
Spencean Appendix (1896)*, p. 16.

" Red Vans ", which sowed literature and lectures broadcast in the rural districts. It is interesting to note that during one of these expeditions Mr. Verinder commented on the seeming apathy of parish clergymen.

After a leisurely tour through some 20 or 30 villages, I am tempted to ask—where are the parish priests of Suffolk? There are a few names which are held in honour among the labouring men, . . . but for aught that one can see, many of the parsons of Suffolk know little and care less about what their parishioners are thinking and saying and doing.[1]

On the roll of the Land Restoration League appeared such well-known names as Sidney Webb, Tom Mann, Bernard Shaw, and Sydney Olivier (now Lord Olivier). Besides Headlam, who was a member of the Executive, and Mr. Verinder, the General Secretary, the Guild of St. Matthew was represented by the Rev. J. E. Symes and H. C. Shuttleworth. The religious tinge of the League is apparent in the name of its magazine, which was borrowed from *The Christian Socialist* of thirty years before. But the permeation was not complete. As the historian of the Fabian Society remarks, " The *Christian Socialist* was established by a band of persons some of whom were not Socialist and others not Christian." It expired, adds Bernard Shaw, owing to a lack of Christians.[2]

From the expropriation of landlords to the chastisement of all capitalists was only a step: through the ante-room of the Land Reform Union one entered the Fabian Society.

[1] *Church Reformer*, 1891, pp. 158-9, 180.

[2] English Land Restoration League, *Reports*, 1892, 1894; *Christian Socialist*, 1883, p. 1; F. G. Bettany, *op. cit.*, p. 135; E. R. Pease, *op. cit.*, p. 25; Archibald Henderson, *George Bernard Shaw, His Life and Works*, p. 48. In 1887 *The Christian Socialist* became the organ of the Christian Socialist Society, also an unsectarian body. (*Christian Socialist*, vol. v, p. 1.)

" We had among our members," says Mr. Sidney Webb
(now Lord Passfield), " not only a large proportion of Christian laymen but also clergy, high and low church." [1] Among
the churchly contingent a little phalanx from the Guild of
St. Matthew was inevitably present: Headlam, Percy Dearmer, Charles Marson, J. G. Adderley, Joseph Clayton—the
last a layman connected at one time or another with almost
every phase of the Labor movement.[2]

It is probable that Stewart Headlam aligned himself with
the Fabians not merely because their social ideology agreed
rather closely with his own but particularly because of their
tolerant attitude toward religion. Frederic Harrison in fact
regarded the Fabian Society as the heir of Christian Socialism: " Out of these efforts of workmen in Trade Unionism
and in Co-operation sprang the literary and spiritual movement of the cultured classes known as Christian Socialism,
which has gradually developed into the intellectual and moral
Socialism of the Fabian and similar societies." The Fabian
Society, in fact, began as an ethical movement, the Fellowship of the New Life. In any case as between Fabianism
and the socialism of the Social Democratic Federation there
could be but one choice for professed Christians. Edward
Aveling sounded a blast on the clarion of the Federation
which associated that body irrevocably with atheism and
anti-clericalism. " Little that is of any real or lasting value,"
he asserted in the first number of *To-Day,* " can be done
until men and women fairly face the fact that the terrible

---

[1] F. G. Bettany, *op. cit.,* p. 137.

[2] Clayton began his career as treasurer of the Oxford Branch of the
Guild of St. Matthew, and was a friend of Keir Hardie, Edward Carpenter, and H. M. Hyndman. He joined the I. L. P. and the Fabian
Society, became secretary of the Leeds Gasworkers' and General
Labourers' Union, and served as election agent for Labor candidates in
1900 and 1924. (Joseph Clayton, *The Rise and Decline of Socialism
in Great Britain,* preface.)

condition of our poor is due, as are so many other ills, to the
two curses of our country and time. These two curses are
Capitalism and Christianity." The article drew vigorous
denials from Marson and Headlam. But when the Scientific
Socialists exhibited a theoretical looseness in sexual matters
and family life, even argument became impossible.[1]

It is difficult to gauge the influence of Christian Socialists
in the Fabian Society. Headlam and Dearmer were perhaps
the most conspicuous recruits, the former serving on the
Executive Committee in 1890-91 and from 1901 to 1911,
the latter, from 1895 to 1898. Each contributed a Tract to
the Fabian series. But, as Bernard Shaw says, " the society
was run so efficiently by a small group of us—Sidney Webb,
myself, Hubert Bland, Mrs. Besant and Graham Wallas—
that there was no room for anyone else." Headlam, in point
of fact, still clung to the land tax as a social panacea, re-
gretted the lack of emotional fervor in the calculating policy
of the society, and (in company with H. G. Wells) was disposed to scoff at the " pseudo-research " it insisted upon
pursuing. Nevertheless he helped to frame the Basis or
platform of 1887, securing the adoption of some of its most
extreme declarations. He also took part in the Fabian campaign of 1890 in Lancashire which resulted in the formation
of many local societies.[2]

The motive selected for this chapter was the growing
tendency of churchmen to organize for social purposes which
manifested itself between 1877 and 1895. The settlement

[1] F. G. Bettany, *op. cit.*, pp. 133-35; Frederic Harrison, *De Senectute,
More Last Words*, p. 158; E. R. Pease, *op. cit.*, pp. 26 *et seq.*; *To-Day*,
vol. i, pp. 30 *et seq.*, 125 *et seq.*, 177 *et seq.*; *Church Reformer*, vol.
vi, pp. 1-2.

[2] F. G. Bettany, *op. cit.*, chap. 13; Fabian Tract No. 42: *Christian
Socialism*, by Headlam. No. 133: *Socialism and Christianity,* by Dearmer;
E. R. Pease, *op. cit.*, pp. 270 *et seq.*

movement, the Guild of St. Matthew, and the Christian Social Union were at once the bearers of an earlier tradition and the product of new economic, philosophical, and religious ideas. These in turn were closely related to contemporary changes in the life of the people both as cause and effect. The Ritualist or High Church party gradually took the lead in formulating a social ethic for the Church. The relation of principles to action, however, was different in each of the Church organizations. The settlement movement achieved practical results without much attention to theory. The Guild of St. Matthew evolved a theory and accomplished some definite results. The Christian Social Union theorized without evolving a theory or producing, as yet, tangible results in keeping with its possibilities. All three, however, helped to guide Church opinion into social channels. This process will be described in the next chapter.

CHAPTER VI

CONQUEST OF THE CHURCH
1877-1914

BETWEEN 1877 and 1914 the influence of the reform societies just dealt with was permeating the Church at large. It the first part of this chapter we shall trace this influence as it appears in the Church assemblies and among the bishops in parliament. Then we shall observe how clergymen applied their principles in the settlement of three important trade disputes. Finally, we shall revert to the later history of the societies themselves, noting important changes in their programs as well as the advent in 1906 of an entirely new organization, the Church Socialist League. All this brings the narrative to the eve of the war.

THE CHURCH ASSEMBLIES AND SOCIAL REFORM

In an earlier chapter the history of the bishops in Parliament was carried to 1875.[1] During the ensuing thirty-eight years taken as a whole there was no marked change in the number of bishops who might be called active parliamentarians. About a third of the ninety-five bishops entitled to sit during that period never raised their voices, and a quarter more, whose terms in Parliament were eleven years on the average, spoke fewer than half a dozen times each.[2] "Owing to a variety of circumstances," said Archbishop Davidson in 1907,

[1] *Supra*, pp. 66-70.

[2] Bishops who held two or more sees in succession are counted separately for each occupancy.

234

it is undoubtedly the fact that the Bishops to-day take a less prominent and constant part in the debates of your Lordships' House than was taken by the Bishops of fifty or a hundred years ago. A reference to *Hansard* would make that clear. The main reason—there are several reasons—is the wholly good one of the vast multiplication of diocesan work which necessitates the Bishops' remaining for the most part in their dioceses.[1]

Leaving aside the conditions a hundred years previously, we may doubt whether the statement is in every sense accurate. From 1875 to 1895 there was, it is true, a marked decline in the activity of the bishops, but the following years saw just as distinct an increase. To Dr. Davidson as bishop of Winchester and then as archbishop of Canterbury belongs much of the credit for this increase. If we compare the decade of the 1850's with that preceding the archbishop's remark, the latter period has the advantage so far as frequency of participation of the bishops is concerned. Relatively to the total activity of the House, however, the statement may still be true.[2]

But it is beyond dispute that the bishops after 1850 displayed a growing alertness when social questions arose in the Lords. Their interest in temperance and education goes without saying, and when Dr. Davidson referred to the greater constancy of the bishops in former times he may have had in mind the unusual vivacity with which they fell upon the education bill of 1906. On the whole the episcopal bench, often speaking through the archbishop of Canterbury, showed a remarkable willingness to set its approval on such schemes of social betterment as appeared in the House, pro-

---

[1] *Hansard*, 1907, vol. 174, col. 3.

[2] Lord Burghclere in 1907 (*Hansard*, vol. 171, cols. 600-603), proposing an enquiry into the rules of debate, called attention to the increased attendance of peers and the growing length of discussions.

vided the interests of the Church were protected. On one occasion, indeed, Lord Beauchamp, a Liberal leader, complained that the bishops were too advanced. The Government, he said, had expected some assistance from them in shaping the Housing and Town-Planning Bill of 1909. " But with the exception of the Bishop of Wakefield, the proposals of the Episcopal Bench were so extreme that a moderate Government like the present were unable to follow them." [1]

In certain cases the bishops themselves took the initiative. They championed as a matter of course bills for preventing Sunday labor, raising the age of consent in cases of seduction, prohibiting traffic in women, and restricting the sale of liquor. They attacked Lord Milner's policy of permitting the importation of Chinese labor into South Africa and supported against government opposition Lord Avebury's various Early Closing of Shops Bills and the duke of Westminster's bill to provide seats for shop assistants. Archbishop Davidson stated in 1907 that during Lord Salisbury's administration he had voted against the government eight out of eleven times and that on two of the other occasions the Liberals had voted with him. " No doubt there is one group of questions," he said,

as to which the Bishops have allied themselves with the party now in Opposition—questions affecting the religious life of England and the continuance of its security. But in regard to another great group of questions, questions of social reform, it is indisputably the case now, whatever it may have been in the past, that the Bishops, who are not infrequently spoken of outside as an appanage of the Tory Party, more frequently give their votes to the Liberal than to the Conservative party.[2]

[1] *Hansard*, 1909, vol. iii, col. 210.

[2] *Ibid.*, 1907, vol. 174, col. 4.

The small parliamentary revolution of 1909-1911 afforded an opportunity of testing both the partisanship and the social attitude of the bishops. In the debate on the Lloyd-George Budget Archbishop Davidson undertook to voice the opinion of " many Bishops who are absent and of a few who are here." He began with a reminiscence:

If I look back along the range of subjects in the discussion of which we Bishops have been privileged to bear a part, and sometimes an important part, during the fifteen years, to take them alone, that I have had the honour of a seat in this House, I find it to include practically all those questions—moral, religious, educational, social—with which this House has constantly to deal. They range from Poor Law Reform and Prison Reform to University or Ecclesiastical Reform, from sweating and overcrowding at home to the treatment of aborigines in Australia and West Africa and elsewhere; while in such matters as temperance and education it goes without saying that the Bishops are expected to be the mouthpiece of many thousands of people.

But of late years the bishops had kept aloof from party allegiance, and the budget seemed about to become a strictly party issue.

The reference [he continued] which I have just made to social questions, and if anybody cares to look at them, the records of my own words and votes . . . will, I think, afford clear evidence that it is not because I and those who think with me are indifferent to the great social questions which are astir in England in connection with the life of the poor that we are taking the line that we do take. I have tried to show that what we are doing we are doing deliberately, in the genuine belief that by adhering to an independent standing we can increase our power of contributing to the solution of some of the greatest, deepest, and most urgent problems which Parliament has continually to consider and to decide.

He and bishops of similar opinions would abstain from voting.[1]   The bishop of Bristol's remarks were decidedly less Olympian.   The honor of the House, he said, was at stake; they must not surrender to the threats of Lord Loreburn, who sponsored a budget that would result in " a dull, monotonous level of poverty without any redeeming features."   The bishop restrained himself with difficulty in referring to the tactics of Mr. Lloyd George, and if incoherence is a mark of sincerity, his speech throughout was sincere.[2]

The other bishops who spoke took a different line.   Dr. Gore, recently become bishop of Birmingham, believed that the budget was

neither revolutionary nor oppressive. . . . We all know that what in a general phrase we call the social question is really the dominant question of our time and when from any reasonable point of view you approach the great social question you are confronted with the requirement of an enormously increased expenditure.

He offered small consolation to Conservatives who objected that the budget placed an unfair burden on the land.

Even if it were the case that there were undue pressure placed on certain interests by the Budget, I should still think that a future Government, more favourably considered by the majority of your Lordships' House than the present Government, might reasonably rectify that undue pressure on one or two interests by raising the pressure on other interests to the same level, because I am certain that it is only by raising the pressure on all classes of the community that we shall be able to obtain the increased amount of money that we shall require for our national expenditure.[3]

[1] *Hansard*, 1909, vol. iv, cols. 939-40.
[2] *Ibid.*, col. 767.
[3] *Ibid.*, col. 799 *et seq.*

Bishop Percival of Hereford spoke with customary direct-
ness. The decision of the archbishop of Canterbury and his
followers he considered unfortunate. To prove that the
budget was not a party issue they had only to vote for it.
" If we who are Bishops have any special function in this
House I venture to think that it is that we may speak and
vote here on behalf of the multitudinous poor whenever
occasion arises." To reject the budget would be to stimulate
the spirit of revolution. " Bloated estimates " were due, not
to expenditures on social welfare, but to excessive armaments, " a continual menace to European peace and . . . a
constant hindrance to all social reform. But your Lordships
who oppose this Budget cannot join me in this protest, because you and your friends are more responsible than the
Government for these bloated Estimates." [1] Archbishop
Lang confessed that since listening to the debate he had
changed his mind about withholding his vote. In an exceedingly able speech he demolished the arguments in favor of
such an unusual proceeding as the rejection of the estimates.
It was the " Celtic temperament " of Mr. Lloyd George, he
said, which led the latter to assert that the present budget
was only a first step. In fact, talk about the dangerous tendencies of the bill

is only our old friend, the thin-end-of-the-wedge argument.
He has been very familiar in all the debates on social legislation
which have taken place during the last fifty years. . . . It is in
an atmosphere of hopelessness and resentment against the social
conditions existing that the extreme and bitter Socialism we all
deplore is engendered and flourishes. Give a man a better
chance, give him a feeling that the social system is not against
him but with him, for him, and on his side, and then his own
individual instincts of energy and enterprise will, I believe, be
a more effectual check against the development of Socialism

[1] *Hansard,* 1909, vol. iv, col. 1080 *et seq.*

than all the arguments that could be argued against it by more
fortunate persons.[1]

The budget was rejected (or, as the Conservatives put it,
" submitted to the judgment of the country ") by a crushing
majority which included the bishop of Lincoln. York, Birmingham, and St. Asaph voted for it.

The sequel was the Parliament Bill of 1911, which reduced
the obstructive possibilities of the House of Lords to a sus-
pensive veto. Most of the bishops except Gore were unwilling to go as far as the government ultimatum although
they favored a drastic reform of the qualifications for membership in the Lords. When it came to the final division,
however, the bishops voted thirteen to two for the bill.
Their decision was almost critical, for without them the bill
would have passed by the narrow margin of six. If their
vote had been reversed the bill would of course have been
defeated.

The social attitude of the bishops appeared to somewhat
better advantage in the Lambeth Conferences than in the
House of Lords. The first two of these assemblies in 1867
and 1878 had dealt with ecclesiastical questions in the narrow
sense. That of 1888, as we have seen, cautiously recognized
the social problem.[2] Stewart Headlam found its report on
Socialism " a curious muddle of sound exhortation with
trivial or ridiculous practical suggestions. . . . ' After all,'
says the report, ' the best help is self-help.' So thought the
anarchist in Paris the other day, who made his own bomb
and threw it at the State policeman on his own responsibility." [3]

The conference of 1897 represented a considerable ad-

[1] *Hansard*, 1909, vol. iv, col. 1234 *et seq.*

[2] *Supra*, p. 210.

[3] *Church Reformer*, Sept., 1888, p. 200.

vance over its predecessor. The references to social matters
both in the encyclical and in the report of the committee on
industrial problems give an impression of greater familiarity
with the social situation and of more appreciation of its complexity. Less prominence was accorded to the time-honored
principle of self-help. The committee believed that the
Church ought not to adopt any particular social theory or
system. But

Christian opinion should be awake to repudiate and condemn
either open breaches of social justice and duty or maxims and
principles of an un-Christian character. It ought to condemn
the belief that economic conditions are to be left to the action
of material causes and mechanical laws, uncontrolled by moral
responsibility. It can pronounce certain conditions of labour
to be intolerable. It can insist that the employer's responsibility,
as such, is not lost by membership in an industrial Company.
It can press upon retail purchasers the obligation to consider
not only the cheapness of the goods supplied to them, but also
the probable conditions of their production. It can speak
plainly of the evils which attach to the economic system under
which we live, such as certain forms of luxurious extravagance,
the widespread pursuit of money by financial gambling, the dis-
honesties of trade into which men are driven by financial competition, and the violence and reprisals of industrial warfare.

The committee recommended industrial co-operation, with
the warning that it would be a failure "if it should degen-
erate into a vast system of joint-stock shopkeeping or industry, conducted on selfish principles, with no dominant
moral purpose pervading it." [1] The Report might have
passed muster as a pamphlet of the Christian Social Union,
and such, no doubt, in part it was, for the chairman and at

[1] *Conference of Bishops of the Anglican Communion, holden at Lambeth
Palace*, 1897, pp. 139, 144.

least four others of the committee were members of the society.

The bishops, in fact, had been specially affected by the progress of the Union. From its foundation in 1889 to 1913 fifty-three episcopal appointments were made.[1] Of these, at least fourteen appointments, mostly to urban or industrial sees, went to members of the Union. Other bishops were more or less favorably disposed toward its doctrines. Domestic influence no doubt made itself felt at Lambeth Palace —Mrs. Davidson was a member of the society. Bishop Mandell Creighton from time to time presided at important meetings of the London Branch.[2] "Oddly enough," said the Rev. Percy Dearmer in 1907, "under the last two Conservative Governments it was rare for any one to be made a bishop who was not keen about social reform."[3] It is perhaps more than a coincidence that all three bishops who spoke in favor of Mr. Lloyd George's budget were members of the Christian Social Union.

The other clerical body which lay open to persuasion by the reform societies of the Church was Convocation. Until 1905, however, nothing remarkable was accomplished in this direction. Convocation continued as in the previous period to expend its social energies on such well-tried themes as temperance and education, but now with an occasional excursion into housing, prostitution, betting and gambling, or industrial conciliation, conducted for the most part on wholly conventional lines. In respect to social reform at least, it was true, as Sir Spencer Walpole wrote, "that the deliberations of the Right Rev. and the Rev. Houses have, in no

[1] Translations are not counted.

[2] C. S. U. (London Branch), pamphlet, 1902, p. 3.

[3] *Commonwealth*, 1907, pp. 294-5. He laments the fact that the opposite is true since the coming of the Liberal Government in 1906.

single particular, affected the history of their country or their Church." [1]

In 1905, however, the president of the Christian Social Union was able to induce the Convocation of Canterbury to give a lead to the Church in the whole matter of social morality. At the request of the Council of the Union Bishop Gore introduced a resolution

That his Grace the President be respectfully requested to direct the appointment of a Joint Committee of Convocation and of the House of Laymen, to consider whether special measures are needed, and if so, what measures, in order to strengthen the moral witness of the Church on certain current abuses of commerce, on gambling, and on certain other offences against the moral law, and take counsel or co-operate with other men of experience in such manner as seems good to them. [2]

In his speech on the resolution Bishop Gore recalled the " salutary and wise " recommendations of the Lambeth Conference Committee of 1897, " but," he said, " I cannot see that we have done anything at all considerable to carry them into effect." What he proposed was a restatement of first principles and the establishment of a machinery for applying them.

I take it that there are no modern moralists who approach the body of moral theology produced by St. Thomas Aquinas without being amazed at the depth and thoroughness of his contact with the actual practices of his own time. . . . I feel quite sure that something of that kind is what the Church ought to be doing now.

The bishops approved the resolution unanimously, al-

[1] *Op. cit.*, vol. v, p. 288.

[2] *Convocation of Canterbury*, 1905, pp. 205 *et seq.*; the resolution is given as it was finally adopted, after slight verbal changes.

though several took exception to Gore's criticism of the inactivity of the Church. Bishop Talbot of Southwark had brought the matter of commercial morality before his diocesan conference and Bishop Percival had quoted the Lambeth Report in charges to his clergy. Bishop Ingram disclosed that in London " for many years now Churchmen and Nonconformists had been formed into a Public Morality Committee," dealing with such questions as " barmaids in public-houses, the state of the streets, temptations to immorality, and we have had experts before us on each subject." [1]

The five diocesan bishops appointed to the new committee were all members of the Christian Social Union.[2] With nine representatives from the Lower House and five from the House of Laymen they drew up a report on the Moral Witness of the Church on Economic Subjects. This was presented to Convocation in 1907. Bishop Gore, convener of the joint committee, also presided as chairman of the subcommittee for drafting " the positive principles which ought to regulate the accumulation and distribution of wealth." In this connection the opinions of a number of business men, social reformers, economists, and representatives of labor were offered and considered.[3]

The Report on Moral Witness was easily the most comprehensive semi-official statement of the Church on social

[1] Talbot, Percival, and Ingram were members of the C. S. U.

[2] The Committee was as follows: Bishops: Gore of Birmingham (convener), Talbot of Southwark, Percival of Hereford, Hoskyns of Southwell, Harmer of Rochester; Members of the Lower House: the bishop of Leicester (Canon Clayton), the dean of Lincoln (Dr. Wickham), the dean of Christ Church (Dr. Strong), Archdeacon Taylor of Southwark, Archdeacon Hodgson of Stafford, Canon Stanton, Canon Bristow, Dr. Argles, Rev. W. E. Pryke; members of the House of Laymen: Messrs. E. A. Ford, Howard Lloyd, C. F. G. Masterman, M. P., A. R. Pennefather, F. Rogers.

[3] *Convocation of Canterbury*, 1907, p. 5.

subjects that had yet appeared. To be sure, it reiterated much that had been said by the Lambeth Conference of 1897, but its language had a new incisiveness, and in one or two instances it pushed well beyond the beaten track. In laying down the " Christian Principles of Society," the committee appealed to the social content of the Old Testament, which it illustrated with a formidable array of texts, and explained how this was deepened, universalized and summed-up in Christ's injunction of duty toward one's " neighbor ". "The Christian ethic," said the report, " is thus essentially social." The old complacency gave way to self-criticism.

We are persuaded that some of the matters which have held, and still hold, the first place in ecclesiastical or clerical interest are such as the New Testament would lead us to believe of quite minor importance. We are further persuaded that the idea of individual salvation has been disastrously isolated in Christian teaching and in current Christian life from the social idea of original Christianity and the teaching of brotherhood.[1]

Several statements of the Report, if taken in conjunction, have quite revolutionary implications. " The first duty of the Christian [it said] . . . is that of work. . . . Idleness, whether it is of the rich or of the poor man, is an offense against God and man." Property being a sacred trust, the employer " must remember that he is responsible for the conditions under which his business is carried on." As to wages, " the fundamental Christian principle of the remuneration of labour is that the first charge upon any industry must be the proper maintenance of the labourer—an idea which it has been sought to express in popular language by the phrase ' the living wage.' " The objection that the individual employer, being in the grip of circumstances, must submit to them, could not be entertained.

[1] *Convocation of Canterbury, Report 412.*

When "the system" makes it necessary for him to do what his conscience condemns, he can, of course, with whatever difficulty, refuse to do it, and suffer the financial loss or ruin involved. We have almost dropped out of our current Christian teaching the idea that a Christian may be called upon to make any great financial or other sacrifice for conscience' sake.

But individual action must be assisted by law. The Church, in fact, "should make clear to itself the great demand for the reconstruction of society which is at present urged upon us," for behind it lies a fundamental moral principle.

Then, in consequence of such deepened reflection, . . . it is undoubtedly the case that we shall need an advance in our present law touching social and industrial problems. It is time, we think, that the Christian conscience of the country voted urgency for all the group of problems which concern the grossly unequal distribution of wealth and well-being; the waste of life and capacity through lack of proper nourishment and training; the sweating of women's and children's labour; the deficiency, in the surroundings of so many, of those things which are the ordinary essentials of physical and moral well-being.

The Report broke cleanly with the orthodox theory of the Church's duty to the poor.

We feel that the existing methods by which the Church relieves the poor—that is, the administration of "charity" . . . , has been shown in its results to be singularly unproductive of permanent good. . . . We have to go deeper to the grounds of the existing misery and want and unemployment; and while we do our best to deal with the present distress, direct our chief attention towards furthering the reorganization of society on such principles of justice as will tend to reduce poverty and misery in the future to more manageable proportions.

Some concessions were offered to the conservative point of view.

We do not desire that the Church as a body should take a side
with this or that political party; nor again, that the Church
should favour any one class. . . . There is perhaps as much
need to teach the workman the duty of conscientious and efficient work, as to teach the employer his responsibility in dealing with his workmen; and there is perhaps quite as much mis-
use of money at the present time among the poor as among the
rich, relatively to what they receive.

The resolutions to which Convocation and the House of
Laymen were asked to agree appear singularly moderate in
view of the Report. They looked toward the instruction of
the clergy and candidates for holy orders in social relations,
the training of church workers in elementary industrial and
sanitary law, more insistence by the Church on " the duty
of the Christian to his neighbor," and, as the Lambeth Conference had suggested in 1897, the formation of a Social
Service Committee in every diocese.

The Report and the resolutions met with almost no opposition from the bishops. Their progress was less tranquil
in the Lower House; there the debate resembled a museum
of antiquities: " criticism of the old economics was founded
on absolute ignorance "; the Report was socialistic; clergymen should not interfere in politics; outsiders would believe
the Report had received the sanction of Convocation. "The
Report," said Canon Henson, " was an extremely able and
clever Christian Social Union pamphlet, which he objected
to floating on the public with more than its due authority."
As for the resolutions, to which alone they were committed,
he offered an amendment that " care should be taken to
guard against the grave risk and profanation involved in any
partisan use of the Christian pulpit." Fortunately the opposition was more vocal than courageous, and the resolutions
were passed with this and a few other slight changes.[1]

[1] *Convocation of Canterbury*, 1907, pp. 90 *et seq.*, 111 *et seq.* Henson's
amendment was rejected by the bishops.

Two subsequent reports of the Committee on Moral Witness supplemented the report of 1907. One issued in 1909 dealt with the question of investments. Recognizing the importance of capital in production, the Committee did not condemn interest as such. But certain investments were at once ruled out, such as property used for immoral purposes or in evasion of the law. Others were conditionally forbidden. In this category fell the liquor traffic—if " we are prepared to say that the use of liquor as a beverage is altogether illegitimate . . . "; the luxury trade, unless in certain cases it was " socially advantageous "; and foreign loans by which " bad governments have been propped up and perpetuated." Investment was discouraged in trades dangerous to the workmen employed or in which unsatisfactory conditions and wages obtained. The effect of an occupation on the consumer must be weighed, but the workman should receive first consideration. Ownership of land involved a special responsibility, for it was not subject to competition.

As it is required of employers that the first charge upon industry should be a living wage for workpeople, so it should be required of landholders that they should provide a " living " house, and of manufacturers that they use " living " workrooms, or, if land is let for building, that they should, to the best of their ability, choose tenants who will carry out these requirements.[1]

Resolutions embodying the principles of the report were agreed to by both houses of Convocation. Canon Pryke informed the Lower House with some satisfaction that 8,000 copies of the first report had been bought by the general public. The realistic Henson " supposed that meant that every member of the Christian Social Union had got one and given another to someone else." [2]

[1] *Convocation of Canterbury*, 1909, *Report 426.*

[2] *Ibid.*, 1909, pp. 27, 30.

In 1911 the Joint Committee reported that every diocese in the province of Canterbury possessed a secretary for social service and that some had also organized or revived committees for this purpose. It also published a lengthy list of reports on social subjects drawn up by the various diocesan committees.[1]

In contrast with Convocation, the Church Congress had very early dealt with a fairly broad range of social subjects.[2] It continued to reflect, somewhat more adequately perhaps, changes in social opinion and to serve, moreover, as a moderately useful center of propaganda for the new reform societies. Critics, however, pointed out defects in its personnel and organization. Stewart Headlam, writing in 1885, declined to regard " the seven and sixpenny self-elected Church Parliament " as in any sense representative. Radicals like himself had been quietly excluded from its platform.[3] But the latter difficulty was rapidly overcome. In later years it was rare indeed that several members of the Christian Social Union, the Guild of St. Matthew, and the Church Socialist League did not appear on the program, and frequently the discussion of certain topics was handed over bodily to them. Fault was also found with the programs of the Congress. They were said to be stereotyped, and to lack boldness, co-ordination, and popular appeal. Responsibility for the arrangements varied from year to year as the Congress migrated from one diocese to another and some of these criticisms continued to be justified. It is worth remarking, however, that the first attempt of the Congress to deal with social problems in a really comprehensive way occurred in 1890, when Bishop Westcott presided over the

---

[1] *Convocation of Canterbury*, 1911, *Report 460.*

[2] *Supra*, p. 95.

[3] *Church Reformer*, 1884, pp. 193, 199; 1886, p. 218; F. G. Bettany, *op. cit.*, pp. 84-5.

meeting at Hull. Even more striking success was achieved by another member of the Christian Social Union, Bishop Percival, at the Brighton Congress in 1913. In general, however, the effectiveness of the Congress was still limited in several ways. Its attention was dispersed over too wide a variety of subjects, few of which could be adequately treated. Too few leading experts and scholars appeared on the program—in the social discussions laymen took less and less part. " Gaiters," said *The Commonwealth,* " are always a bright and cheering feature at a congress; but it does sometimes seem as if the Committee looked at speakers' shins rather than at their heads." [1]

The appeal of the Congress to workingmen does not always seem to have been of the happiest description. Most of the sessions being held during the daytime, workmen were necessarily prevented from attending, and provision was made for them *en masse* at night. Not until 1905 were these assemblies customarily called " Men's Meetings " instead of " Workingmen's Meetings ". The speakers at these assemblies—clergymen for the most part—were almost without exception eminently safe. From time to time the suggestion was put forward that workingmen should be given an opportunity to speak for themselves. The experiment was tried in 1887 with not very encouraging results. Their discourses were if possible less enlightening than those of the usual orators. In the course of years, however, a number of trade-union leaders were called to the platforms both of the regular and of the workingmen's meetings with better results. But generally speaking such radical flights as the middle-class visitor at other sessions was forced to endure

---

[1] *Church Reformer,* 1885, p. 271; Rev. W. M. Ede, *The Attitude of the Church to Some of the Social Problems of Town Life,* preface (by Bishop Westcott) ; *Church Congress,* 1908, preface, pp. viii-ix; *Commonwealth,* 1911, p. 338.

were more than balanced by the moderate sentiments dealt
out to workingmen.   Occasionally a man like Bishop Kempthorne put forward " subversive " opinions, but the speakers
usually contented themselves with impressing upon their
audience the dangers of intemperance, thriftlessness, sexual
immorality, infidelity, and secularism, and defending the
establishment, the ritual, and the revenues of the Church.

We shall return to some of the details of the Congress's
deliberations later on.   However, on at least one point they
deserve special notice, for the Congress seems to have been
the first Church body to discuss old-age pensions.   Canon
J. W. Blackley claimed to have originated the idea of compulsory insurance against sickness and old age.   The plan
had been considered in a committee of Parliament where it
had been opposed by the Friendly Societies before Canon
Blackley brought it to the attention of the Church Congress
in 1889.   He was supported by Canon W. More Ede, later
Bishop Westcott's coadjutor in social matters at Durham.
Again in 1892 and 1899 Canon Blackley spoke to the Congress on the subject.   Principles similar to those he advocated were embodied in the Old Age Pension Act of 1908
and the National Insurance Act of 1911.[1]

Enough has perhaps been said to indicate the virtues and
the shortcomings of the Church Congress.   It had its crass
moments.   As late as 1905—which should have been well
within the age of enlightenment—a business man naïvely
upheld the tithe:

Where will you get such a proposition as that from anyone in
the world . . . ? [he inquired] . . . Out of every pound I get,
one-tenth goes to the credit of my tithe account in my ledger
and in the bank.   Now mark this: the more strictly I adhere
to and faithfully keep this law of God, the more increase I get.

[1] *Church Congress*, 1889, pp. 424 *et seq.*, 438; 1892, p. 369; 1899, p. 347.

Do not forget it. I want every business man in this hall to open an account to-morrow and try it.[1]

The Congress also had its moments of timidity. The campaign which the Christian Social Union had been waging against lead poisoning reached the Congress in 1911. The occasion was appropriate, for the meeting was held that year at Stoke-on-Trent, the center of a great pottery manufacture. Miss Gertrude Tuckwell, a leader and expert of the Union, advocated the use of leadless glaze as the only means of eliminating plumbism among workers. Yet none of the three clergymen of the city who spoke supported her without qualification. They dwelt upon the difficulty of educating the public in the use of leadless-glazed ware and the economic damage to the workers that would result if its use were made compulsory. At the same time they indignantly repudiated the charge that the clergy of the district had been remiss.[2]

The judgment of *The Commonwealth* on Church Congresses at the end of our period, while it recognized advances that had been made, was tinged with irony:

How curiously responsive and open a Church Congress has become! It cheers everything. It welcomes every conceivable opinion. It especially enjoys criticism of itself. . . . This novel temper of the normal Churchman, however delightful to recognize, has its alarming side. Have we all become so tolerant, because we know that we still find ourselves doing nothing? . . . Once long ago, no thorny matter could be trusted to show up in a Church Congress without provoking wild shrieks of protest. Now, we are rather nervously asking for some one to show some sign of dissent.[3]

Finally, a few words must be said of three other Church

[1] *Church Congress*, 1905, p. 86.

[2] *Ibid.*, 1911, pp. 71 *et seq.*

[3] 1913, p. 321.

assemblies. The diocesan conferences have already been alluded to.[1] They continued to meet and discuss a variety of social matters. Their activity in this respect no doubt depended largely on the social inclinations of the bishops who called them together.[2]

The laity were still unsatisfied with the position they held in the counsels of the Church. An ineffective attempt had been made to admit them to Convocation, and after long deliberation a compromise was reached in 1886 by which an unofficial House of Laymen took its place beside the Convocation of Canterbury. A similar body met at York in 1892. In 1904 the two Houses of Laymen and the provincial Convocations united to form a (still unofficial) Representative Church Council. Its constituent bodies also of course continued to hold independent sessions.

The Houses of Laymen were elective but hardly representative assemblies. In the London diocese only a few hundred churchmen voted. Both the Representative Church Council and the Houses of Laymen seem to have devoted less attention to social matters than the purely clerical Convocations.[3] Nevertheless the Canterbury House of Laymen considered the question of old-age pensions in 1892, and issued next year a report on the co-ordination of efforts to relieve poverty and unemployment. In 1907 the Representative Church Council ratified the work of the Committee on Moral Witness and resolved in favor of diocesan social service committees. Again, during the coal strike of 1912 the Council

---

[1] *Supra*, pp. 65-6.

[2] Archidiaconal and parish conferences supplemented on a still more local scale the work of the Church Congress and the diocesan conferences.

[3] I have been unable to examine the official debates of these bodies, but have used the *Church of England Year Book* for summaries, and the fuller reports of some of their proceedings in *The Guardian* and *The Church Times*.

passed a resolution, moved by the archdeacon of Rochester and couched in somewhat general terms, sympathizing with the aspirations of the workers. In the debate on the resolution few laymen spoke—a fact which was commented upon by Archbishop Davidson—and those who did were noticeably more cautious than the clergy.[1] Thus, while the new bodies could not insulate themselves completely from what had formerly been called secular things, they were still too busy with Church polity and doctrine to spare much time for inquiry into social problems.

THE BISHOPS AND STRIKES

After 1875 it was the clergy and not the laity who took the lead in extending and diversifying the social action of the Church. Hughes, Ludlow, and Lord Shaftesbury had no lay successors of equal prominence, but Maurice and Kingsley inaugurated a whole line of clerical reformers. The latter differed among themselves as to the exact social function of the Church, but most of them agreed that it included, in an imperfect world, the recognition of trade-unionism and the right to strike. Acceptance of a principle and interference by clergymen in specific industrial disputes are of course two quite different things. Nevertheless many of the clergy were logical enough to assume the latter and more difficult responsibility. We remember that Canon Girdlestone and others had supported the agricultural laborers in 1874, that Bishop Fraser had acted as a referee in trade disputes on several occasions, and that the Christian Social Union had helped to form unions among the workingmen of Oxford. Three later and more important instances of clerical intervention must now be considered.

The great London dock strike of 1889 heralded the advent of the " new unionism ". The strategy of Ben Tillett, John

[1] *Church Times*, 2 July, 1912.

Burns, and Tom Mann was a brilliant departure from the dull mercantilism of the older unionism.   The immediate issue was one of simple justice.   The dock laborers were expected to live on a starvation wage of 4d. to 5d. an hour for casuals or 3s. 8d. to 5s. a day for regulars.   " The dock gates of the East End," says a government report of 1890, " might almost be described as the very cesspool of London, if not, indeed, the national labour market.   The men to whom, from whatever cause, all other avenues to employment seemed closed, turned almost as a last resort to the docks." [1]   Thus the revolt of a body of unskilled laborers had a quality of daring and an aspect of righteousness which caught the imagination and sympathy of the British public.

Among the clergy who rallied to the dockers' support were members of the Guild of St. Matthew and the group just then projecting the Christian Social Union.   Tillett, in his history of the strike, mentions particularly the Rev. J. G. Adderley, who collected £700 to feed the strikers—and lost a peer's subscription to his mission of £50.[2]

No one knew better than Tillett the value of a moral appeal where Englishmen were concerned.   Even before the strike he had therefore sought the support, " for organizing reasons ", of the arch-custodians of morals, Cardinal Manning and Bishop Temple.   The latter's response was " a malignant letter, abusing the docker generally," and when the strike finally occurred the bishop was conveniently absent on a holiday in Wales.[3]

But Dr. Temple was not permitted to escape thus easily. An emissary of the London clergy set off posthaste for

---

[1] C. 6176, p. 6.

[2] Ben Tillett, *A Brief History of the Dockers' Union*, p. 24; J. G. Adderley, *In Slums and Society*, p. 197.

[3] Ben Tillett, *op. cit.*, p. 15.

Wales and returned triumphantly with the quarry. This stroke was followed by the calling of a conference at the mission rooms of Canon Mason, the Lord Mayor being invited to attend at Temple's request. There Ben Tillett and John Burns laid the dockers' case before Cardinal Manning, Bishop Temple, Mr. Sydney Buxton, and the Lord Mayor. The demands of the strikers were moderate: a minimum wage of 6d. an hour and at least four hours' employment at a time. Agreement on these points was reached without difficulty. But a stipulation that the new regulations should be postponed for three months threatened to wreck the negotiations. Tillett and Burns had consented to the delay but when the decision was made known to the dockers they promptly rejected it. Bishop Temple made the most of this incident: " Tillett and Burns were roundly accused of bad faith and of double dealing," and the bishop washed his hands of the whole affair.[1] The interlude has been described with bitter irony by Ben Tillett.

The play of passion and personal interests was centered in the fight the square-jawed, hard-featured Temple put up against the aesthetic and spiritual-faced Cardinal Manning; he would have sacrificed the whole of the dockers to win for his Church. Apart from my contempt for Temple, remembering his brutal letter to me about the dockers, it was interesting to me, tired as I was, to watch the combat of the Churches over the bodies of the dockers. But the older man was more human and subtle, his diplomacy that of the ages and the Church. He chided, did this old man, chided the pomp of the Lord Mayor, the harshness of Bishop Temple, the pushfulness of Burns.[2]

To the despair of his subordinates, Bishop Temple re-

[1] E. G. Sandford (ed.), *Memoirs of Archbishop Temple*, vol. ii, pp. 145 *et seq.*; S. Paget, *op. cit.*, p. 170.

[2] Ben Tillett, *op. cit.*, p. 29.

sumed his broken holiday in Wales. Cardinal Manning, on the other hand, was more conciliatory. Taking up the broken threads of the negotiations, he quickly brought about a settlement acceptable to the men.

Once more the Church had suffered a tactical defeat. During the strike of 1874, the stupidity of two obscure clerical magistrates and the indiscretion of a bishop had overshadowed the outspoken sympathy of many churchmen. In 1889 Temple's spectacular retirement outweighed the quiet efforts of the Christian Socialists. Thus trade unionism passed its crisis without full benefit of clergy. But the Church's honor was to be partially retrieved by Bishops Creighton and Westcott even though a great opportunity had been missed.

Mandell Creighton became bishop of Peterborough in 1891. Four years later the man who as a historian had judiciously held the balance between popes and Protestants was called upon to perform a like service for antagonists in the boot trade. At the beginning of 1895 a lockout in Leicester and Northampton threw 120,000 men out of work. Just a year before, Creighton in a charge to his clergy had observed that

the clergy are, as a rule, little suited to decide economic questions. . . . I believe that what men of all kinds of opinion would all join in advising [them to aim at] is benevolent neutrality in trade disputes, constant helpfulness in alleviating inevitable distress, outspoken criticism of all unfairness, and unswerving maintenance of the great principle of justice.

On the present occasion, therefore, he at first tried only to open the way for an understanding by clearing the air of suspicion and antagonism. With this object he agreed to the holding of prayer meetings, and published a letter dwelling upon the better motives of both parties to the dispute.

But every effort at negotiation failed until Creighton himself undertook to break the impasse. He first sounded out the masters' federation and the trade council as to their willingness to resume the discussions with a view to arbitration. The response was favorable. He then visited the Board of Trade and induced the Permanent Secretary, Sir Courtenay Boyle, to act as arbitrator. Meanwhile he listened to the arguments of both sides and suggested to them points which might be safely referred to the arbitrator. In Boyle's absence the bishop kept him informed of difficulties as they arose and advised him as to the proper means of meeting them. These negotiations occupied more than two weeks, but Creighton had his reward and all differences were ultimately adjusted. " The Bishop," says his biographer,

succeeded in keeping his part in helping to bring about an agreement in the background, and his action was never referred to by the public press; but Sir Courtenay Boyle wrote to him: " My own efforts were largely helped by your information and counsel, which enabled me to see where danger lay and where safety was to be sought." [1]

Except momentarily during a strike, Temple and Creighton had little personal experience of the labor movement. Westcott also passed through a trade conflict, but this was only an incident in his relations with labor. As a Christian Socialist and a believer in Co-operation he considered it his duty not only to act as peace-maker in the midst of hostilities, but to discourage any threat of force whatever. As one alternative he advocated boards of conciliation. Conferences, in fact, were his favorite social implements, and many were held at Auckland Castle during his residence as bishop of Durham. John Wilson, an official of the Durham Miners'

[1] Mrs. Creighton, *Life and Letters of Mandell Creighton*, vol. ii, pp. 119-130.

Association, faithfully attended these gatherings. " When he [Westcott] first came to the diocese," said Mr. Wilson,

> he adopted a course somewhat peculiar to himself as a Bishop. His custom was at certain intervals to invite a number of gentle-men to his castle. It was a mixed gathering: leading em-ployers, literary men, clergymen, economists and trades union leaders. As one of the last class I was always invited. . . . These meetings were of immense benefit to all who took part.[1]

Westcott had been at Durham scarcely more than a year when the clouds of industrial strife began to gather. As early as April, 1891, the mine owners of that district an-nounced that the state of the coal market required a cut of 15 per cent in wages. The workers, thanks to the diplomatic parleying of John Wilson, were able to evade this demand until January, 1892. The employers then offered the alter-native of a 10 per cent reduction or reference to arbitration. Contrary to the advice of their leaders the men rejected these terms and began the most costly struggle in the history of the Durham union—at least up to that time. The lockout involved between 75,000 and 100,000 men and continued for three months (9 March to 3 June).

Toward the middle of April Bishop Westcott wrote a letter to the Miners' Federation. The only response was a circular to the effect that the men wanted no outside inter-ference. Time worked for the employers, however, and their demands rose as the resources of the workers fell. Westcott meanwhile published a statement announcing his complete neutrality and explaining that his first duty was to help re-store peace.

As the end of May found the miners in a more receptive mood, Westcott again stepped in. He appealed to both par-

[1] Arthur Westcott, *op. cit.*, vol. ii, pp. 111, 135, 377-8; John Wilson, *Memories of a Labour Leader*, pp. 218 *et seq.*

ties in similar terms. There appeared, he said, to be " an agreement as to the substantial reduction in wages which is required, and as to the methods to be employed for the settlement of future difficulties as to wages." Though the owners were now demanding a 13½ per cent reduction, he proposed one of 10 per cent and reference of any further reduction to a Wages Board. He invited both parties to meet at Auckland Castle " to discuss details ".

The owners agreed to a conference without committing themselves to Westcott's terms. The miners also consented to attend, stating that they had already offered to accept a cut of 10 per cent. On May 30th the meeting took place. After luncheon (the bishop always began his conferences with a meal) the parties separated to consider their problem. Westcott passed back and forth between them. He praised the fortitude of the men and insisted that they should not be starved into complete submission. Reason finally prevailed; the owners accepted a 10 per cent reduction and pronounced themselves in favor of conciliation.[1]

The settlement was obviously a truce; Westcott had therefore steered the negotiations with an eye to future emergencies. But it was a long step from pious wishes to the actual machinery of conciliation, and he did not consider his responsibility at an end. Early in 1894, therefore, he met a group of masters and workmen at Auckland Castle to discuss practical measures. All present were favorably disposed toward conciliation but doubted whether the trade as a whole would co-operate. They suggested that the bishop call a public conference as a means of testing sentiment throughout the whole northern area. Westcott acted on the proposal at

[1] Arthur Westcott, op. cit., vol. ii, pp. 115 et seq.; Sidney Webb, The Story of the Durham Miners, p. 74. For the correspondence between the owners, miners, and Bishop Westcott before the final conference see Reports of Commissioners, 1893, vol. 32, pp. 385-94.

once, and such was the interest aroused that almost every prominent trade-union leader in Northumberland, Durham, and North Yorkshire was present. The bishop presided. He pointed out that committees of conciliation for local purposes already existed and that the benefit should be extended to matters of general interest. Following this conference the question was thrashed out in the local unions. "Four months later," says Canon More Ede, " the Conciliation Board was an established fact in the Northumberland coal trade, and Durham did not long lag behind." Canon More Ede, the right-hand man of Bishop Westcott in all his dealings with labor, himself acted as chairman at various meetings for the settlement of industrial disputes.

Success came almost too easily, however, and the promoters of conciliation had to pass through a time of trial. A period of trade depression set in. The boards awarded further reductions, and the unpopularity of this action added to the opinion which existed in some quarters that the boards were an obstacle to agitation for a minimum wage and a hindrance to a national federation of mine workers proved to be temporarily overwhelming. In 1896 the miners voted to discontinue the boards. But the decision was not irrevocable. In 1899 the machinery was again set up and conciliation became a fixture in the northern mining industry.[1]

Too much stress should not be laid upon the part which Temple, Creighton, and Westcott played in the settlement of strikes. Though uncommon, it was not an entirely novel proceeding. Nor were the bishops over-bold. In the case of Bishop Temple, the credit for intervening belongs not to him but to a group of London clergy. Bishop Creighton waited until the situation was not only mature but almost

---

[1] *Church Congress*, 1896, pp. 386 *et seq.*; Arthur Westcott, *op. cit.*, vol. ii, pp. 381-3; Sidney Webb, *The Story of the Durham Miners*, p. 75.

over-ripe before he acted.   Westcott alone interfered during
the heat of a struggle, suffered a rebuff, and was gallant
enough to overlook it.   Nevertheless it was something that
from time to time the official Church put its fluent generalizations to the test of practice.   If, as all were coming to
agree, the Church had a function to perform in the economic
sphere, it was courageous to touch that structure at its sorest
point.   And, considering the publicity it sometimes evoked,
successful mediation was good politics.

LATER HISTORY OF THE CHRISTIAN SOCIAL UNION

From the late '70's to 1914 the propaganda of the reform
societies, and most obviously that of the Christian Social
Union, had powerfully affected the minds of churchpeople.
The permeation had been seconded by all those forces which
are often called " the spirit of the age ", and while no revolutionary change in sentiment had occurred, an alteration
was visible to the most thoroughgoing pessimists.   The
Union had its spokesmen on the bench of bishops, and could
make itself heard in the House of Commons, while the Church
assemblies surrendered eagerly to its logic, swallowed its
proposals wryly, or listened to them with what resignation it
was possible to muster.   But this was only one aspect of the
Union's activities; it also participated in the settlement movement and made its influence felt in government administration.   The following pages will show how this varied program was carried out, from about 1895 to 1914.

Certain of the old methods continued to be utilized.   The
Union still issued " white lists," and urged preferential trading in connection with its campaign for leadless glaze.   But
when a trade was unorganized and no standard conditions had
been fixed, or when the stages and processes of manufacture
were so complicated that the conditions of labor were not

fully known, it became apparent that the white list had little
or no value.[1]

Study and investigation had been a main object of the
Union from the beginning. It became the practice to issue
an annual study-topic such as " Unemployment " or " Child
Labor ", the branches being urged to examine local conditions for themselves. The results would then be summed up
in a general report, as was the case in 1913, when the Union
issued a pamphlet on Housing and Town-Planning. Here
certain branches had done work of a very practical kind. In
some instances they had been conducting limited-dividend
housing companies for a number of years and were projecting
others, or had taken action for the improvement of dwellings
under the act of 1909.[2]

Books, magazines, and pamphlets remained an important
part of the propaganda. Every subject of current social interest was bound to find its way into one or all of these publications. One of the most ambitious undertakings of the
Union was the issuance in 1911-1913 of a series of eight
handbooks under the editorship of Canon Holland which
dealt with a number of social topics from the Christian point
of view.[3]

Shortly before 1900 a new orientation began to appear in
the activities of the Union. " During its tenth year," said
the Report of 1900, " the London Branch has developed in

---

[1] C. S. U. leaflet, 1910 (Oxford Branch), signed by Gore and Carter;
Commonwealth, 1907, p. 145; 1914, p. 126.

[2] C. S. U., *Report on Housing and Town Planning*, 1913; *Report on
Unemployment*, 1910.

[3] The list follows: W. E. Chadwick, *Christianity and Citizenship*;
Spencer J. Gibb, *The Boy and his Work*; A. W. Jephson, *Municipal
Work from a Christian Standpoint*; A. J. Carlyle, *The Influence of
Christianity upon Social and Political Ideas*; the same, *Wages*; H. S.
Holland, *Our Neighbors*; Cyril Jackson, *Outlines of Education in
England*; C. E. B. Russell, *Social Problems of the North*.

several directions : its activities are a good deal more complex than they were five years ago, and its preaching is now less marked a feature then its endeavours to press forward practical reforms." [1] The change was one rather of emphasis than of direction, and it answered at least in part the charge that the Union liked better to talk than to act, and that even its talk was marred by a confusion of tongues.

As an evidence of this new trend, Maurice Hostel came into being in 1899. " The Settlement was started," said the Report of the London Branch,

to give further scope to the practical side of our work. . . . It is easy to discuss social problems, and listen to lectures and speeches on social problems, but to live amid the problems, to meet them face to face in our daily life, and feel called upon to strive and struggle at some solution, brings us to a keener sense of the vastness of the task that lies before the Christian Social Union if it is to carry out its special mission.[2]

The Rev. H. R. Wakefield, later bishop of Birmingham, was a large contributor to the settlement, but the inspiration and much of the financial support came from Canon Holland. A site in Hoxton was chosen which had been the scene of Holland's earliest work in the slums. Eventually the settlement added a Women's House and maintained vacation homes for girls and boys.[3]

Perhaps the clearest example of the Union's progress from theory to practice is the growing prominence of the Research Committee. This Committee, set up in 1895, ultimately became the leading authority of the Union in matters of social legislation. Any member was eligible to join it, but few or none rendered as valuable service as Miss Constance Smith

[1] C. S. U. (London Branch), *Annual Report*, 1900, p. 3.

[2] *Ibid.*, p. 12.

[3] *Ibid.*, 1899, p. 3; 1902, p. 12.

and Miss Gertrude Tuckwell.   The latter was already known
as honorary secretary of the Women's Trade Union League,
an office which she held from 1892 to 1904.   Being a niece of
Lady Dilke, Miss Tuckwell belonged by birth as well as interest and ability to the " Dilke coterie ", whose members had
something to do with almost every phase of the industrial
legislation of the period.[1]

As its special field the Research Committee undertook to
investigate, and if necessary, to reform, the conditions of
labor in unorganized, sweated, and dangerous trades employing chiefly women.   Inquiries were conducted and reports
issued with regard to laundries, artificial-flower making, fish-
curing, fruit-preserving, tea-packing, brush-making, and
piece-work.   The attempt of Parliament to regulate laundries
had led to rather peculiar complications.   Many hospitals and
other institutions supported by religious bodies operated laundries for their own convenience or as means of employing
the inmates.   The factory bill of 1901 for the first time included a provision for the inspection of these laundries but
the clause encountered such opposition from the Irish Catholic members that it had to be dropped.   The Anglican bishops
in the House of Lords, on the other hand, expressed their
entire willingness to accept it, and for several years thereafter laundries operated by Church institutions voluntarily
submitted to inspection.   Their experience apparently removed the apprehensions of Roman Catholics, for a new
measure was accepted without protest in 1907.[2]

One of the most important matters which engaged the Research Committee was the campaign against lead-poisoning
in the manufacture of pottery.   The problem was not new—

[1] H. A. Mess, *Factory Legislation and its Administration*, 1891-1924,
pp. 188-9.

[2] H. A. Mess, *op. cit.*, pp. 23 *et seq.*; *Hansard*, 1901, vol. 99, cols. 876,
878, 882.

it had been the subject of agitation since 1842—and some ineffective attempts had been made to deal with it by acts of Parliament and Home-Office regulations.   In 1898 members of the Hanley Labor Church,[1] revived the question and the Women's Trade Union League followed it up with a vigorous campaign to secure remedial legislation.   As a result, no doubt, of Miss Tuckwell's connection with the latter organization the Research Committee interested itself in the matter. The Committee and the Christian Social Union as a whole centered their efforts on an attempt to popularize the use of leadless-glazed ware with the buying public.   To this end appeals were issued and white lists of tradesmen handling the ware were circulated.   As it turned out, pressure of this kind did not, apparently, have much effect upon manufacturers, but in any event it helped to keep the question alive.   In 1908 a departmental committee of the Home Office began an extensive inquiry into the danger to health arising from the use of lead in pottery and lithographic processes.   Miss Tuckwell was named of the committee.   It had been proposed that the use of lead in the making of certain enumerated articles should be forbidden and that the Home Office should have power to extend the list at its discretion.   But after hearing the evidence of manufacturers as to the unsatisfactory character of leadless glaze the majority of the committee appeared to be convinced that a prohibited list was impracticable, and recommended simply more stringent regulations for the protection of the workers engaged.   Miss Tuckwell alone re-

---

[1] " Labor churches " were organized in the late 1890's by groups of socialists who thought a religious atmosphere was necessary to the success of socialism but who objected to ordinary Christian doctrines.   As *The Labour Church Record* put it, " When they say ' As Socialists we should do so-and-so,' they mean much what our good Guild of St. Matthew friends mean when they say ' As Christians we should do so-and-so.' . . . The Labour Church folk do not bother much about God." (*Labour Church Record*, April, 1899.)

mained firm. As specially representing the women employed, who were the chief sufferers from lead-poisoning, she could not, she said, assent to the proposals of the majority; the only effective remedy was a prohibited list. The government followed the advice of her colleagues, however, and promulgated a new set of regulations in 1912. [1]

The Research Committee in other ways sought to influence public opinion in general and governmental action in particular. At its suggestion the *Daily News* sponsored an Exhibition of Sweated Industries in 1907. Members of the Committee contributed articles based on its investigations to the *Fortnightly* and *Saturday Reviews*. Memorials and reports were constantly being laid before the Home Office, where they received practical consideration or at least civil acknowledgment. On at least two occasions members of Parliament interested in factory legislation were invited to attend special meetings under C. S. U. auspices at the opening of Parliament, and information as to the industries examined by the Research Committee was regularly supplied them. From time to time this material formed the substance of debates in the House of Commons; the Union could always depend upon a number of M. P.'s to state its views. In this respect the Rt. Hon. J. G. Talbot, Mr. H. J. Tennant, and Sir Charles Dilke were useful. [2]

Only a few developments in industrial legislation can be traced directly to C. S. U. intervention. On two occasions the Union was able to improve the regulations governing the fruit-preserving trade. In 1899 it defeated an attempt to lengthen the hours of women's labor in this industry. [3] Again, the Factory and Workshops Act of 1901

[1] H. A. Mess, *op. cit.*, pp. 51 *et seq.*; Cd. 5219 (1910), p. 129; C. S. U. (London Branch), *Annual Report*, 1902, p. 16.

[2] *Economic Review*, 1905, p. 349; 1908, p. 2; C. S. U. (London Branch), *Annual Reports*, 1898, 1899, 1902.

[3] *Church of England Year Book*, 1900, p. 512.

provided, by a clause which the Rt. Hon. J. G. Talbot, M. P., acting as the spokesman of the C. S. U. was successful in getting inserted at the committee stage, that the Secretary of State shall have power to prescribe by administrative order the conditions under which the special exceptions as to the hours of women and young persons engaged in the process of cleaning and preparing fruit are to be permitted. Accordingly, an order laying down rules on such points as the amount of cubic air space to each worker, drainage of floors, provision of fans to carry off steam in boiling-rooms, and breaks for meals, was issued in 1902.[1]

The Union's agitation in behalf of piece-workers was also rewarded in 1907 by the issuance of an order which entitled large numbers of these workers in various occupations to a ticket determining before-hand the price of their work.[2] All this was preliminary to an attack on the sweating system from a new angle.   In 1907 the Union began to advocate the establishment of wage-boards for the fixing of minimum wages in unorganized trades.   Members were assured by Mr. G. N. Barnes that labor would support the proposal.[3]   It seems reasonable to conclude that a share of the credit for the Trade Boards Act of 1909 belongs to the Christian Social Union.

But while the hands of the Christian Social Union were busy, its mind was not at peace. The fate of movements which have passed their first bloom seemed to be overtaking it. The leaders complained of a decline in enthusiasm, of the inactivity of numerous branches, of a failure to enlist the masses of the laity. The Union was no longer a novelty. But the cause of its short-comings seemed to lie deeper than this. Writing in 1905, the Rev. T. C. Fry said that the

[1] *Economic Review*, 1905, pp. 349-50.

[2] *Commonwealth*, 1907, p. 112.

[3] *Ibid.*, p. 170.

Union suffered from a general reaction in progressive thought which dated from the Boer War. Imperial questions having little to do with social welfare had thrown reformers into rival camps.[1] Some years later the Rev. Reginald Tribe asserted that the ethical appeal was being neglected: nothing distinguished the Union from a crowd of other enthusiasts clamoring for particular reforms. Even when they discovered a germinal principle the society made no use of it. Such had been the fate of Bishop Gore's precept that wages should be the first charge upon industry.

> Not only do we keep our separate problems in compartments and pull them out one at a time for an airing [he said] but our remedies for these problems vary from year to year. This shows that we have no grip of the underlying principles, whereas if we examine the Bishop of Birmingham's [Gore's] dictum we find that it is applicable not only to sweating, but to many other problems also.[2]

In point of fact, this anarchy of principles and methods was inherent in the composition of the Union. It was a microcosm of the Church, which had sacrificed uniformity of belief to comprehensiveness. The members frequently trod on each other's toes—to avoid doing so they had to be ridiculously careful. " The remedy [for the decline in vitality] most frequently proposed is that the Union should be more cautious of utterance than of old," said an editor of *The Commonwealth*.

> It must be carefully explained on every possible occasion that we have no connexion with Socialism. . . . No subject must be introduced which might be likely to " set class against class ". The unfortunate death of Leopold II removed a very safe subject from the list. . . . The City Branch may safely discuss

[1] *Economic Review*, 1905, pp. 385 *et seq.*

[2] *Commonwealth*, 1911, p. 331.

rural housing: the rural Branch will do well to discuss town planning in cities. . . . This policy is surely the main cause of our weakness. A society which starts in alarm at each fresh enumeration of its own principles can never grow in usefulness or power.[1]

In a sense all this was nothing new. Schisms in the counsels of the Union had existed from the beginning. What alarmed moderates was a persistent drift toward the left which affected the very pillars of the society. Gore's principle as to wages struck at the foundations of capitalism. Holland's empiricism at last began to harden into dogma. " The State," he said in 1911,

must take up our task of neighborly responsibility or it can never be taken up at all. But this is Socialism, you cry. Exactly. This is the irresistible verity on which Socialism has seized. This is the fixed and certain experience which has given Socialism its immense impetus. . . . Socialism, in emphasizing the moral significance of the State, has got hold of the real trend of things, under which we are all inevitably and rationally moving.[2]

In 1908 two articles in *The Economic Review* defined the issue with special clarity. The Rev. William Temple (now archbishop of York) fired the first gun. The gospels, he said, taught nothing less than evolutionary socialism. Competition was " inherently a principle of selfishness, and, indeed, of hatred . . . The alternative stands before us— Socialism or Heresy; we are involved in one or the other." No middle ground was tenable. To preach the " stewardship " of wealth involved an economic and a moral fallacy; it would destroy the incentive to accumulate and would entrust to the rich the sole guardianship of the public good. " The

[1] *Commonwealth*, 1912, p. 326.
[2] *Our Neighbors*, p. 85.

New Testament theory of the effect of riches upon character would not lead us to suppose that mere possession bestows upon a man unbounded insight." Churchmen must therefore recognize the aims of labor as essentially their own. So doing they became not the tail of a political movement but the guardians of its ideals. For the chief need of the labor movement was a symbol—"an appropriate ritual, such as may embody the ideal of the movement and restore enthusiasm when it flags." The sacrament of communion precisely met this need.[1]

Temple's manifesto drew a searching and closely reasoned reply from a professional philosopher. The Rev. Hastings Rashdall had also examined the gospel. Far from discovering therein Mr. Temple's brand of socialism he had actually found tolerance for self-love and competition. Properly regulated, these motives inured to the well-being of society. "Mr. Temple's argument is one which (however little intended to do só) seems to me calculated to encourage an interpretation of Christian ethics . . . which denies all value to any side of human life or character except a sentimental, extravagant, and socially pernicious self-sacrifice or altruism." Socialists and non-socialists were agreed as to ends and divided as to means. But they could co-operate to remove proximate evils. Let the socialists beware that their dogmatism did not make this co-operation impossible. "Even a socialistic State would be none the worse for a little toleration in matters of opinion." Yet Mr. Rashdall admitted that these deplorable sentiments were rapidly gaining ground:

Not so very long ago it would have seemed to many people a bold proposition to affirm that the Christian may be also a Socialist. . . . Of late years the progress of definitely socialistic opinions—particularly among the younger clergy in our large towns—has been so rapid that the assertion " A Christian may

[1] *Economic Review*, 1908, pp. 190 *et seq.*

not be a Socialist" has come to seem in many quarters less paradoxical, less in need of defence, than the contrary proposition "A Christian may be a non-Socialist".[1]

But the moderates had little real cause for alarm. There was as much likelihood of the Christian Social Union's pledging itself to economic socialism, said *The Commonwealth*, " as of the Lower House of Convocation joining the Fabian Society." An official statement issued in 1910 by Bishops Gore, Talbot, and Chavasse confirmed this opinion: " We . . . are determined to continue to ask no questions as to the politics of our members; and to leave them free as individuals (not as representing the Union) to take action with any political party. . . . The Union remains uncommitted by such action of its individual members."[2]

THE CHURCH SOCIALIST LEAGUE

The demand for a reconsideration of C. S. U. principles had been rendered less urgent by an event which occurred in 1906. This was the founding of the Church Socialist League. Like its predecessors the League grew out of discontent with the Church's relation to labor. The feeling was particularly keen among a group of clergymen whose charges lay in the north of England. They had been stimulated by the social policy followed by Westcott after his accession to the bishopric of Durham. The north, moreover, was (and is) the stronghold of the labor movement; to be familiar with its ambitions bred approval and respect. Emotionally also churchmen had a good deal in common with labor leaders. The Independent Labor Party, says a recent writer, was then a party of idealists. " Its leaders were, for the most part, religious men, trained in the Sunday Schools, P. S. A.'s and chapels of Nonconformity." Labor's sudden access of

[1] *Economic Review*, 1908, pp. 315 *et seq.*

[2] *Commonwealth*, 1910, pp. 185, 188.

strength in the election of 1906 semed to promise great things; it won over still more clergymen. To the latter the time now seemed ripe for action.

The first step was taken by a group of clergymen engaged in a preaching mission at Morecambe. An exchange of views made it clear that most of the group considered the existing reform societies inadequate to present needs. " The C. S. U. for obvious reasons did not lend itself to the kind of action we had in view. The G. S. M. on the other hand had a splendid record, but was in a moribund condition with an ever dwindling membership." The ritualistic bias of the Guild also, it was feared, would not commend itself to the North. What was wanted was " a society which would link up those clergy and laymen who were supporters of labour ", and specifically, of the labor movement. " At the time of the 1906 election we realized that in all parts of the country clergy and other members of the Church of England were actively supporting Labour and Socialist candidates and regarded it as their religious duty to do so." [1]

The discussions led to the calling of a formal conference. In June, 1906, some sixty priests and a few laymen, mostly from the North, assembled at Morecambe under the chairmanship of the Rev. Algernon West. Most of them belonged to one or other of the existing Church societies— more than half of the speakers were members of the Christian Social Union. The Rev. Conrad Noel tried to persuade the conference to support the Guild of St. Matthew, " which can claim to antedate every secular socialist society in this country." Stewart Headlam urged the importance of a Catholic and sacramental basis. The Rev. Percy Widdrington wished an explication of a " Christian sociology " to be included among the aims. All three proposals were de-

---

[1] *Commonwealth*, 1927, pp. 118-19: "The Church Socialist League," by Rev. P. E. T. Widdrington; *ibid.*, 1923, p. 153: "The Church Socialist League," by C. L. Smith.

feated.   The conference determined to form a new organization under the name of the " Church Socialist League."
Failure to take proper account of the last two proposals was
the cause of later dissensions—many of the most influential
members of the League were dissatisfied with its basis from
the beginning.   " The League," wrote Conrad Noel in 1906,
" . . . is to consist solely of people, clerical and lay, who
have found what they believe to be *the* remedy most con-
gruous to the Church's work and development in these times;
that remedy is *Socialism,* as defined in dictionaries and understood by Socialist societies."   " Many of those present," said
Mr. Widdrington long afterward, " seemed to hold that Socialism provided us with a ready made sociology. . .   It
made the danger that we might find ourselves tied to the
chariot of the Labour Party a very real one." [1]

Those who reproached the Christian Social Union for the
vagueness of its principles were bound to be explicit; the
basis of the League as ultimately formulated left little to be
desired in this respect.   Members

accept the *principles of Socialism,* viz: The political, economic,
and social emancipation of the whole people, men and women,
by the establishment of a democratic commonwealth in which
the community shall own the land and capital collectively, and
use them co-operatively for the good of all.   [The League]
works upon the following principles, (1) The Church has to do
with the whole of human life, social and industrial, material
and spiritual; (2) the Church can best fulfill this mission in its
corporate capacity; (3) the Church and State, each in its own
proper sphere, have essentially the same aim, viz., the attainment of the fulness of life for all.

Letters of congratulations arrived from Keir Hardie and
Ramsay MacDonald.[2]

[1] *Commonwealth,* 1927, pp. 120-21; 1906, pp. 209, 223; 1922, p. 134.
[2] *Ibid.,* 1906, p. 223.

The rise of the Church Socialist League was accompanied by the disappearance of the already moribund Guild of St. Matthew. The latter survived for three troublous years during which Stewart Headlam was pressed to convert it into a definitely socialist body. He agreed to give the Church Socialist League a clear field in the north of England, but to repudiate his past and to weaken the sacramental basis of the Guild was unthinkable. Headlam's principles belonged to the age of Henry George; they had been too visionary for the Christian Social Union—they were now too antiquated for his younger followers, who had decided opinions of their own. As it became likely that his opposition might be overridden by the newer members, among whom the most dangerous were Messrs. Gilbert Chesterton and Edgerton Swann, he suggested that the Guild be dissolved. " All we do," he said, " is to talk about a definition of Socialism." The proposal was adopted and the Guild closed its eventful career in 1909. But though the Guild of St. Matthew had passed away, its spirit lived on to influence and even to embarrass the Church Socialist League.[1]

Meanwhile the League set out energetically to win a place for the Church in the labor movement and to bring home the logic of socialism to fellow members of the Church. A simple method of achieving the first was, in the opinion of some members, to affiliate the League with the Labor Party on the same basis as the I. L. P. or the Fabian Society. But this solution never was adopted; the League preferred independence to borrowed prestige. The step was also less imperative because some of its most prominent members already belonged to the socialist parties. Contact with the labor movement was maintained in other ways. The League for some years employed a paid organizer, and the Rev. Conrad Noel and C. S. Smith, who successively held the

[1] *Commonwealth*, 1927, p. 120; F. G. Bettany, *op. cit.*, p. 92.

office, were well known in labor circles. It was their business not only to gain members for the League but to make it plain that churchmen could be quite as good socialists as were dissenters or atheists. " No priest in the country could claim so wide and intimate a knowledge of the Labour movement," says Mr. Widdrington of Conrad Noel. " In I. L. P. branches and Labour churches his lectures and debates created a deep impression and a friendliness which did much to remove the suspicion in Labour circles that the Church was hostile to the claims of Labour." During the winter of 1907-1908 it was estimated that members of the League addressed at least a thousand socialist meetings.[1]

Another mode of League propaganda directed toward the same objects was the organization of public demonstrations during industrial crises. Thus the Rev. F. L. Donaldson in 1906 led a band of unemployed on a pilgrimage from Leicester to London. Again, during the coal strike of 1912 the League held a public meeting in the Church House at Westminster, after which some five hundred of those present marched in solemn procession to Lambeth bearing a petition to the archbishop of Canterbury.[2]

In otherwise attempting to influence Church opinion, the League proceeded along well-tried lines. Petitions to the bishops, sermons from the pulpit, and addresses to the Church Congress, clerical conferences, and Sunday schools were employed. If earlier manifestoes of the Church such as pronouncements of the Lambeth Conference had been colored by C. S. U. doctrine, later ones showed the hand of the Church Socialist League. Branches sprang up all over England, and for some years the membership steadily increased. By 1909 no less than 35 branches had been established with a total

---

[1] *Commonwealth*, 1922, p. 134; 1927, p. 121; Fabian Tract 87, p. 15.

[2] *Commonwealth*, 1927, p. 219; *Church Socialist*, May, 1912, p. 18.

membership of about 1,200.   In 1911 London, the most powerful center of the League, had 17 groups at work.

The Church Socialist League was characterized by the Rev. Arnold Pinchard (chairman from 1909 to 1912) as " an association of Socialists who are also Churchmen." (The fortuitous combination of interests implied in this statement did not, of course, remain unchallenged.) Within those limits it contained a group of persons better known and representing a more complete cross-section of the intellectual class than any other Church society could boast.   On the roll appeared Mr. George Lansbury and Mr. (now Sir) Henry Slesser, both active in the affairs of the League and later members of the Labor Government, Messrs. R. H. Tawney, A. J. Penty, G. K. and Cecil Chesterton, M. B. Reckitt, and Frances Evelyn Countess of Warwick.   The conduct of the League rested chiefly, however, on its clerical members, among the most valuable in this respect being the Rev. Conrad Noel, Paul Stacy, P. E. T. Widdrington, Paul Bull, G. C. Binyon, and Arnold Pinchard.   It seems that, in contrast with the Christian Social Union, only one member of the League ever attained episcopal rank; the Rev. W. H. Frere became bishop of Truro in 1923.

Dr. Frere for many years previous to his elevation had been Superior of the Community of the Resurrection at Mirfield.   Other personal and intellectual ties bound the League to the Community, as will shortly appear.

The Community had also a social history of its own. Founded by Charles Gore in 1892 it realized his idea of " a community of celibate men, living simply . . . a life of combined labour, according to different gifts, on a strongly developed background of prayer and meditation, and with real community of goods." [1]   The order as a whole never espoused a definite political program, and the members were

[1] *Economic Review*, 1892, p. 159.

free to employ themselves in scholarly or other pursuits. Many of them, under the influence of Dr. Gore, naturally devoted themselves to the social question and often found answers to it at variance with his own. Some joined the Church Socialist League. Mirfield not only had a branch of the League but in course of time gave the League a chairman —Father Paul Bull.

It was at Father Bull's instance that two conferences were held at Mirfield, independent of the League but designed to promote the same ends—intercourse between laymen identified with the labor movement and socially-inclined churchmen. At these gatherings the sharp edge of religious and class prejudice was somewhat blunted by mutual contact and the urbane ministrations of the chairman, Father Frere. Some of the speakers felt called upon to begin their remarks with a proclamation of infidelity. But Father Frere was unruffled. All of us, he assured them, were agnostics at birth and became less so year by year. Between 500 and 600 persons, for the most part delegates from the socialist societies of Lancashire and Yorkshire, attended the second conference in 1907.[1]

The Community of the Resurrection reaches a more impressionable group through its educational work. It maintains a free college for a limited number of boys who lack the means to continue their schooling in the ordinary institutions. Needless to say the social viewpoint of the instructors has not been suppressed. Father Bull manages, he says, to make his pupils " good socialists ", and a number of them have become agents of the Industrial Christian Fellowship—which is not, perhaps, exactly the same thing.[2]

The work of an inmate of Mirfield helped to produce a revolution in the philosophy and consequently the action of

[1] Private information; *Commonwealth*, 1907, p. 184.
[2] Private information.

the Church Socialist League. J. N. Figgis gave up a rich
living to enter the Community of the Resurrection. There
he worked out a pluralistic conception of the State whose
leading ideas have been appropriated by a whole school of
political scientists. " Figgis' importance for Catholic Democrats," wrote the Rev. Paul Stacy,

lies largely in his later works, beginning with " Civilization at
the Cross Roads." . . . In " Churches and the Modern State "
Dr. Figgis has not only helped Catholic Democrats, but has
immensely stimulated even non-Christian Democrats in their
thinking. . . . It is in the very spirit of National Guilds, and
Figgis gave it its finest and clearest expression.[1]

The new orientation of the League was, in short, toward
guild socialism. In 1912 the first number of *The Church
Socialist* appeared, and in the same year the guild movement
" made its formal début." From then on the new organ of
the League was almost as completely devoted to guild
propaganda as *The New Age*. Guild socialism was much
like a gasoline engine: it moved by a series of internal
explosions. The controversies of Messrs. Penty and Reckitt
supplied *The Church Socialist* with enough combustible yet
enlightening material to make any crusade attractive.

The mechanism of the guild state need not detain us here.
The reason why it appealed so powerfully to many Church
Socialists is more to the point. Naturally they laid stress
upon its spiritual and moral value. " The Guild," wrote Mr.
Reckitt, " is indeed the only barrier against economic tyranny,
but it is much more—it is the social unit in which the
average man may hope to recapture something of the joy of
mutual intercourse that once made ' Merrie England '."
Guild socialism also seemed to place a greater value upon the

[1] *Church Socialist*, 1919, p. 196. Dr. Figgis never became a member
of the C. S. L.

individual than either capitalism or collectivism, and Christians were bound to consider not only the virtues of fellowship but the claims of single souls. "Man's real life," said a Church Socialist,

. . . is concerned above all with his labour, his freedom to pursue it in his own way, and to enjoy the fruits of it with the circle of his closest associates whom he terms his family. By means of this circle and the wider circle of his fellow-labourers and friends, he develops his individuality and seeks through it to glorify the God Whom at the altar and beyond he learns to know and serve.

One might exaggerate the communist idea to the detriment of Christian individualism, thought Conrad Noel. "With this *self-dignity in fellowship,* which has been undoubtedly an orthodox Christian principle from the very beginning, there naturally goes a condemnation of the heresies of avarice on the one hand and extreme communism on the other." The Rev. F. L. Donaldson saw the Great State with its co-operating yet autonomous groups as a reflection, in the industrial sphere, of the Catholic Church, whose systems of province, diocese, and parish affirmed " the sacred character and rights of the 'imperia in imperio.' " [1]

With the adoption of guildism, Church Socialists had completed a cycle. In many of its essentials the new gospel was merely producers' co-operation rejuvenated. J. M. Ludlow died in 1911 but Mr. Maurice Reckitt carried on. Not that there was an avowed apostolic succession. Yet Hughes, Maurice, Ludlow, Bishop Westcott, and others had kept alive, against Fabian and Marxian alike, the notion of producers' co-operation, making easier than might have been the case the revival of that idea by the guildsmen. [2] The doctrine

---

[1] *Church Socialist,* August, 1913, p. 13; Feb., p. 14; June, p. 4; *Commonwealth,* 1914, p. 208.

[2] Niles Carpenter, *Guild Socialism,* pp. 24-25, 39.

now involved a theory of the state and looked toward the
complete destruction of capitalism, but the similarities between the old and new movements are more striking than
their differences.   Even the revisions which a friendly critic
of guild socialism considers necessary to its temporal success
were urged in behalf of its ancestor.   Though he does not
mention the fact—is perhaps unaware of it—Mr. Niles Carpenter in suggesting that the co-operative distributors finance
the guilds and act as their marketing agents only repeats
what J. M. Ludlow preached with almost tiresome insistence
at one Co-operative Congress after another.   Mr. Carpenter's
further advice to guildsmen that they abandon political theor-
izing would, if adopted, make them indistinguishable from
co-operators.[1]

Mr. Reckitt himself has no illusions as to the originality
of guild doctrine.   He laments, however, the fatal absence
of logic which hampered earlier efforts.

The establishment of National Guilds involves the abolition of
the wage system, the attainment of self-government in industry,
and the modification of State sovereignty.   There is nothing
novel about these ideas. . . . But there is something novel in
their being accepted as the essential standard by which all social
change is tested.   Doubtless many social reformers of the last
century would have been brought to agree that these ideals were
quite desirable, when reforms had cleared the way for them.
But such a condition was really fatal, since the reforms contemplated did not clear the way for the realization of these
ideals; indeed, they postponed them.[2]

Whether the reforms of the nineteenth and twentieth centuries have merely added a few rivets to the shackles of labor

[1] Carpenter, *op. cit.*, p. 316.

[2] Reckitt and Bechhofer, *The Meaning of National Guilds*, introduction,
p. xii.

is still an open question. The time limit for a revolution has not expired, and piecemeal reforms are perhaps as productive of further discontent as of a slave psychology. Even the Christian Social Union may have had a reason for existence.

It is a striking coincidence that both the early Christian Socialists and the Church Socialists arrived at almost the same destination, though by different roads. What significance attaches to this fact is not entirely clear. Some will conclude that Christian ethics demands a commonwealth of autonomous producers' organizations and that the Church must sooner or later teach guild socialism as a dogma. But before this happens a large number of clergymen must be converted or pass away.

CHAPTER VII

WAR AND RECONSTRUCTION

THE war opened to the Church a prospect of increased usefulness and power. It also brought temporary confusion to the old modes of social thought and action. These, if not repudiated, were in many cases transformed. But war itself is a social phenomenon. We must therefore pause to note how the Church adapted itself to the conflict.

PROBLEMS OF WAR AND PEACE

Before 1914 the Church's attitude toward war was on the whole realistic. " Without denying that there are just wars and that we cannot prevent their recurrence entirely, yet we are convinced that there are other and better ways of settling the quarrels of nations than by fighting." Thus ran the Lambeth encyclical of 1897. Similar views were expressed at the Church Congress of 1900 : war is evil, but righteousness is a higher end than peace. Less caution and unanimity were to be found in the Christian Social Union. During the siege of Ladysmith, Scott Holland preached an anti-war sermon at St. Paul's which (says Mr. Nevinson) " aroused some indignation." But Bishop Westcott, who defended arbitration in industry, denied it to South Africa. " It was impossible," he held, " for us to submit to arbitration the fulfilment of our imperial obligations." Holland also felt that England had a mission. " She cannot shrink up behind her white cliffs, and throw the reins down," he wrote in 1907. ". . . The Home, the seat of the principal authority, must retain its right to speak, to control, to review. . . It is

283

England's charge—to lift these black races to self-control and freedom." [1]

In Parliament the bishops were usually neither warlike, pacific, nor neutral. They merely said nothing. A few exceptions must be noted. In 1902 Bishop Percival criticized the " spectacular executions " in South Africa and refused to vote confidence in the government because he feared it meant pushing the Boers to unconditional surrender. In 1909 he pointed out that the unexampled size of the budget was due not to social legislation but to excessive armaments. Yet like many others he favored universal military training. " I must confess," he said in 1902, " that I have no liking for the stream of tendency which is turning our freedom-loving, industrial nation into a military empire, with the taint of commercial greed in it; but we must have an Army. Let us, then, make it efficient; and to make it efficient we must make it democratic." On the ground of its disciplinary and physical value Bishops Robertson and Kennion supported Lord Roberts's National Service Bill. " The country," said Bishop Williams in 1914 (just before the war) " is in a thoroughly defenceless position; . . . whereas our fathers depended for the defence of the country on God and their own good swords, we are dependent on the forbearance of some Powers and on a fragile, delicate alliance with other Powers." [2] In short, pacifists found the episcopal bench rather hard and uncomfortable.

Discussion in the Church Congress of 1911 was little more encouraging. The arrangements committee had thoughtfully provided a man of straw, Sir R. Hardy, for the occa-

---

[1] *Report of the Lambeth Conference*, 1897, pp. 17-18; *Church Congress*, 1900, pp. 179 *et seq.*; H. W. Nevinson, *op. cit.*, p. 250; Arthur Westcott, *op. cit.*, vol. ii, p. 287; *Commonwealth*, 1907, p. 50.

[2] *Hansard*, 1902, vol. 101, col. 938; vol. 111, col. 487; 1909, vol. i, col. 309; vol. ii, col. 350; vol. iv, col. 1080; 1914, vol. 15, col. 544.

sion. His address was rich in phrases about " war, God's
highest instrument in the development of man's higher qualities," " combativeness, a natural propensity," and great nations " moulded not by inglorious sloth but by deeds that
were golden." This brought the expected reaction. But to
hear speakers dwell upon the manifold incitements to war,
unrighteous though they were, must have led those present
to doubt more than ever the feeble resources of peace. Some
words of friendship were addressed to Germany, and a
former ambassador to Berlin, Sir F. C. Lascelles, was almost
hopeful. No ground of war, he said, existed between England and Germany. " If . . . any means could be found
for persuading people in both countries that they were not
in danger of being attacked, I think a great step would be
taken towards the maintenance of peace." [1] Speakers at the
Congress of 1913 laid more stress on the need of cultivating
the factors of international comity. England and Germany,
said Mr. M. J. Rendall, are united by a common religious and
historic tradition, yet they are " spurring themselves to a war
which they almost regard as inevitable." Canon W. L.
Crane gibed at " our faked invasions and idiotic Dreadnought
competitions." [2] Next year the Congress did not meet; war
had passed beyond the realm of conversation.

Officially the Church fell quickly into line when war was
declared. A statement of the archbishop of Canterbury probably represents the feeling of both Convocations:

I imagine that there is not one of us who entertains any doubt
of this, that our nation could not, without sacrificing principles
of honour and justice more dear than life itself, have stood and
looked idly on. Fearful, devilish, calamitous as a great war
must be, there would be something, there is something, yet

[1] *Church Congress*, 1911, pp. 180 *et seq.*

[2] *Ibid.*, 1913, pp. 194 *et seq.*

worse. To stand selfishly idle while vile wrong is perpetrated in a matter wherein we are concerned would, if I may use the phrase, debase the moral currency of a people more, far more, than to join in warfare, terrible as it is, for rolling the wrong back.

The bishop of London's fortitude was boundless and perhaps unique. "Death," he said, "was still looked upon as a great calamity, even by many Christian people. They sang beautiful hymns " about it,

but his experience was that that was not really thoroughly believed by Church people, and perhaps they themselves needed to have a firmer grip of it. They needed a brighter view of death as the mourners poured into their rooms.[1]

In the Christian Social Union there was a disposition to take a more mundane view of the war and its causes. The president (Bishop Kempthorne), it is true, believed it to be "ultimately a war of ideals;" but it came of "selfishness and forgetfulness of God." For Scott Holland the invasion of Belgium was decisive. Yet from his analysis of the catastrophe he might with equal reason have become a conscientious objector. Generally speaking, members of the Union seem to have accepted the war as a vile necessity from which, possibly, some good might spring.[2]

It is impossible to generalize about opinions in the Church Socialist League. Two discussions of the Executive early in 1915 exhibited "a strong cleavage of opinion and it was found impossible to issue an agreed statement of the causes and merits of the war." [3] Socialism everywhere displayed

---

[1] *Convocation of Canterbury*, 1915, p. 4.

[2] *Letter from the President* (pamphlet), 1914; *Commonwealth*, 1914, p. 257; for other expressions on the war see *ibid.*, p. 282 and *Economic Review*, 1914, pp. 361-2.

[3] *Church Socialist*, 1915, p. 62.

a strong nationalistic bias and a certain group within the Church Socialist League was not peculiar in this respect. The consecrated fervor of the bishop of London paled before that of Mr. Egerton Swann. He flew off into regions of ecstatic fury whither it is unnecessary to follow.[1] According to Mr. Maurice Reckitt the aspirations of small nations could only be realized by a victory of the allies. Besides, the trade-union movement in England was more constructive than elsewhere—it must continue unhampered the struggle against the wage system. "The English Trade Unions," wrote Mr. Reckitt, ". . . are the hope of the world. English industrial effort and English democratic aspirations are worth preserving, and who can doubt that they would lose by a victory of Germany and her militarist ideals?"[2] Poles removed from Messrs. Swann and Reckitt stood another group, pacifists to the core. An article in *The Church Socialist,* bearing the initials S. P. and entitled "Murder in the Thieves Kitchen", is a counterpiece to Mr. Swann's tirade.[3] Mary Phelps, later editor of *The Church Socialist,* was no less resolute:

I am unmoved in my conviction that killing is sinful and war altogether forbidden to Christian people. It would have been madness on the part of the English government to choose any war cry but such as would attract the enthusiasm and gallantry of the people. . . . Had Belgium been less like the vestibule to our own land, the plea would have sounded more disinterested. But the war has been a certainty for years, the question of entering upon it did not come up afresh for decision a few weeks ago. We in company with other nations have been preparing for it long enough.[4]

[1] *Church Socialist,* 1914, p. 195.
[2] *Ibid.,* 1915, pp. 6 *et seq.*
[3] *Ibid.,* 1914, p. 197.
[4] *Ibid.,* 1914, p. 212.

Eventually the Church Socialist League possessed a new branch. "Dartmoor Prison Branch," wrote Mr. Charles Record, its honorary secretary, "was formed in May last [1917], and consists entirely of men who have been court-martialled and imprisoned—and in one case sentenced to death in France—for refusing military service on pacifist and anti-militarist principles."[1] Between these extremes stood a group who neither apologized for the war nor turned their backs upon it. Deplorable as it was, the war had created an emotional disturbance which, they believed, might be turned to the profit of social reconstruction.[2]

After all, dissent in war time is usually futile and, if the government is wise, impossible. To the clergy still remained their ancient duty of mitigating a conflict they had done little to prevent. The whole religious organization at the front can only be noticed here. At home the rôle of the clergy was less highly wrought but quite as important. In Parliament several of the bishops helped to keep alive a spark of reason and humanity. The question of conscientious objectors was a delicate one, but the archbishop of Canterbury, Bishop Talbot, and Bishop Gore often spoke in favor of greater leniency.[3] Archbishop Davidson pelted the government with questions as to the exchange of civilian prisoners. Internment, he said, meant intolerable hardship for the older men in Germany and "in not a few cases in this country."[4] He also rigidly opposed a policy of military reprisals and was supported in this attitude by the Canterbury Houses of Bishops and Laymen.[5]

[1] *Church Socialist*, 1917, p. 239.

[2] *Ibid.*, 1914, p. 188, the opinion of Rev. F. L. Donaldson.

[3] *Hansard*, 1916, vol. 21, col. 904, 922; vol. 22, cols. 488, 538, 722; 1917, vol. 25, col. 330; vol. 26, col. 1000; 1919, vol. 34, col. 69.

[4] *Ibid.*, 1916, vol. 23, cols. 493, 1085; vol. 24, cols. 227, 639; vol. 29, col. 334; vol. 30, col. 1108; vol. 31, col. 726, vol. 33, col. 880.

[5] *Ibid.*, 1916, vol. 24, col. 1013; *Guardian*, 12 July, 1917, p. 538.

Activities of this sort naturally raised some doubts in the minds of super-nationalists as to the bishops' patriotism. The earl of Denbigh placed " ex-ministers of the crown, ex-Lord Chancellors, . . . members of the episcopal bench" in the same category. The insinuation was baseless: that Lord Curzon defended the bishops is ample proof.[1] But the archbishop of Canterbury time and again made it abundantly clear that the clergy knew their obligations. "It has been suggested," he said, speaking on a military service bill in 1916,

. . . that we Bishops and others who further this want the clergy to evade the obligation of bearing their part and doing their share in this mighty effort to roll back a great wrong and to establish what is right. . . . The nation has, I believe, recognized to the full that there is something other than physical force required for the successful conduct of this war—moral earnestness in our corporate life, deliberate self-denial and self-discipline in our homes, quiet and buoyant courage in hours of distress, anxiety and sorrow.

It was the function of the clergy, he said, to strengthen these qualities in the people.[2] The archbishop also had nothing but praise for the progress that had been made during the past twenty years in teaching patriotism in the schools. If this advance was doubted,

let any one read the circulars which have been issued by the Director of Education . . . year after year . . . giving guidance and direction how to teach patriotism, what should be the meaning of Empire Day, how our Empire came to be what it is, and instructing them [the teachers] to give this information through geography, through history, through other various lessons which lead up to the character basis on which it is desired to build.

[1] *Hansard*, 1918, vol. 29, cols. 1013, 1046.

[2] *Ibid.*, 1916, vol. 20, col. 1038; also *cf. ibid.*, 1918, vol. 29, col. 725.

He referred with approval to the patriotic observances in American schools. Nor did he anticipate any undesirable consequences:

The idea . . . that this movement was essentially the teaching of a militarism which must be mischievous has, I believe, been merged in the larger thought of a patriotism which hardly anybody will call mischievous. . . . That patriotism and militarism do not mean the same thing is now so clear to everybody that it is unnecessary to say anything about it.[1]

Pacifists might denounce the war as wholly evil, but many churchmen expected great things of it. Now, if ever, schemes of reconstruction might be put forward with some prospect of success. The British public lived for the moment in an atmosphere of heroism; it had become callous to change. The old land-marks of individualism were fast being submerged under defence of the realm acts and an empirical, but very thoroughgoing, state socialism. Would their classic outlines ever reappear? Portents of a domestic cataclysm loomed on every side. Peace might prove to be a more tremendous adventure than even war. To forestall a débâcle while time remained was no less politic than humane.

On three occasions Archbishop Lang uttered pointed warnings in the House of Lords.[2]

It seems to me [he said in 1917] that what is surprising is not that there is so much disquieting unrest . . . but that there is so little. . . . It is only what would be expected, that men to whom the country had given a goodly heritage, of advantage and education, should have been ready to come to her aid in time of need; but what perhaps could hardly have been expected is that vast numbers of men to whom this country had

[1] *Hansard*, 1915, vol. 20, col. 426; 1916, vol. 21, col. 613.

[2] *Ibid.*, 1917, vol. 26, col. 914 *et seq.*; 1918, vol. 31, col. 1146; 1919, vol. 33, col. 307.

given apparently nothing but an obscure place in a vast industrial machine and an over-crowded house in some slum or
grimy street should have been at the outbreak of the war among
the first to come forward to the help of the country to which
they apparently owed so little.

Again in 1919:

It is not enough for us at the present time to analyze the causes
of unrest and disturbance, or to remedy isolated grievances,
but to recognize plainly, frankly, and courageously that the
time has come when we must prepare the way for the introduction of a new spirit and system into industry as a whole.
. . . The utmost possible good-will . . . between masters and
men does not in the least blunt the determination of the men
to do what they can to change a system which is quite independent of the kindlier personal relations.

There must be joint control in industry; Whitley councils
were only a step in the right direction.

I share the hope that there might be evolved from them . . .
a League, a permanent Industrial Council, representing the
employers, the workers, and the government of the country.
. . . While the employer must keep ultimately his right to lock
out and the worker retain his right to strike, for you cannot
deprive free men, compulsorily, of the right to withhold their
work or labour as they please, I hope that there will be less
and less recourse to force before there has been an appeal to
a permanent and abiding tribunal. . . .

Revealing discussions took place in the Convocation of
Canterbury during 1917 and 1918. Bishops Woods and
Kempthorne—both members of the Christian Social Union
—called upon the Church to raise the standard of revolt.
" They did not exist as a Church," said Woods, " merely to
express mild hopes that some day there would be some im-

provement, but to announce authoritatively the plan of God."
He did not give the economic details of this plan except to
intimate that it involved an " Industrial Peace Conference "
representing capital and labor, a certain measure of nationalization, and the limitation of profits.   He also glanced
favorably at guild socialism.   Bishop Kempthorne was more
specific and intrepid.   The " first lines of advance " which
he advocated would in themselves have constituted a transformation of industry, but he went on, quoting Bishop Westcott, to predict the disappearance of the whole wage system.
" It was well," he concluded,

to recognize that they needed a revolution, a radical change in
their way of thinking if they were to avoid the revolution which
meant civil war.   They belonged to that Divine Society whose
leaders were once described as those who had turned the world
upside down.   The Church should be more militant than the
Prussian, and more revolutionary than the revolutionist.[1]

The composure with which these subversive opinions were
received is as striking as Bishop Kempthorne's radicalism.
Many bishops spoke but only two protested.   One was the
bishop of Exeter, Lord Rupert Cecil, and the other, as might
have been expected, the bishop of Hereford, Dr. Hensley
Henson.   The latter defends an economic creed which is now
almost extinct in episcopal circles.   But more than one of
his hearers must have felt their emotions congeal as he
coolly surveyed the economic obstacles to reform, for Bishop
Henson is exceedingly wise in his generation.   He agreed
that they must make large concessions to the spirit of the
age.   But there was a tendency to applaud grandiose projects of social reform without much thought of the expense
involved.   A great part of the money must come from

[1] *Convocation of Canterbury*, 1917, pp. 192 *et seq.*; 1918, pp. 215 *et seq.*,
265-68.

foreign trade, but would competing nations accept a British definition of the Christian law? Then, striking home, he asked whether the clergy expected to apply the new morality to themselves.

They . . . represented a Church which was endowed with the two kinds of property against which mainly the conscience of the community was being actively directed. The tithes represented a form of rent. The great accumulations of property which the Ecclesiastical Commissioners administered represented types of property which were most invidious at that moment. Of course it was obvious that if there were intrinsic wrongfulness in that kind of property, *cadit quaestio*, at all hazards they must repudiate it entirely. But he did not wish them to forget that they themselves held types of property which did not leave them free to discuss quite as freely as some of them would like to do the questions which the Bishop had raised. He apprehended they were committed as a Church to the principle of private property.[1]

His objections remained unanswered.

Similar discussions took place in the Lower House. There, however, the pleas of Canon Garbett and the Rev. William Temple (now archbishop of York) met with a comparatively cool reception. Dean Inge more than adequately took the place of Bishop Henson. But either the silent majority was favorably disposed or the opposition did not care to commit itself too deeply, for a resolution was passed, 49 to 2, urging churchpeople to support the minimum wage, unemployment relief, and " recognition of the status of workers in the in-industries in which they are engaged." [2]

Obviously the southern Convocation was progressing— at least from the viewpoint of reformers. There was a disposition to grapple with fundamental economic questions and

---

[1] *Convocation of Canterbury*, 1918, p. 271.

[2] *Ibid.*, 1918, p. 361.

an amount of plain speaking on both sides which clearly revealed the sincerity of the protagonists. Bishop Woods was convinced that an advance had taken place in the Church as a whole. " Sentiments were openly applauded now in Church gatherings," he said, "at which five years ago they would have held up their hands in horror." [1] At the same time the result is somewhat meager if conversation, no matter how animated, leads only to a resolution buried in the records of a church assembly. What was wanted was at least a thoroughgoing, well-advertised program of reconstruction.

Such a plan was formulated by the Labor Party in 1918. The London Branch of the Christian Social Union hastened to evaluate it. With the principle of a national minimum wage the Branch found itself in hearty agreement. It doubted, however, whether labor could yet dispense with the employer, and looked to the Whitley councils to supply a means of democratic control. As to the conscription of wealth, there were "practical difficulties involved in the transfer to the State of a great mass of unrealisable securities." The utilization of surplus wealth for the common good, on the other hand, was an essentially Christian principle. Incomes, however, ought not to be taxed down to a subsistence level—it would endanger the nation's productive power, which depended on capital accumulated through saving. The nationalization of basic industries—" subject to the adequate compensation of all legitimate interests "—was approved. State control in the interest of the community would suffice for other industries unless efficiency could be promoted by nationalization. Certain proposed items of social legislation were welcomed, but " we desire to add a word of warning against the tendency to regard the State as a kind of universal provider. The voluntary organizations that the workers have built up for their own protection

---

[1] *Convocation of Canterbury*, 1918, p. 222.

have had a great social and educational value, and we fear that a vast extension of State action might lead to a loss of initiative and even self-respect among the workers." On the whole, " while we are not prepared to assent to all the suggestions of the Report we recognize the moral idealism that underlies its proposals, and we believe that men of all political parties might give a general support to the scheme of reconstruction outlined in it." [1] Thus the London Branch accepted with not too serious qualifications a left-wing manifesto of the labor movement.

The Church for the past two years had been incubating a program of its own. Early in 1916 a National Mission of Repentance and Hope was initiated by the two archbishops for the purpose of stimulating and directing the emotional forces generated by the war. Retreats for the clergy, Pilgrimages of Prayer, Quiet Days, served the needs of worship. Welfare work and mass meetings for the discussion of social questions emphasized the material concerns of religion. After the Mission had been in operation for a year there was much inconclusive discussion as to whether it had been a success.[2] Those who expected a reformation or even a renaissance were perhaps bound to be disappointed. Others might well have been satisfied with the Mission's literary results alone. Five committees were appointed to draw up reports on various problems confronting the Church.[3] The Fifth Committee dealt with " Christianity and Industrial Problems " and included a majority of laymen. Among those who served were Bishops Talbot (chairman), Gore, Kempthorne, and Woods, Miss Constance Smith, and Messrs. W. C. Bridgeman (later First Lord of the Admiralty),

[1] *C. S. U. Papers*, no. 4, London Branch.

[2] *Convocation of York*, 1916, p. 95; 1917, pp. 10 *et seq.*

[3] On the Teaching Office, Worship, Evangelistic Work, Reform of the Church, Industrial Problems.

Albert Mansbridge, R. H. Tawney, and George Lansbury.[1] Their Report appeared in 1918.

The volume (it was nothing less) must take rank as the most comprehensive statement that had yet appeared under the auspices—though not the official sanction—of the Church. Besides a thorough exposition of Christian principles it contained an extraordinary number of particular applications. The Committee, said the chairman, " have strongly felt their duty in a time like this, to err on the side of too much rather than too little practical suggestion." [2]   The Report was also comprehensive in the sense that it attempted a harmony of the gospels—of socialism and of benevolent individualism— for the committee represented many shades of opinion. Thus, the Church must proclaim principles " which are always pressing, by the force that is in them, for fuller embodiment and application ", .e g., " for more complete equality, both of opportunity and consideration ", and at the same time such as " make any social arrangement, *while it lasts,* work humanely, and as fairly and respectfully to each human being concerned as its limitations will allow."   We have met these principles before—the sanctity of personality, the duty of service expressed in co-operation rather than in competition, the stewardship of wealth.

By these standards the present system was held to be " gravely defective ", but the large changes necessary must be carried out in a spirit of tolerance. Adequate leisure for the workingman and a living wage, the first charge on industry, were essential.   Unemployment must be eliminated or its burdens distributed by proper organization.   This might be achieved by a system of dual occupations (work in the factory supplemented by work on the land) ; the concentration of public purchases in times of business inactivity,

---

[1] There were twenty-eight members in all.
[2] P. x.

and the maintenance of labor in slack periods out of the accumulations of prosperity. While capital should receive a fair return, there must be full publicity of profits, and no one should receive an income who rendered no public service. The government of industry presented greater difficulties. The Committee differed as to whether questions of policy and organization should be decided by the employer alone or increasingly devolved upon the organized workers. All agreed that it was immediately possible to associate workers with the management for the discussion of " matters affecting their [the workers'] livelihood and comfort, and the welfare of the business, such as the fixing and alteration of piece-rates ", etc. This, of course, was strongly suggestive of the Whitley scheme.

Other sections of the Report dealt with housing, education, and the safe-guarding of women in industry. " The aim of education," it declared, " must be not merely to offer special opportunities to those who are specially gifted, but to provide for all members of the community the education needed to develop their personality and to fit them for social life, irrespective of their social class, income, or occupation." Full-time attendance at school should ultimately be extended to the age of sixteen and continued by compulsory part-time attendance to eighteen.

The Report also suggested ways of increasing the efficiency of the clergy. Candidates for the ministry ought to be drawn from every class, and better opportunities afforded to working-class boys particularly. The clergy should receive some training in economics and sociology, though in practice many matters requiring expert treatment had better be left to the laity—" it is, for example, only in rare instances that the clergy can successfully act as mediators in trade disputes." The parish priest was often over-burdened with administrative duties. Some of these could be devolved upon the laity, to afford him more time for prayer and thought.

The Report aroused mixed emotions among churchpeople. Bishop Headlam in a sermon before Cambridge University criticized the " crude and half-thought-out " economic ideas of the Report and professed to regard it as " one of the most harmful documents which have been issued in the name of Christianity since the days, perhaps, when the Stuart divines taught the divine right of kings." [1] Mr. George Lansbury was a skeptic of a different hue. " We struggled for months about formulas," he writes, describing the work of his committee.

Nobody denied capitalism and landlordism were of the devil, but all, except Tawney, jibbed at Socialism. So we compromised by declaring the first charge on industry was the decent, adequate maintenance of the workers and their dependents. Events have proved that this is unattainable within the capitalist system. [2]

On the other hand the Lower House of York Convocation recommended the Report to the attention of masters and men, [3] and the Church Socialist League adopted it, with reservations, as a basis of propaganda. More significant still was the cautious approval bestowed upon it by the Lambeth Conference of 1920. A committee of this body emitted a report on " The Church and Industrial Problems ", and announced themselves to be substantially in agreement with the Report of 1918—" they would, however, desire to emphasize the fact that while individual groups within the Church may rightly advocate some specific programme or policy, the Church should never, as a Body, concern itself with a political issue unless it involves a clear moral issue." [4]

[1] *Guardian*, 6 Feb., 1919.
[2] George Lansbury, *My Life*, p. 221.
[3] *Convocation of York*, 1919, pp. 50 *et seq.*
[4] *Conference of Bishops of the Anglican Communion*, 1920, p. 67.

THE REFORM SOCIETIES AFTER 1914

Although members of the Church Socialist League were finding it difficult to agree upon any concerted action of their own, they at once accepted the challenge of the National Mission. *The Church Socialist* printed articles dealing with the Mission and a Message was drawn up, some 1,500 copies of which were distributed among the clergy. The League postponed further action until the publication of *Christianity and Industrial Problems* in 1918. Though the League had been represented on the committee charged with framing that document, it was not entirely satisfied with the result. The annual conference of 1918 declared itself opposed to any plan of reconstruction based on capitalism and the maintenance of the wage system. The conclusions of the Report left room for both. Mr. Widdrington, chairman of the League, dismissed them as " utterly inadequate " and " such as might be drawn up by any body of worthy progressives." The remainder of the Report, however, gave them " an admirable instrument of propaganda." [1]

At that juncture, not propaganda, but the fate of their own society, engrossed the members of the League. Controversies rising out of the war and the Russion revolution had disturbed the none too peaceful currents of the society. The membership in 1923 was only a quarter of its former strength. This no doubt partly reflected a decline in interest on the part of the branches which had been evident since a paid organizer ceased to be employed.

But a fundamental divergence of opinion had been present from the very beginning. It gradually assumed the form of a dispute as to the exact relationship between the political activities and the religious principles of the League. The connection between the two was of course assumed, but at least until 1912 there was little to distinguish the propaganda

---

[1] *Church Socialist*, 1917, p. 118; Dec., 1918-Jan., 1919, p. 148.

of the League from that of the labor movement. The question arose whether members of the League were merely Christians *and* Socialists or Christians and *hence* Socialists. Was current Socialism really an epitome of Christian teaching? To many members it appeared that the Church had something distinctive to contribute toward the regeneration of society—something which was not expressed completely or perhaps at all in the philosophy of the labor movement. That fact ought to be made more evident in the League's propaganda.[1] Guild socialism seemed to be a step in the right direction. " It removed some of the stumbling blocks which Collectivist Socialism presented to many sincere democrats," says Mr. Widdrington. " It placed a welcome emphasis on personality, and asserted the right to initiative and control as belonging to the ordinary man. Its philosophy was distinctively Christian."[2]

Numerous attempts were made to revise the League's Basis in accordance with these ideas, but they resulted in compromises which satisfied no one. Meanwhile individual members undertook to lay the basis for a new Christian Sociology. In 1922 a volume of essays called *The Return of Christendom* appeared. The contributors were Messrs. Reckitt, Slesser, Widdrington, A. J. Carlyle, Penty, Niles Carpenter, and Paul Bull, and the book was furnished with an introduction by Bishop Gore and an epilogue by Mr. G. K. Chesterton. The main point stressed was the need of restoring the authority of Catholic dogma. The prevalent order was the fruit of a false philosophy and with the possible exception of guildism no existing scheme could harmonize or, better, synthesize the spiritual and material needs of human nature. The Church, said Father Bull, should claim absolute dominion over the whole life of man; " dogma, discipline,

[1] *Church Socialist*, 1914, p. 242.
[2] *Commonwealth*, 1927, p. 221.

and devotion" were the counterparts of "faith, freedom, and fellowship".

The two parties in the League were rapidly becoming irreconcilable. After a warm but inconclusive discussion at the Birmingham conference in 1916 the first important schism occurred when the Rev. Conrad Noel withdrew from the League. In 1918 he organized the Catholic Crusade. Its aims revealed in part at least his reasons for withdrawal:

To create the demand for the Catholic Faith, the whole Catholic Faith, and nothing but the Catholic Faith. To encourage the rising of the people in the might of the risen Christ and the Saints, mingling heaven and earth that we may shatter this greedy world to bits, and remould it to the heart's desire. To demand that portion of common with personal ownership as shall encourage our self-expression as free people in fellowship. To fight the soul saving gang and their glory-for-me religion.[1]

By 1923 the apologists of the old Basis were no longer strong enough to avert a crisis even by compromise. The Rev. Claude Stuart Smith, a founder and early organizer of the League, made one last appeal. The times, he said, were critical for Socialism and Labor. " It is not at such a time that we can desert our allies. We propose, therefore, that we should take the step of applying for affiliation to the Labour Party." He considered the new Christian Sociology both too vague and too tolerant. It was also too closely identified with Anglo-Catholicism. "What of those who cannot toe the Anglo-Catholic line? To confine the Society to Anglo-Catholics is to narrow its scope most seriously and to invite the repetition of the Guild of St. Matthew." [2]

The Church Socialist League was easier to kill than to

[1] These are the objects only in part. *Church Socialist*, 1918, p. 108.

[2] *Commonwealth*, 1923, p. 154.

reform.   At the Birmingham conference of 1923 (May 22 and 23) it was quietly laid to rest and a new society formed out of the old membership.   Those who mourned its passing raised no objection; having foreseen the inevitable they simply remained aloof.[1]   The " League of the Kingdom of God ", as the new body called itself, therefore began life with a somewhat contracted membership.   In 1927, groups were reported at work in Birmingham, Cardiff, Coventry, Leeds, Leicester, Manchester, Liverpool, and London.   There were also centers of influence at Kelham, Mirfield, and Lincoln Theological College.[2]   *The Christian Socialist* had been discontinued in 1921.   *The Commonwealth,* formerly the organ of the Christian Social Union, then became the medium of the Church Socialist League.   It now represents the League of the Kingdom of God.

The Basis of the new League was Catholic and anti-capitalist; within those limits its socialism was undogmatic.

The League [it stated] is a band of Churchmen and Church-women who believe that the Catholic Faith demands a challenge to the world by the repudiation of capitalist plutocracy and the wage system, and stands for a social order in which means of life subserve the Commonweal.   The League, insisting on the Faith as the Church's primary aim and care, and as the only satisfactory basis of life for all people, declares its devotion to the liberation of the poor and oppressed as a cause specially dear to God.   The League believes that a holy, just, and free society—Christendom—will come first and chiefly through faith and thought and sacramental power—personal loyalty to Christ and His cause—and that it must express itself in jealous endeavours after fellowship in industry, commerce, citizenship and culture.

[1] *Commonwealth*, 1923, p. 178.   Some members of the old school joined the new League.   Rev. T. C. Gobat, its first chairman, and Mr. George Lansbury were of the number.

[2] *Commonwealth*, 1927, p. 317; 1928, p. 30.

The " objects " of the League are:

1. The insistence on the prophetic Office of the Church and the Kingdom of God as the regulative principle of theology.   2. The awakening of Churchmen to the lost social traditions of Christendom and the recreation of a Christian sociology consonant with the needs of the age.   3. The restoration of the Eucharist as the central act of Christian values.   4. The recognition and enforcement of the Church's social discipline over her own members.   5. The winning of those indifferent or hostile to the Catholic Faith while standing for justice in the common life, and those within the Church who resist the Christian ordering of society.   6. Co-operation with other bodies, religious or secular, on occasions when fundamental issues of social righteousness are at stake.

In contrast with the Church Socialist League, the new society has spent more effort in indoctrinating the Church than in direct political agitation.   And since its spiritual home is in the Anglo-Catholic movement, the latter has been its first object of conquest and also—as this progresses—its vehicle of propaganda.   None too gently Mr. Widdrington flicked his brother Catholics.   " For years past," he wrote in 1920,

Anglo-Catholicism has been " gloriously aloof from the dead present ".   Here and there individual priests have interested themselves in the Labour Movement, but the party as a party has given no lead in social matters.   It has lagged behind even the Roman Catholics in this country. . . . It is not surprising that it cannot claim a single Labour M. P. amongst its members.

He took it as a good omen that the first Anglo-Catholic Congress announced " The Church and Labour " as a topic of discussion.[1]   In 1925 the idea was carried still further.   A joint committee of delegates from the L. K. G., the Anglo-

[1] *Church Socialist*, 1920, p. 15.

Catholic Congress, the Fellowship of Catholic Priests and the English Church Union sanctioned the establishment of an annual summer-school. (The Church Socialist League had also conducted such a school for several years before its dissolution.) The Summer School of Sociology, held at Keble College, Oxford, has therefore become a permanent feature of the Anglo-Catholic movement and of course is largely under the direction of L. K. G. members.[1]

The Summer School, says Mr. Widdrington, has done more to place before Catholics the general principle that Christianity involves social obligations than the Church Socialist League did throughout its whole existence. The authoritative Christian sociology is as yet unformulated however. One gathers that it will remain so until a larger section of the Church is convinced of its necessity. Intimations of its character may be gleaned from discussions in the Summer School and from writings of members of the League. All unite in repudiating the existing capitalistic order. In his annual address as chairman of the League in 1928 Mr. Reckitt observed that not only orthodox socialism but all varieties of distributivist doctrine are equally

incompatible with the monopoly, centralised initiative, and widespread underconsumption that are the characteristic features of contemporary capitalism. But . . . I would urge that what is needed to-day is less a whole-hearted idolatry of any of them than a single-minded and sustained effort at discrimination . . . with the object of hammering out a synthesis that shall be sufficient to the complex needs and opportunities of to-day. For it is a melancholy characteristic of most programmes of reform to be a quarter of a century too late, and to be contending vigorously· upon battlefields from which the enemy has already disappeared.[2]

[1] *Commonwealth*, 1925, p. 229; 1927, p. 317.
[2] *Ibid.*, 1928, p. 107.

Discussions in the Summer School of 1927 were favorable to guild socialism. One study circle concluded that the wage system was unjust chiefly because it prevented free choice of employment and that a bare living should be assured every one regardless of his contribution to society. Another decided that the distributivist ideal was valid, but that to be in harmony with the corporate idea of Catholicism, distributivism must be co-operative: " This would require some system of guilds." [1] A cynic might conclude that the " old gang " were taking advantage of innocent fellow-Catholics, for confirmed guild socialists led the discussions. On the other hand it is possible that Christian principles actually demand a revival of the guild.

While the Church Socialist League was being partially reincarnated in the League of the Kingdom of God, a similar fate had already overtaken the Christian Social Union. The activities of the Union were of course badly crippled by the war. Annual study-topics continued to be given out, but in 1916 the Research Committee was compelled to suspend operations. The publication of pamphlets also ceased due to a lack of competent writers, and an attenuated *Gazette* issued quarterly and then at longer intervals testified to the waning vitality of the society. Instead of disbanding the Union, however, it was decided to merge it in a stronger organization. " The Navvy Mission [founded in 1877] was an old-fashioned evangelistic society of the familar type," writes Father James Adderley.

. . . [But] the " hot gospel " had become chilly. The navvy and the working man generally if they were to have use for religion must find it guiding their everyday social aspirations and providing them with a rule for everyday life. . . . This was the gospel of the C. S. U., but it had never succeeded in holding the working man, or, for that matter, the business man either.

[1] *Commonwealth*, 1927, pp. 269 *et seq.*

What could be better than to amalgamate the Navvy Mission, on the lookout for a social gospel and the C. S. U., in despair about capturing the men.

Early in 1920, therefore, the Union and the Mission combined to form the " Industrial Christian Fellowship ". Not all the members of the Union followed "the ' goodwill ', a small library of books, office furniture, and many unsold pamphlets " into the fold of the Fellowship. Some of the groups continued to work along the old lines. But the Union disappeared as a separate entity.[1]

The Industrial Christian Fellowship has won a varied following. It is more catholic even than the Christian Social Union in this respect. Thus the three archbishops are its presidents, while many members of the L. K. G. have places on the Executive Committee and the Council.[2] The explanation of this ability to draw support from many quarters seems to be that the Fellowship proclaims no fixed economic theories which might alarm the more diffident, and at the same time has a more direct contact with the rank and file of labor than any other Church movement since early Christian Socialism. The latter point is perhaps what chiefly attracts members of the L. K. G. The Fellowship works for such limited objects as improved housing, etc., but it does not ignore the possibility of a fundamental reorganization of society, and by means of study circles, lectures, correspondence courses, and publications (including a monthly magazine, *The Torch*) seeks to spread information concerning theories of reform. It holds that such proposals must conform with Christian ideas. In a word, the Fellowship stands for brotherhood in industry and believes that a large measure

[1] *The C. S. U. Gazette*, April, 1916, p. 7; C. S. U., *Annual Report*, 1917; Industrial Christian Fellowship, *The History of a Remarkable Year, 1920-1921*, p. 5; *Commonwealth*, 1927, p. 46.

[2] *I. C. F. Report*, 1925-6.

of it can be attained within the present order. It declares, moreover, that Christianity is at once the supreme expression of brotherhood and a necessary part of the personal experience of the individual. Thus no social order can be perfect unless it is also Christian. The propaganda of the Fellowship is therefore frequently couched in language which strongly recalls the society's semi-evangelistic origin. A great deal of attention is given to combating secularism.

The work of the Fellowship is carried on mainly by paid field-workers, both clerical and lay. " Clerical directors " travel about given areas preaching in churches, addressing workmen and employers, speaking before clerical conferences, chambers of commerce and rotary clubs, social gatherings, schools and colleges. They also visit the resident lay agents, secure openings for them, and raise funds. Contributions amounted to over £19,000 in 1925-1926 and to almost £15,-000 in 1927-1928. The Fellowship has recently (8 March, 1929) lost its most successful and best-known speaker. The late Rev. G. A. Studdert Kennedy attained popularity for his work at the front and won a nick-name which survived the war for his energy in distributing cigarettes. " If the C. S. U. was Holland in action," wrote Father Adderley, "the I. C. F. was and is Studdert Kennedy, or 'Woodbine Willie ', on the war path. . . The I. C. F. has been fortunate in getting the most popular preacher of the day to be its mouthpiece." [1]

The use of lay agents is the most interesting feature of the I.C.F. The agents are all former workingmen (in one or two instances, women) who have been given a course of training in social subjects and then sent to represent the Fellowship in various industrial centers throughout the country. In halls, in factories (if the employer is willing), and at open-air meetings wherever workmen gather they preach the

[1] *Commonwealth*, 1927, p. 46.

doctrines of the Fellowship and encourage questions and discussion. Very often they set up a pulpit in some public place where it is necessary to compete with quack doctors, missioners, and political saviors for the attention of a volatile and not too polite audience. The agents also visit the sick and perform other friendly offices for those who call upon them.

I. C. F. workers have co-operated with the local clergy in conducting numerous " crusades ". The crusade was first used by Bishop Hough at Woolwich in 1919 and is an intensive effort to arouse the interest of the public and promote the work of the Church. An elaborate syllabus and program are prepared beforehand and all parishes of the town or rural district are expected to take part. The crusade usually lasts two weeks, being opened with a demonstration and procession of the churches. Outside speakers are called in and several open-air mass-meetings are held daily. The crusade in some respects resembles a mission, but it attempts to convey more than a spiritual message. " A crusade," says Bishop Hough, " is rather an effort to break down barriers; to induce those who are outside Church organization, but not necessarily antagonistic to religion, to hear the way in which Christianity may bring light to bear on the complex problems of to-day. In this way it may be possible to remove prejudices, and make those who hear willing to learn more at a later stage."

The total influence of the I. C. F. is of course impossible to measure. In 1925 its agents spoke to perhaps a million or more workingmen. Since industrial conciliation is a primary object of the Fellowship one of the main duties of the clerical directors has been to act as intermediaries when disputes arise. The Fellowship had an opportunity to demonstrate its effectiveness in this respect in 1926 during the so-called general strike and the coal lock-out. That it fulfilled the expectations of its friends was largely due to the energy of the General Director, the Rev. P. T. R. Kirk. The activity of Archbishop Davidson and Bishop Kempthorne during the crisis also reflected credit on the Fellowship: both were officers of the society. These matters will be spoken of at length later on.[1]

One other Church body concerned with social problems remains to be mentioned: the Social and Industrial Commission of the National Assembly. In 1920 a " National Assembly of the Church of England " was constituted by act of Parliament. It replaced the Representative Church Council and like that body is composed of the members of both convocations and of elected representatives of the laity. The National Assembly in 1923 appointed a Social and Industrial Committee which it enlarged into a Commission in 1924. The Commission acts as a connecting link between many of the social, welfare, and missionary societies of the Church, being represented by delegates in the I. C. F., the Church Tutorial Classes, the Church of England Missionary Society, and others. It has also issued several reports, for the information of the National Assembly, on emigration, the problems of young people, and housing, and circulated a questionnaire on the social effects of betting and gambling. Lord Hugh Cecil and others opposed the establishment of the Commission on the ground that the sole business of the Assembly was Church legislation and finance, and this attitude continued to act as a drag on the effectiveness of the Commission. After three years of the Commission the honorary secretary, Sir Wyndham Deedes (head of Oxford House), was of opinion that its usefulness was lessened by the shortness and inconvenience of its sessions. He believed further that the Commission should be more used as a means

---

[1] This account of the I. C. F. is based on a number of leaflets and other publications of the society and a personal interview with the General Director.

of gathering information.[1]   A leader of one of the Church reform organizations has said that the Commission is not of very much importance and that in any body set up by the National Assembly the conservative point of view is sure to predominate.

The progress of interdenominational action in social matters is one of the most encouraging developments of recent years, and the Church of England has been strongly represented in this movement.   An early undertaking of the kind was the Interdenominational Conference of Social Service Unions, founded in 1911 under the chairmanship of Bishop Gore.   This body comprised members of the Christian Social Union, the (Roman) Catholic Social Guild, and seven Free Church societies.   It held a summer school and set up a central Council of Christian Witness and local councils of social service in some fifty-seven towns.   The war, however, interrupted many of its activities.[2]

One of the best advertised and most ambitious inter-church projects was formally launched in 1924.   It is known as " Copec ", signifying " a Christian order in politics, economics, and citizenship.   Preparation for it began in 1920 with the formation of a council of 350 men and women. This group distributed 250,000 questionnaires, which were considered and reported on by hundreds of study circles all over the country.   The results were then formulated in a series of twelve reports embodying the principles which should govern Christians in dealing with social problems. The reports were considered by 1,500 delegates representing many denominations at the Birmingham Conference of 1924. No Roman Catholics, however, attended.   The interest

[1] *National Assembly Report*, 1921, vol. ii, no. 3, pp. 87 *et seq.* Most of this account comes from an interview with Sir Wyndham Deedes.

[2] C. S. U. *Annual Report*, 1912, p. 10; *Convocation of Canterbury*, 1924, p. 227.

created by the reports furnished enough momentum to carry
on the work of propagating the ideas set forth. It was
hoped that ultimately the movement would receive the official
backing of the churches. Meanwhile a continuation committee headed by Bishop Temple, who had presided over the
conference, went forward with the work of organization and
propaganda. This included the formation of local Groups,
the inauguration of a summer school, the founding of a
League of Youth, and the holding of regional conferences
and public meetings. Special committees have also dealt
with rural conditions and the promotion of the Christian
social viewpoint in schools and colleges. The Information
Bureau has undertaken a Welfare of Youth enquiry.[1] In
view of its broad interdenominational basis and the nature
of its work, some disappointment was expressed that Copec
was not made the mouthpiece of the churches during the
great strike of 1926. This would doubtless have raised the
prestige and helped to maintain the impetus of the movement.

In 1924, shortly before Copec announced itself, another
group made a bid for inter-church support. Certain members
of the defunct Church Socialist League—among them the
Rev. C. S. Smith and Messrs. Fred Hughes and Charles
Record — who had been unable to accept the Christian
Sociology of the L. K. G.—decided to continue the principles
of the old League in a new organization. It was agreed,
however, that the addition of yet another to the list of
strictly Church bodies could scarcely be justified. The
"Society of Socialist Christians", therefore, welcomed
members of all denominations. The name, says Mr. Hughes,
stresses "the primacy of our Christianity and the undiluted
character of our Socialism." The society is affiliated with
the Labor Party although it does not commit itself to everything said or done in the name of the party. It has also

---

[1] *Copec News*, July, 1926; *Copec in Action*, a pamphlet.

established relations with two continental organizations—the Federation of Christian Socialists in France, Belgium and Switzerland and the Union of Religious Socialists in Germany. In 1927 the executive committee of the society was composed of seven Anglicans, five Free Church members, and one member of the Society of Friends.[1]

THE COAL CRISIS AND THE GENERAL STRIKE

Industrial crises test the sincerity and practicality of reformers; mere generalizations are out of place in a trade dispute. One must either take sides or be a peace-maker. And while it takes one form of courage to take the unpopular side, it requires another and not necessarily lower form to act as a mediator. Stepping into the midst of a mêlée with the hand of peace outstretched and at the same time dodging missiles from two directions may lead to nothing but a loss of dignity. Fraser, Creighton, and Westcott, as we have seen, accomplished the feat successfully: Bishop Temple fled discomfited to Wales. For many years after Westcott's interposition in the northern coal dispute no dignitary was willing or able to follow his example. It was even asserted that the time had passed for such heroic measures. With so many expert agencies at work, said the archbishop of Canterbury in 1912, interference would probably be an anachronism.[2] So when a delegation from the Church Socialist League twice waited upon the archbishop during that troublous year in the hope of moving him to action they met with no response.[2]

Reformers were perhaps encouraged that Convocation took notice of the miners' strike of 1912, something that it

[1] *Commonwealth*, 1924, p. 71; 1927, pp. 242-3.

[2] *Convocation of Canterbury*, 1912, p. 148; also *cf.* the bishop of Wakefield to the same purpose, *Convocation of York*, 1912, pp. 82-3.

[3] *Commonwealth*, 1927, p. 220.

had never done before under similar circumstances. In February when the strike seemed imminent both Houses of Bishops passed resolutions expressing the hope that a peaceful settlement might be reached, but they made little attempt to examine the claims of either side. The bishop of Wakefield repeated the aphorism that the first charge upon industry ought to be the proper remuneration of the worker, but he held that the employers also had just claims. It was generally agreed that the complicated nature of industrial problems made it impossible to take sides. However, the workers were admonished as to the sacredness of duty, the limited nature of profits, and the dangers of syndicalism.[1] Convocation also passed resolutions favoring the living wage, one of the main issues of the coal dispute.[2]

Industrial hostilities were virtually suspended during the war. They recommenced immediately after the armistice, and Convocation again interjected its comments. Resolutions invoking a spirit of conciliation were passed. These could alarm no one; but the attendant discussions were much more lively. The customary warnings were addressed to labor, and the " whither-are-we-drifting " group denounced socialism. But it was something new to hear technical economic questions discussed as moral issues in the midst of a strike. It was also new to hear the government's policy roundly criticized in Convocation. Both occurred in 1919 and again in 1921.[3] During the coal strike (or lock-out) of 1921 the Canterbury House of Bishops debated the question of remedies for the mining industry. Bishops Furse and Garbett favored a national pool. They joined Kempthorne,

---

[1] *Convocation of Canterbury*, 1912, pp. 144 *et seq.*; *Convocation of York*, 1912, pp. 81 *et seq.*

[2] *Convocation of Canterbury*, 1914, pp. 319 *et seq.*; *Convocation of York*, 1912, pp. 270 *et seq.*; 1914, pp. 202 *et seq.*

[3] *Convocation of Canterbury*, 1919, pp. 134 *et seq.*; 1921, pp. 241 *et seq.*

Woods, and Talbot in censuring the government for insisting on decontrol before a constructive plan had been adopted. These opinions were of course challenged not only by the bishop of Exeter but by others less immobile. They may also have inspired Lord Bryce's letter to President Lowell:

It [the strike] is more revolutionary, and even more communistic than other countries seem to have realized. I am daily amazed at the extent to which quasi communistic principles have spread among the educated and well-to-do classes. Even the Bishops are permeated by them, and still more the average clergy, even of the Church of England.[1]

" The coal question," says Mr. G. D. H. Cole, is " the symbolic issue of the post-war labour struggle." The lock-out of 1921 ended in a reduction of wages which was reflected in other industries. A temporary trade revival in 1923 together with the moral effect of a labor government in 1924 enabled the miners to negotiate an agreement calling for an increased minimum wage. The agreement expired in 1925 but before that time business had resumed its normal downward curve and both parties were girding themselves for a continuation of the struggle. The owners talked of reduced wages and increased hours; the miners appealed to the General Council of the Trade Union Congress for support. In July, 1925, the Congress pledged itself to uphold the miners, if necessary by a general strike. The government took alarm and offered its famous subsidy in aid of wages, to continue until yet another Royal Commission should investigate the industry. The Samuel Report was presented early in 1926 but neither side would accept its recommendations voluntarily and the government refused otherwise to put its own authority behind the report. Negotiations reached a deadlock. The

[1] H. A. L. Fisher, *James Bryce*, vol. ii, p. 260. The letter was written less than two weeks after the debate referred to.

miners appealed to the General Council which renewed its strike pledge. Last moment conversation abruptly halted when the government made a constitutional issue of the refusal of employes of the *Daily Mail* to print an article hostile to the strike. The subsidy was thereupon withdrawn and the mine-owners announced new and lower wage rates effective 1 May. The miners accordingly struck work. The General Council responded by calling out the railway and transport workers, the iron and steel workers, the builders, and the printers.[1]

During the tense period following the Samuel Commission's Report, while negotiations were still in progress,[2] a "Call to Prayer" was issued signed by thirty-nine diocesan and other bishops, the heads of eight Free Churches, and representatives of the Fellowship of Reconciliation and the Salvation Army. "If all sides approach the issue in the right spirit," said this manifesto,

the recommendations contained in the recent official Report give ground for hope that, provided a better bridge can be built, the way to peace and prosperity will be found, and the coal industry will be able to adapt itself to the new conditions obtaining in the commerce of the world. Meanwhile, let us also commit to God, with fellow-feeling, the human needs of those who, in the service of the community, are engaged in the perilous task of coal-mining, remembering that His Will for them and their families—as for all His children—is a standard of life compatible with the essential dignity of human personality.

On 4 May, however, the great strike began. Two days later the bishop of London offered Fulham Palace as a neutral ground for further negotiations. Speaking at a

---

[1] G. D. H. Cole, *A Short History of the British Working Class Movement*, vol. iii, pp. 203 *et seq.*

[2] At least this seems to be the date. *The Torch*, May, 1926.

public meeting of intercession he said that a higher standard of living was a worthy object, not to be attained, however, by any short cut.[1]   In the House of Lords, the archbishop of Canterbury saw neither black nor red.   He commended the good humor and friendliness of the " poorest classes ".

But I do not think that among thoughtful people there is a very great difference of opinion as to its [the strike's] unwisdom and its mischievousness.   To my mind it is simply shocking that it should be possible at this time of day in our country for a set of men [the General Council] who are a kind of oligarchy chosen in such a way that it is not very obvious that it rests upon a broad popular basis, to make the extraordinary claim to exercise the powers of the Government as regards the control of the Press, the control of the country's communications, and the ordinary living and well-being of the people.

He recognized, however, a justifiable fear on the part of the workers that " legislation or lack of legislation " might reduce the standard of living, and indicated a course of action which might end the struggle.

The Government would have behind them an overwhelming weight of public opinion if they felt it to be possible, even at the risk of doing something illogical, something that appears inconsistent, to explore yet further the possibility of averting the growth which must arise soon of a spirit very different from that which prevails at this moment.[2]

The Government ignored this rather vague suggestion, but the archbishop was meanwhile " day and night immersed in interviews, correspondence, and efforts to secure peace." [3] Pressure was being exerted upon him even by non-Anglicans

[1] *British Gazette*, 6 May, 1926.

[2] *Hansard*, 1926, vol. 64, col. 49.

[3] *Yorkshire Post*, 10 May.

to take some independent action.[1] He was in touch with Cardinal Bourne.

On 8 May, therefore, the archbishops of Canterbury and York made public an appeal to end the strike, whose terms had been " settled after full conference between the Archbishop and the Christian Churches of the country." Briefly, it advocated a return to the status quo of 1 May and the resumption of negotiations. " Our proposal should be interpreted as involving simultaneously and concurrently (1) The cancellation on the part of the T. U. C. of the General Strike; (2) Renewal by the Government of its offer of assistance to the Coal Industry for a short definite period; (3) The withdrawal on the part of the mine-owners of the new wage scales recently issued." [2]

The appeal encountered difficulties from the start. The archbishop had complained of one oligarchy; he quickly felt the weight of another. *The British Worker,* organ of the General Council, and certain other private newspapers which managed fitfully to survive printed the proposal, but neither the government broadcasting station nor *The British Gazette,* the government newspaper, accepted it. Yet the latter interesting publication—edited by Mr. Winston Churchill— found space for a virulent attack on trade unionism, for sports news, and for Cardinal Bourne's sermon denouncing the strike as a " sin ".[3] When Mr. Lloyd George sharply questioned the government's attitude toward the archbishop's appeal, Churchill disclaimed any covert motives but his defence was extremely thin.[4] However, the next morning the churches' message was broadcast through the government radio station.[5]

[1] Private information.

[2] *British Worker,* 8 May.

[3] *British Gazette,* 5, 10 May.

[4] *Hansard* (Commons), 1926, vol. 195, col. 707.

[5] *Daily News and The Star,* 12 May.

"The Archbishop was made very angry (and he did well to be angry) by the stupid effort to suppress the call of the Churches," writes a Labor journalist.[1]   His supporters used every means to give the appeal publicity.   Copies were distributed broadcast and sandwich men were pressed into service.   The general director of the Industrial Christian Fellowship circularized the clergy.[2]

Labor and moderate opinion were distinctly sympathetic. "During the week-end meetings were held all over the country calling upon Baldwin to end the strike on the terms of this appeal."[3]   But the government, and particularly Mr. Churchill, insisted on unconditional surrender, while the General Council became more and more anxious to end the strike on any terms.   When Sir Herbert Samuel, therefore, suggested a compromise somewhat more favorable to the miners than his own Report, the General Council recommended settlement to the miners.   The latter unhesitatingly rejected it. Without further parley the General Council called off the strike (12 May), leaving the miners to fight it out alone.[4]

Of all parties concerned with the strike, the Church perhaps came off best.   "Nothing has been more significant," said *The Manchester Guardian,*

than the action taken by the Archbishop of Canterbury and the manifesto issued by the several Masters of Houses and Fellows at Oxford.   In the nineteenth century the Church and the old universities represented a body of opinion that was stiff and uncompromising on all questions in which the claims of property were challenged.   There were, of course, distinguished exceptions, but for the most part these institutions respected

[1] Hamilton Fyfe, *Behind the Scenes of the Great Strike,* p. 51.

[2] Private information.

[3] H. Fyfe, *op. cit.,* p. 63.

[4] G. D. H. Cole, *op. cit.,* vol. iii, p. 210.

the fixed conservative view and the traditional prejudices of the governing class. The workers never looked to them for sympathy in an acute struggle. . . . Their bold leadership in this crisis has been a powerful influence in keeping the nation from the catastrophe of a class war. . . . It will have a profound influence on the future.[1]

Some felt, however, that the Church had condoned an act of violence. It is interesting to find Father Cyril Bickersteth, an original member of the Christian Social Union, aligning himself with the egregious *Daily Mail:*

In the dock strike [of 1889] our sympathies were wholly on the side of the men and what seemed to us the Christian point of view was expressed with greater clearness and emphasis by a Roman Catholic Cardinal than by the Bishops of our own Communion or any other religious leaders. . . . Personally I am sorry that this time it was left again to a Roman Catholic Cardinal to apply Christian principles to the question of a general strike. I should have liked the I. C. F.'s having said plainly that the Trade Union Council were guilty not only of a blunder, but of a crime.[2]

The government met the coal strike as it had the general strike—by a policy of no concessions. But the churches had not yet given up hope of a peaceful issue. While the archbishop of Canterbury disappeared from the scene, Bishop Kempthorne, supported by a group of bishops and Free Church leaders, initiated a new peace movement. One of Kempthorne's chief aides was the Rev. P. T. R. Kirk of the Industrial Christian Fellowship. Believing " that the solution of the coal problem lies in the adoption of the Coal Commission Report in its entirety," the group early in July sounded out the coal-owners' association. They met with

[1] 21 May, 1926.
[2] *Torch,* June, 1926, p. ii.

no encouragement. " Sir Adam Nimmo, and others, gave us a lengthy explanation of their views on the present situation, but indicated that the recommendations of the Report did not provide a solution." On 14 and 15 July conferences were held with representatives of the Miners' Federation. The miners had so far steadfastly opposed the solutions offered by the Samuel Report. Nevertheless their attitude at present was conciliatory. The intervention of the churches was indeed more welcome than a new gesture of the T. U. C. " I believe that there will be new negotiations next week," said a member of the Miners' executive, "but if they come about, it will be through the intervention of the Bishops and the Free Church leaders. . . The T. U. C. General Council have been told pretty bluntly that the miners are not going to permit them to butt in in regard to negotiations." The proposals as finally agreed on were transmitted to the Prime Minister on 16 July. They provided for an immediate return to work under pre-strike conditions, with a government subsidy for not more than four months to permit the negotiation of a national agreement. The terms of the latter were to be drawn up by the authors of the coal report and if disagreement existed at the end of four months the disputed points were to be settled by a joint arbitration board with powers of final decision. In his covering letter Bishop Kempthorne stated the view of the church group that the attitude of the miners' representatives showed a distinct advance toward the Samuel Report. He asked whether the Prime Minister would receive a deputation of churchmen.[1]

Mr. Baldwin's reply was polite but unbending. He would, of course, grant an interview. But the terms of an agreement must be settled between the owners and the miners. And since the churchmen stood upon the coal report they were reminded that " one of the emphatic recommendations

[1] *Times,* 17, 19 July.

of the Commission was that there should be no more subsidy." "This is a suggestion to which the Government
could not possibly assent, and it would therefore be useless
for me to communicate the present proposals to the owners." [1]

Under these unpropitious circumstances the meeting took
place. Mr. Baldwin and his advisers would not talk of a
subsidy. The delegates then suggested that a loan to the
industry would answer the same purpose, but this alternative
aid was likewise denied. It was gathered that the government would be willing to name a neutral chairman for conferences between the parties. This marked its limit of
intervention. [2]

For several days the possibility of a loan by private interests was talked of. That hope, too, eventually faded and
the gloomy prospect of a settlement by attrition once more
loomed ahead. Four months longer the strike dragged on.
The end came in November. Faced by a gradual drift back
to work, the Miners' Federation resigned its powers into the
hands of the local unions to make what individual terms they
could.

The part played by churchmen in the events of 1926 gave
meaning to the sentiments they had freely expressed during
and after the war. The feeling that talk should eventuate
in action, however, led them not only to interfere in a national
crisis, but less spectacularly, to organize the Industrial Christian Fellowship and to co-operate with other denominations
for concrete social objects. Yet the Church as a whole is
still unable to agree as to what, exactly, Anglican doctrine
demands in the way of social action and how ceremonies and
ritual affect the social conscience. Practical action appears
to be hampered because these preliminary questions remain

[1] *Times*, 19 July.
[2] *Ibid.*, 21 July.

unsettled. The conflict goes on not only between reformers and apologists of the present order but among reformers themselves. The career of the Church Socialist League has been described in considerable detail because it so well illustrates this conflict. The League was formed to preach and practice socialism. It was disrupted because some of the members reached the conclusion that no one could be a good socialist unless he was also a thorough Anglo-Catholic and that his Anglo-Catholicism determined the kind of socialism he would profess. This conception may have enlarged the meaning of religion for Catholics. It unquestionably narrowed the ground of appeal to non-Catholics.

CHAPTER VIII

CONCLUSION

THE activities of churchmen during the strikes of 1926 are some measure of the distance which the Church has travelled since 1850. It would have been difficult to imagine the archbishop of Canterbury recommending conciliation to the government and praising the motives of workingmen during, say, the Chartist agitation of 1848. Perhaps the contrast is too flattering to the Church as a whole, for undoubtedly average opinion is at present more radical among the bishops than among the lower clergy and the laity. Nevertheless the old idea has been losing ground that the Church is first of all a corporation to preserve a body of ceremonies and privileges and that its social action should be confined to the traditional fields of sexual morality, education, temperance, and charity. For if one admits that the Church can speak authoritatively upon these latter topics there is really no logical halting-place, and every phase of social conduct becomes its legitimate concern.

This broader conception of religion does not mean that those who hold it must of necessity range themselves on the side of social reform. It may mean that religion will be invoked to consecrate the status quo. Yet it usually happens that those who talk most about the social function of the Church are also dissatisfied with the existing order. From criticism to the advocacy of remedies is only a step, and, as we have seen, churchmen often find themselves co-operating with secular reformers.

This co-operation sometimes has its difficulties. For one

323

thing it arouses the suspicion that the religious sanction is an after-thought rather than a source of inspiration, and that the Church may be made simply the tail of a secular reform movement which it can never hope to dominate.   Even some churchmen who firmly believe that Christianity is fundamentally social and who support guildism or the Labor Party from religious conviction hesitate to demand that the Church officially adopt the philosophy of either movement.   Radicals and conservatives thus find themselves in agreement.

The root of the difficulty seems to be that every comprehensive reform movement whether it be syndicalism, collectivism, guildism, or what not, arouses emotions in its adherents and expresses itself in formulas which are akin to those of orthodox religion.   If the Church were to sanction any of these movements it would run the risk of having its own theology and rites supplanted or rendered superfluous by those of the adopted movement.   The alternative would be to induce the labor movement, for example, to formulate its aspirations in terms of Anglican doctrine and to release its enthusiasm through the forms of Anglican ritual.   Under these circumstances the Church might be induced to sanction, officially, a new ordering of society.   But what Bishop Gore says of the Christian Social Union is also true of the whole reform movement of the Church: it " entirely failed to raise up in the ranks of the Church a sufficient body of trade unionists who were also Churchmen to make any effective impression on the Labour movement as a whole." [1]   The Industrial Christian Fellowship may have better success with the policy of penetration.   There remains the possibility that the Church itself will evolve a comprehensive social philosophy of which its own ritual and theology will be an organic part.   The Christian Sociology of the L. K. G. will be designed to fit these requirements.

[1] S. Paget, *op. cit.,* p. 250.

Although responsible leaders have hesitated to commit the Church to any social or economic theory their individual sympathy and co-operation with new movements have helped to soften the attitude of non-Anglican reformers toward the Church. The incident which Tom Mann records in his memoirs could scarcely have occurred a century ago: early in his career he seriously considered entering the Anglican ministry in order more effectually to serve the working class.[1] Even such a joyous revolutionist as Mr. Lansbury appears to have succeeded in reconciling his allegiance to socialism with his loyalty to the Church.

The direct contribution of the Church to social reform during the past seventy-five years has been by no means negligible. It has been made, however, not usually by the Church as a body but by individuals and groups. We may recall some of the main achievements. There is of course Lord Shaftesbury's multifarious activity, which continued far into the period. There is the later work of the first Christian Socialists—especially of Hughes, Ludlow, and Neale—in promoting co-operation and in improving the legal status of trade unions and friendly societies. There are the devoted labors of clergymen and laymen in the slums and the local reforms they were able to effect. There are the modifications in the factory code which the Christian Social Union helped to bring about, the mediation of bishops and other churchmen in industrial disputes, and the successful efforts of Bishop Westcott and his co-workers to establish central boards of arbitration in the northern coal trade. There is the legislative contribution of certain bishops in the House of Lords. Churchmen also originated what is said to have been the first English socialist society, the Guild of St. Matthew. A clergyman, Samuel Barnett, was the pioneer of the settlement movement.

[1] *Tom Mann's Memoirs*, pp. 118-19.

The indirect effect of the Church social movement has been to help create a public opinion favorable to reform. The propaganda of the Guild of St. Matthew, the Christian Social Union, the Church Socialist League, and other organizations, the writings of prominent churchmen such as J. N. Figgis, A. J. Carlyle, M. B. Reckitt, and R. H. Tawney, the manifestoes of later Lambeth Conferences and the reports of the Committee on Moral Witness and of the Archbishops' Committee on Industrial Problems, all these have appealed to a wide public.

But the appeal, grounded as it usually is upon the social implications of Christianity and the doctrines of the Church, has been aimed more directly at the mass of churchpeople, and its effects are apparent in their changed attitude toward reform. This change can be traced in the discussions which have taken place in the Church assemblies, where there is a growing tendency to deal with matters once considered outside the province of religion. The conversion is of course by no means complete. Bishop Gore's opinion delivered in 1921 is probably still true: " Whatever may be said of the central or official church, the Church as a whole, whether clerical or lay, remains, I fear, a body which as a whole the social reformer or the Labour man regards as something which is alien to his ends and aims, and which he finds irresponsive and dull." [1]   Considering what has already been done the prospect is less discouraging than these words imply. Seventy-five years ago bishops would have been regarded as the last possible converts to radical reform. Many of them are now far in advance of their flocks and a few are nothing less than agitators. This is a lesson which should cheer those who hope for a real revolution in sentiment among the rank and file of the Church.

" I used to think," said H. M. Hyndman toward the end of

[1] S. Paget, *op. cit.*, p. 250.

his life, " that Social Democracy would take the place of religion, but I now see that human beings want something more. Religious belief, in one shape or another, will be necessary for hundreds of years yet, and we shall have to find it for them somehow." It used to be thought that " religion " could take the place of social democracy, but it is now clear that human beings want something more. Social reform will be necessary for hundreds of years yet, and religion will have to find a place for it in its own scheme of the universe.

BIBLIOGRAPHY

NOTE.—The writer received personal information from the following churchmen, most of whom have participated in social reform movements dealt with in this book: Bishop Charles Gore, Dr. Percy Dearmer, Fr. Paul Bull, formerly chairman of the Church Socialist League; the Rev. P. T. R. Kirk, general director of the Industrial Christian Fellowship; Dr. W. R. Matthews, dean of King's College, London; Sir Wyndham Deedes, head of Oxford House; the Rev. Claude Jenkins, librarian of Lambeth Palace Library; and Miss Maude Royden.

The following list contains only works named in the course of this book. Unless otherwise noted, the place of publication is London.

REPORTS AND PROCEEDINGS OF CHURCH ASSEMBLIES

Convocation of Canterbury, *The Chronicle of Convocation* . . .
Convocation of York, *The York Journal of Convocation* . . . York, [etc.].
Church Congress, *Reports.* Cambridge, London, etc.
Lambeth Conferences:
> R. T. Davidson (ed.), *The Lambeth Conferences of 1867, 1878 and 1888.* 1889.
> *Conference of Bishops of the Anglican Communion.* 1897, 1908, 1920.

National Assembly of the Church of England, *Report of Proceedings.*

OTHER OFFICIAL OR SEMI-OFFICIAL CHURCH PUBLICATIONS

Crockford's Clerical Directory.
Official Yearbook of the Church of England.

GOVERNMENT PUBLICATIONS

Parliamentary Debates. Referred to as *Hansard.*
Parliamentary Papers:
> *Reports of Royal Commissions:*
>> Popular Education (England), 1861, vol. xxi.
>> Organization and Rules of Trade Unions, 1867, vol. xxxii; 1867-8, vol. xxxix; 1868-9, vol. xxxi.
>> Employment of Children, Young Persons and Women in Agriculture, 1867-8, vol. xvii; 1868-9, vol. xiii; 1870, vol. xiii.
>> Friendly and Benefit and Building Societies, 1871, vol. xxv; 1872, vol. xxvi; 1873, vol. xxii; 1874, vol. xxiii.

328

Working of the Master and Servant Act and Criminal law
Amendment Act, 1874, vol. xxiv; 1875, vol. xxx.

Housing of the Working Classes, 1884-5, vol. xxxi.

Reports of Parliamentary Committees:

Labouring Poor (Allotments of Land), 1843, vol. vii.

Bill to Prevent Sunday Trading, 1850, vol. xix.

Deficiency of Means of Spiritual Instruction, 1857-8, vol. ix.

Intemperance, 1877, vol. xi; 1878, vol. xiv; 1878-9, vol. x.

Sunday Trading, 1906, vol. xiii.

Accounts and Papers:

Religious Worship (England and Wales), 1822-3, vol. lxxxix.

Population (Great Britain), 1852-3, vol. xc.

Committee of Council's Reports on Education, 1862, vol. xlii;
1863, vol. xlvii; 1865, vol. lii; 1866, vol. xxvii.

Education (National Society), 1868-9, vol. xlvii, p. 269.

Clerks in Holy Orders in Commission [of the Peace], 1873,
vol. liv.

Correspondence Respecting the Magistrates of Chipping Norton,
1873, vol. liv.

Industrial and Provident Societies, 1877, vol. lxxvii.

Return of Magistrates Appointed from 1 January, 1900, to 21
December, 1905, 1906, vol. xcix.

Lead in Pottery and Lithographic Processes, 1909, vol. xxxix
(Cd. 5219).

Education Department:

Special Reports on Educational Subjects, 1896-7: M. E. Sadler and
J. W. Edwards, *Public Elementary Education in England and
Wales, 1870-1895.*

PERIODICALS AND NEWSPAPERS

Church:

British Magazine
Christian Observer
Church of England Magazine
Church of England Temperance Magazine
Church Reformer
Church Socialist
Church Times
Commonwealth
Economic Review
Guardian

Secular:

Times

Newspapers published in Great Britain during the General Strike of
1926, including *The British Worker, The British Gazette*, etc.
(A two-volume collection in the New York Public Library.)

LITERATURE

Adamson, J. W., *A Short History of Education*. Cambridge, 1919.
Adderley, J. G., *In Slums and Society*. 1916.
——, *Looking Upward*. 1891.
Arch, Joseph, *The Story of his Life*. 1898.
Archbishops' Fifth Committee's Report, *Christianity and Industrial Problems*. 1918.
Ashley, Sir William, *The Christian Outlook, being the Sermons of an Economist*. 1925.
——, *An Introduction to English Economic History and Theory*. 1888.
——, Memoir of, *Economic History Review*, 1928, pp. 319-21.
Ashwell, A. R. and Wilberforce, R. I., *Life of the Right Rev. Samuel Wilberforce*. 1880.
Baernreither, J. M., *English Association of Workingmen*. 1897.
Bain, W. J., *A Paper on the Early History of Sunday Schools Especially in Northamptonshire*. Northampton, 1876.
Barnett, Mrs. H. O., *Canon Barnett, his Life, Work and Friends*. 1918.
Barnett, S. A., and Mrs., *Practicable Socialism, New Series*. 1915.
Bentham, Jeremy, *The Book of Church Reform, containing the Most Essential Part of Mr. Bentham's "Church of Englandism Examined"*. Edited by One of his Disciples. 1831.
Beresford Hope, A. J. B., *The Place and Influence in the Church Movement of Church Congresses*. 1874.
Bettany, F. G., *Stewart Headlam*. 1926.
Binns, H. B., *A Century of Education*. 1908.
Birchenough, Charles, *History of Elementary Education in England and Wales from 1800 to the Present Day*. 1914.
Black Book, The. 1835.
Booth, Charles, *Life and Labour of the People in London. Third Series: Religious Influences*. 1902.
Bosanquet, H., *Social Work in London, a History of the Charity Organization Society*. 1914.
Bowden, Witt, *Industrial Society in England towards the End of the Eighteenth Century*. New York, 1925.
Bready, J. W., *Lord Shaftesbury and Social-Industrial Progress*. 1926.
Brentano, Lujo, *Christlich-soziale Bewegung in England*. Leipzig, 1883.

British Association for the Advancement of Science, *Report of the Thirty-eighth Meeting.* 1869.

Burne-Jones, G., *Memorials of Edward Burne-Jones.* New York, 1906.

Burns, Dawson, *Temperance Ballads.* 1884.

——, *Temperance History.* 1899.

Carpenter, Niles, *Guild Socialism.* New York, 1922.

Chamberlain, Montague, *The Church Army.* Boston, 1897.

Christian Social Union:
 Annual Reports, leaflets (Oxford Branch), papers (London Branch), handbooks, etc.

Clarke, J. J., *The Housing Problem.* 1920.

Clayden, Arthur, *The Revolt of the Field.* 1874.

Clayton, Joseph, *The Rise and Decline of Socialism in Great Britain, 1884-1924.* 1926.

Cobbett, William, *Legacy to Parsons.* 1830.

Cole, G. D. H., *Robert Owen.* 1926.

——, *Life of William Cobbett.* 1924.

——, *Short History of the British Working Class Movement,* vol. iii. New York, 1927.

Cook, W. G. H., Electoral Reform and Organized Christianity in England. *Political Science Quarterly,* vol. xxxix, p. 485.

Co-operative Congress, *Reports.*

Copec, *Reports.* 1924.

——, *Copec in Action.*

——, *Copec News.*

Cornish, F. W., *The Church of England in the Nineteenth Century.* 1908.

Creighton, Mrs., *Life and Letters of Mandell Creighton.* 1904.

Cunningham, W., *Growth of English Industry and Commerce.* 1912.

——, Memoir of, *Proceedings of the British Academy,* 1919-20, p. 466.

Davies, J. Ll., *The Working Men's College, 1854-1904.* 1904.

——, Memoir of, *Contemporary Review,* vol. cix, p. 782.

Dawson, W. H., *The German Empire.* 1919.

Dearmer, Percy, *The Beginnings of the Christian Social Union.* 1912.

Dent, J. J., *J. M. Ludlow.* Manchester, 1921.

Dewsnup, E. R., *The Housing Problem in England, its Statistics, Legislation and Policy.* Manchester, 1907.

Draper, W. H., *University Extension, a Survey of Fifty Years, 1873-1923.* Cambridge, 1923.

Ede, W. More, *The Attitude of the Church to Some of the Social Problems of Town Life.* Cambridge, 1896.

Edwards, George, *From Crow-Scaring to Westminster.* 1922.

Encyclopedia of Sunday Schools and Religious Education. New York, 1915.

English Land Restoration League, *Annual Reports.*

Fabian Tracts:

    No. 42: *Christian Socialism,* by Stewart Headlam.

    No. 133: *Socialism and Christianity,* by Percy Dearmer.

Faulkner, H. U., *Chartism and the Churches.* New York, 1916.

Fisher, H. A. L., *James Bryce.* New York, 1927.

Ford, F. M., *Ford Madox Brown.* 1896.

Froude, J. A., *Short Studies on Great Subjects. Fourth Series.* New York, 1883.

Fyfe, Hamilton, *Behind the Scenes of the Great Strike.* 1926.

George, Henry, [Jr.], *Life of Henry George.* New York, 1900.

George, M. Dorothy, *London Life in the XVIIIth Century.* New York, 1925.

Girdlestone, E., The National Agricultural Labourers' Union. *Macmillan's Magazine,* vol. xxviii, p. 426.

Glasier, J. Bruce, *William Morris and the Early Days of the Socialist Movement.* 1921.

Gore, Charles, *The Incarnation of the Son of God.* New York, 1891.

Graham, Harry, *Splendid Failures.* 1913.

Grandmaison, Ch. le Cour, Mundella et les Conseils d'Arbitrage en Angleterre. *Revue des deux Mondes,* April, 1898.

Gray, Albert, and Fremantle, W. H., editors, *Church Reform.* 1885.

Guedalla, Philip, *Palmerston.* New York, 1927.

Halévy, Elie, *A History of the English People in 1815.* 1924.

Hammond, J. L., and Barbara, *The Town Labourer.* 1917.

——, *The Village Labourer.* 1920.

Harrison, Frederic, *Autobiographic Memoirs.* 1911.

——, *De Senectute, More Last Words.* 1923.

Hasbach, Wilhelm, *A History of the English Agricultural Labourer.* 1908.

Headlam, Stewart, *The Guild of St. Matthew.* 1890.

Heath, F. G., *The English Peasantry.* 1874.

Henderson, Archibald, *George Bernard Shaw, his Life and Works.* 1911.

Hervey, Lord Arthur, *A Suggestion for Supplying the Literary, Scientific and Mechanics' Institutes of Great Britain and Ireland with Lecturers from the Universities.* 1855.

Hill, G. B., *Letters of Dante Gabriel Rossetti to William Allingham.* 1897.

Hodder, Edwin, *Life and Work of the Seventh Earl of Shaftesbury.* 1886.

Hole, James, *An Essay on the History and Management of Literary, Scientific and Mechanics' Institutions.* 1853.

Holland, H. S., *Brooke Foss Westcott, Bishop of Durham.* 1910.

——, *A Bundle of Memories.* 1915.

——, *Our Neighbors.* 1911.

Holyoake, G. J., *Bygones Worth Remembering.* 1905.
——, *The History of Co-operation in England.* 1906.
Hovell, Mark, *The Chartist Movement.* Manchester, 1918.
Howell, George, *Labour Legislation, Labour Movements, and Labour Leaders.* 1902.
Hudson, J. W., *The History of Adult Education.* 1851.
Hudson, T. H., *Christian Socialism Explained and Enforced and Compared with Infidel Fellowship, especially as Propounded by Robert Owen, Esq.* 1839.
Hughes, Thomas, *James Fraser, Second Bishop of Manchester.* 1887.
——, and Neale, E. V., *A Manual for Co-operators.* 1881.
Hutchins, B. L., and Harrison, Amy, *History of Factory Legislation.* 1911.
Hutt, W. H., The Factory System of the Early Nineteenth Century. *Economica*, March, 1926, p. 78.
Hyndman, H. M., *The Record of an Adventurous Life.* New York, 1911.
Illingworth, A. L., *Life and Work of John Richardson Illingworth.* 1917.
Industrial Christian Fellowship: various pamphlets and leaflets.
Jones, Benjamin, *Co-operative Production*, Oxford, 1894.
Kingsley, Charles, *Village Sermons and Town and Country Sermons.* 1884.
Kingsley, F. E., *Charles Kingsley, his Letters and Memories of his Life.* 1876.
Lansbury, George, *My Life.* 1928.
Leslie, T. E. Cliffe, *Essays on Political and Moral Philosophy.* 1879.
Liddon, H. P., *Life of Edward Bouverie Pusey.* 1893-7.
London County Council, *The Housing Problem in London, 1855-1900.* 1900.
Lovett, William, *Life and Struggles.* 1920.
Lucas, Sir Charles, Llewelyn Davies and the Working Men's College. *Cornhill Magazine*, 1916, p. 421.
Ludlow, J. M., Guilds and Friendly Societies. *Contemporary Review*, April, 1873.
Ludlow, J. M., and Jones, Lloyd, *Progress of the Working Classes, 1832-1867.* 1867.
Lux Mundi. 1891 (fifth ed.).
Macdonnell, J. C., *The Life and Correspondence of William Connor Magee, Archbishop of York.* 1896.
McEntee, G. P., *The Social Catholic Movement in Great Britain.* 1928.
Malthus, T. R., *Essay on the Principle of Population.* 1806.
Mann, Tom, *Memoirs.* 1923.
Marshall, Alfred, *Principles of Economics.*
Marson, Charles L., *God's Co-operative Society.* 1914.
Masterman, C. F. G., *Frederick Denison Maurice.* 1907.
Mathieson, W. L., *English Church Reform, 1815-1840.* 1923.

——, *England in Transition, 1789-1832.* 1920.

Maurice, Frederick, *Life and Letters of Frederick Denison Maurice.* 1884.

Mess, H. A., *Factory Legislation and its Administration,* 1891-1924. 1926.

Mill, John Stuart, *Principles of Economics.*

Milman, H. H., *Savonarola, Erasmus and Other Essays.* 1870.

Molesworth, W. N., *The History of England from the Year* 1835. 1874.

Monypenny, W. F., and Buckle, G. E., *The Life of Benjamin Disraeli, Earl of Beaconsfield.* 1910-20.

More, Hannah, *Works.* 1830.

Morley, John, *Life of William Ewart Gladstone.* 1903.

National Association for the Promotion of Social Science:
     Trades' Societies and Strikes. 1860.
     Transactions, 1872. 1873.

Neale, E. V., *The Principles, Objects and Methods of the Labour Association.* 1907.

Nevinson, H. M., *Changes and Chances.* New York, 1923.

Newman, J. H., *The Arians of the Fourth Century.* 1871.

——, *Letters and Correspondence.* 1890.

Newton, John, *Letters, Originally Published under the Signatures of Omicron and Virgil.* Edinburgh, 1781.

Nicholls, Sir George, *A History of the English Poor Law.* 1898.

Overton, J. H., *Christopher Wordsworth, Bishop of Lincoln.* 1890.

Paget, Stephen, *Henry Scott Holland, Memoir and Letters.* 1921.

Paris, M. le Comte de, *The Trade Unions of England.* 1861.

Pease, E. R., *History of the Fabian Society.* 1916.

Philpott, H. B., *London at School, the History of the School Board.* 1904.

Picht, Werner, *Toynbee Hall und die Englische Settlement-bewegung. Archiv für Sozialwissenschaft und Sozialpolitik,* ix, 1913. Translated in 1914.

Pigou, A. C., *Memorials of Alfred Marshall.* 1925.

Podmore, F., *Robert Owen.* 1906.

Postgate, R. W., *The Builders History.* 1923.

Prothero, R. E., *English Farming Past and Present.* 1912.

Prothero, R. W., and Bradley, G. G., *Life and Correspondence of Dean Stanley.* 1893.

Rait, R. S., *Memorials of Albert Venn Dicey.* 1925.

Raven, C. E., *Christian Socialism, 1848-1854.* 1920.

Reason, Will, *University and Social Settlements.* 1898.

Reckitt, Maurice, and Bechhofer, C. E., *The Meaning of National Guilds.* New York, 1918.

Redfern, Percy, *C. W. S., the Story of the Co-operative Wholesale Society, Limited, 1863-1913.* Manchester, 1914.

Reichel, O. J., *The Elements of Canon Law.* 1887.

Return of Christendom, The, by a Group of Churchmen, with an Introduction by Bishop Gore and an Epilogue by G. K. Chesterton. 1922.

Richmond, Wilfrid, *Christian Economics.* 1888.

Roberts, Henry, *The Dwellings of the Labouring Classes.* 1850.

Robinson, M. F., *The Spirit of Association.* 1913.

Rogers, J. E. T., *Six Centuries of Work and Wages.* 1886.

Rose, Henry, *Henry George, a Biographical, Anecdotal, and Critical Sketch.* 1884.

Ruskin, John, *Praeterita*, vol. iii.

Sandford, E. G., *Memoirs of Archbishop Temple.* 1906.

Selley, Ernest, *Village Trade Unions in Two Centuries.* 1919.

Slater, G., *The Making of Modern England.* New York, 1915.

Smith, Frank, *The Life and Works of Sir James Kay-Shuttleworth.* 1923.

Sockman, R. W., *The Revival of Conventual Life in the Church of England in the Nineteenth Century.* New York, 1917.

Stanhope, Earl, *Life of the Right Honorable William Pitt.* 1861.

Stanley, A. P., *The Life and Correspondence of Thomas Arnold.* 1844.

Stephen, Sir James, *Essays in Ecclesiastical Biography.* 1850.

Thomson, E. H., *Life and Letters of William Thomson, Archbishop of York.* 1919.

Tillett, Ben, *A Brief History of the Dockers Union.* 1910.

Torrens, W. M., *Memoirs of the Rt. Hon. William, Second Viscount Melbourne.* 1878.

Toynbee, Arnold, *Lectures on the Industrial Revolution in England.* 1884.

Toynbee Hall, *Annual Reports.*

Tracts for the Times.

Venn, Henry, *The Complete Duty of Man.* 1811.

Verinder, Frederick, *Land for the Landless: Spence and Spence's Plan with Neo-Spencean Appendix.* 1896.

Victoria, Queen, *Letters, Second Series.* 1926.

Wallas, Graham, *Life of Francis Place.* 1898.

Walpole, Sir S., *History of England from the Conclusion of the Great War in 1815.* 1907.

Webb, Beatrice Potter, *The Co-operative Movement in Great Britain.* 1891.

Webb, Beatrice Potter, *My Apprenticeship.* New York, 1926.

Webb, Catherine, *Industrial Co-operation.* Manchester, 1907.

Webb, Sidney, *The Story of the Durham Miners, 1662-1921.* 1921.

Webb, Sidney and Beatrice, *English Local Government: The Parish and the County.* 1906.

——, *The History of Trade Unionism.* 1920.

Wesley, John, *Works.* 1829.

Westcott, Arthur, *Life and Letters of Brooke Foss Westcott.* 1903.

336 BIBLIOGRAPHY

Westcott, Brooke Foss, *Social Aspects of Christianity*. 1887.
Wilkinson, J. F., *The Friendly Society Movement*. 1891.
Williams, J. B., *Guide to the Printed Materials for English Social and Economic History*. New York, 1926.
Wilson, John, *Memoirs of a Labour Leader.* 1910.
Woods, R. A., and Kennedy, A. J., *The Settlement Movement, a National Estimate*. New York, 1922.
Woodworth, A. V., *Christian Socialism in England*. 1903.
Working Men and Religious Institutions: Full and Extended Report of the Speeches at the Conference at the London Coffee House. 1867.
Yeaxlee, Basil, *Spiritual Values in Adult Education*. 1925.

INDEX